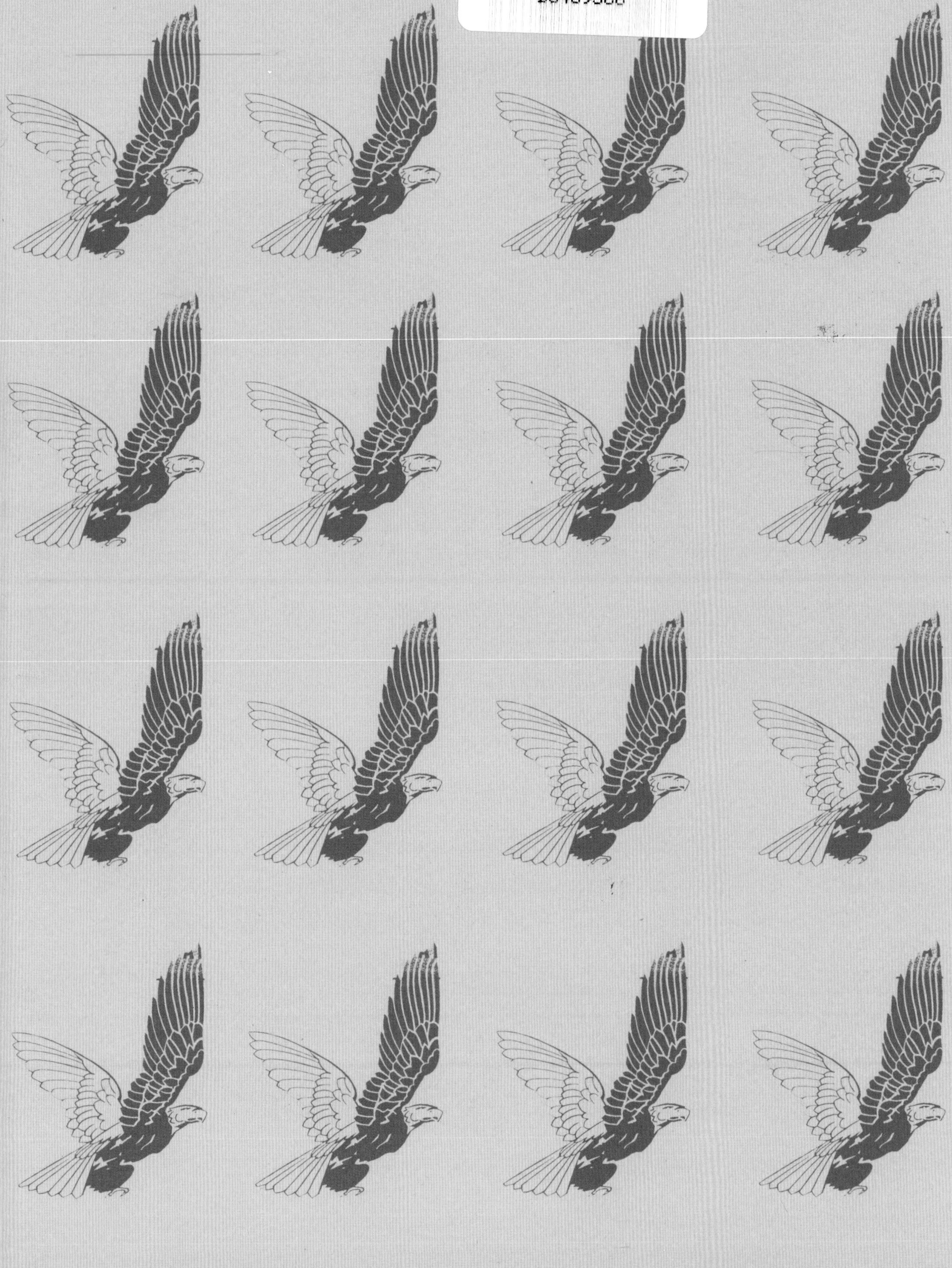

EAGLE
ANNUAL
THE 1950s

EDITED BY

DANIEL TATARSKY

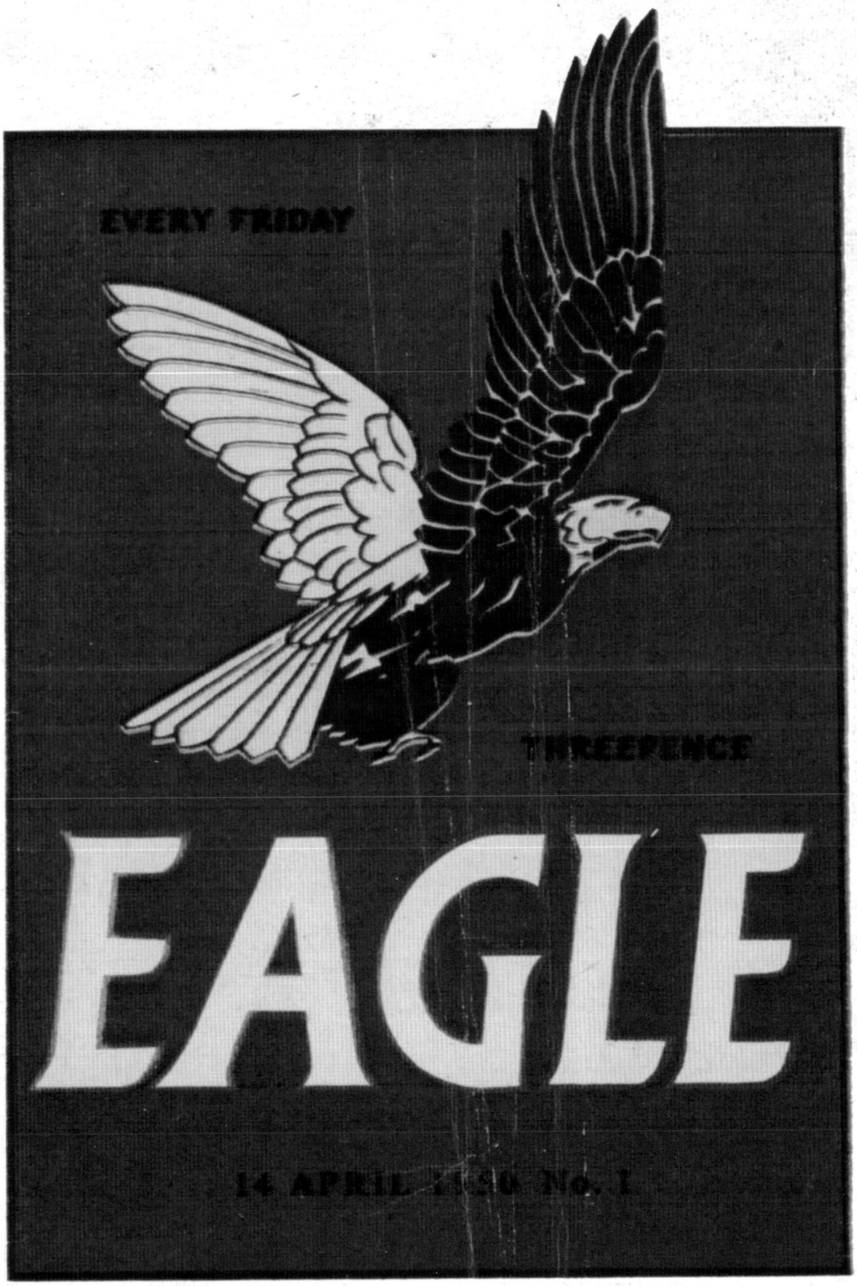
EVERY FRIDAY
THREEPENCE
EAGLE
14 APRIL
No. 1

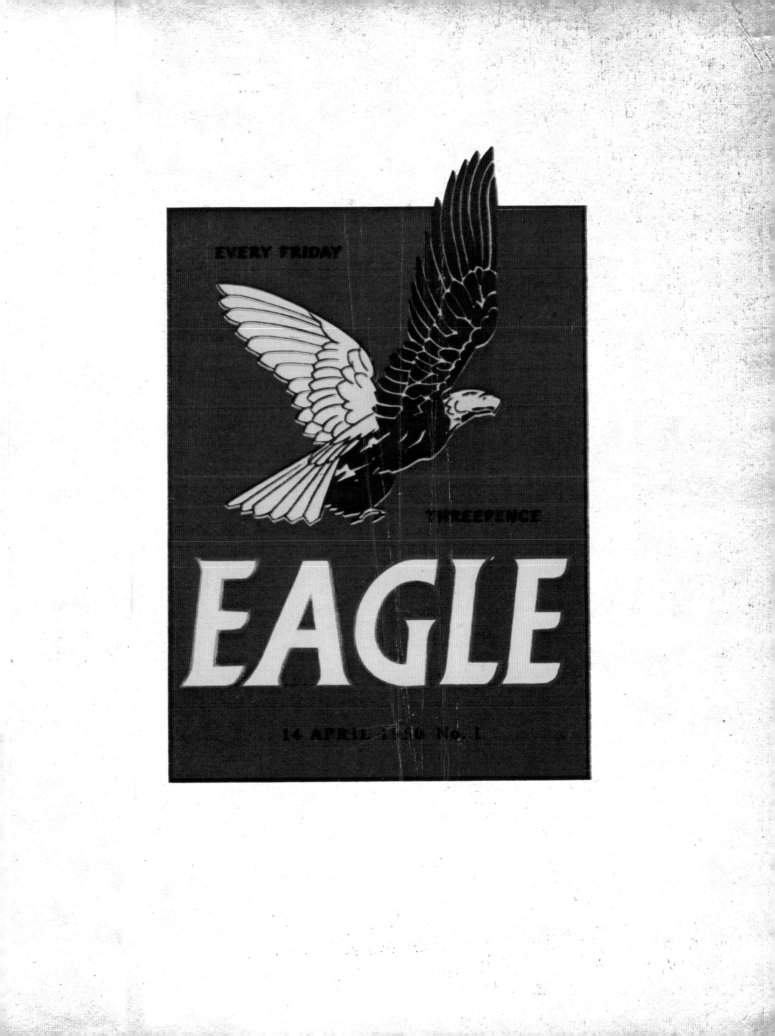

This book belongs to:

EAGLE ANNUAL

THE BEST OF THE 1950S COMIC

FEATURES *DAN DARE*, THE GREATEST COMIC STRIP OF ALL TIME

First published in hardback in Great Britain in 2007
by Orion Books
an imprint of the Orion Publishing Group Ltd
Orion House, 5 Upper St Martin's Lane,
London WC2H 9EA
An Hachette Livre UK Company

1 3 5 7 9 10 8 6 4 2

A CIP catalogue record for this book is available
from the British Library.

ISBN: 978 0 7528 8894 1

Printed and bound in Italy by Rotolito Lombarda

The Orion Publishing Group's policy is to use papers that are natural, renewable
and recyclable and made from wood grown in sustainable forests. The logging and
manufacturing processes are expected to conform to the environmental regulations
of the country of origin.

Every effort has been made to fulfil requirements with regard to reproducing copyright
material. The author and publisher will be glad to rectify any omissions
at the earliest opportunity.

www.orionbooks.co.uk

EAGLE

When *Eagle* first hit the streets on 14 April 1950 it was, to paraphrase an infamous split infinitive of the next decade, boldly going where no strip comic had gone before. It cost 50 per cent more than its rivals but over half the pages were full colour and in Dan Dare, it was to create one of the most popular and most enduring heroes of them all.

Coming just five years after the end of the Second World War the *Eagle* landed in a United Kingdom still struggling with rationing and trying to cope with wide-ranging social changes. For the adults who had come through the war life was, in the main, still looking pretty grim. The economy was suffering, trying to recover from the large spending required for warfare, jobs were sparse, and the shops could not provide all that was required. Much of this though was outside the thoughts of the average child. The war brought stories of heroism and derring-do, and while a bombed out housing estate was just that to an adult, to a child it was an adventure playground. With a blast of colour, *Eagle* shone amidst the grime and while war has its devastating effects, it is also a time when invention

and technology thrives, and this spirit of discovery and limitless possibilities underpins every page of the comic.

If *Eagle* was the baby born on that spring day, then its parents were undoubtedly Marcus Morris and Frank Hampson. Many others were involved in what was a painful and protracted gestation period, but it was these two men with their unique drive and vision who are ultimately credited with bringing the *Eagle* into the world. Reverend Marcus Morris, to give him his clerical title of the time, had been serving his parish in Southport for just a few years when he decided to improve the efforts of his church magazine to spread the word. He changed its name to *Anvil* and, with the aim of it becoming a national mouthpiece for his views, set to work on redesigning its look.

Morris discovered Frank Hampson at the local school of arts and crafts. Having served with the Royal Army Service Corps during the war Hampson was trying to support his young family by making a living as an artist. Like most meetings of this sort – Lennon and McCartney, or Morecambe and Wise – there were no fireworks or bolts of lightning. Neither man could possibly have guessed that together they would change the face of the comic strip for ever.

Working first on *Anvil*, it was not long before Morris and Hampson turned their attention to the requirements of their younger readers. It has been well documented that Morris wrote an article for *The Sunday Dispatch* entitled 'Comics that bring horror into the nursery'. It was here that he, in effect, laid out his manifesto for what he thought was a suitable publication for young boys. While the American comics which Morris was so against brought death, destruction and low morals, his *Eagle* was to soar above that and take the high ground. 'Wholesome' is a word that has often been used to describe how *Eagle* would be different but a more accurate one is 'decent'.

Having met in 1947, it was two years before they had a dummy issue of *Eagle*, and Morris began to look for a publisher. The effort and detail that went into producing this blueprint for the comic should not be underestimated. To make the strips as detailed as possible, models were painstakingly built and costumes designed from which the artists could work. It is almost an insult to some of the work to merely refer to them as comic strips; many could be seen as works of art in their own right.

With the dummy under his arm, Morris pounded the streets of London, knocking on the doors of likely publishers. Eventually it was Hulton Press who took the risk on *Eagle*, and it was a risk. Taking on a publication with an editor whose day job was as a vicar, with artists and writers, many of whom had never worked on a published comic before,

never mind one that would be a national magazine coming out every week, was going to be no easy task.

Hindsight allows 20/20 vision and so it can be easy to forget this risk. To devise, produce, and promote a comic with a circulation going from zero to nearly one million in its first week was a mammoth task, and it is a credit to all involved, that *Eagle* quickly established itself as a must have in the satchel of schoolboys up and down the country. Out of this effort came iconic characters and features which have held their place in the memories of millions of fans the world over. These include, just from the first issue, strips such as 'The Adventures of PC49', 'Seth and Shorty', and 'Rob Conway', L. Ashwell Wood's 'Cutaway', features about sport, nature and science and, last but not least, 'Dan Dare'.

Why was *Eagle* so successful? Vibrant colours, great stories, incredible detail all went into the mix, but maybe it was the very simple title of the first story, on the first page, of the first issue: 'Dan Dare – Pilot of the Future'. He and *Eagle* represented the unwritten future and the reader was part of it, right in the middle of it.

This collection from the Fifties attempts to bring together the best, the most beautiful and the most exciting elements of the *Eagle*. It's almost impossible to recreate the raw excitement of running down to the newsagent to grab the new issue off the shelves to see where Dan Dare and his crew were heading next, but it is hoped that these pages come mighty close.

Daniel Tatarsky

EAGLE – THE NEW NATIONAL STRIP CARTOON WEEKLY

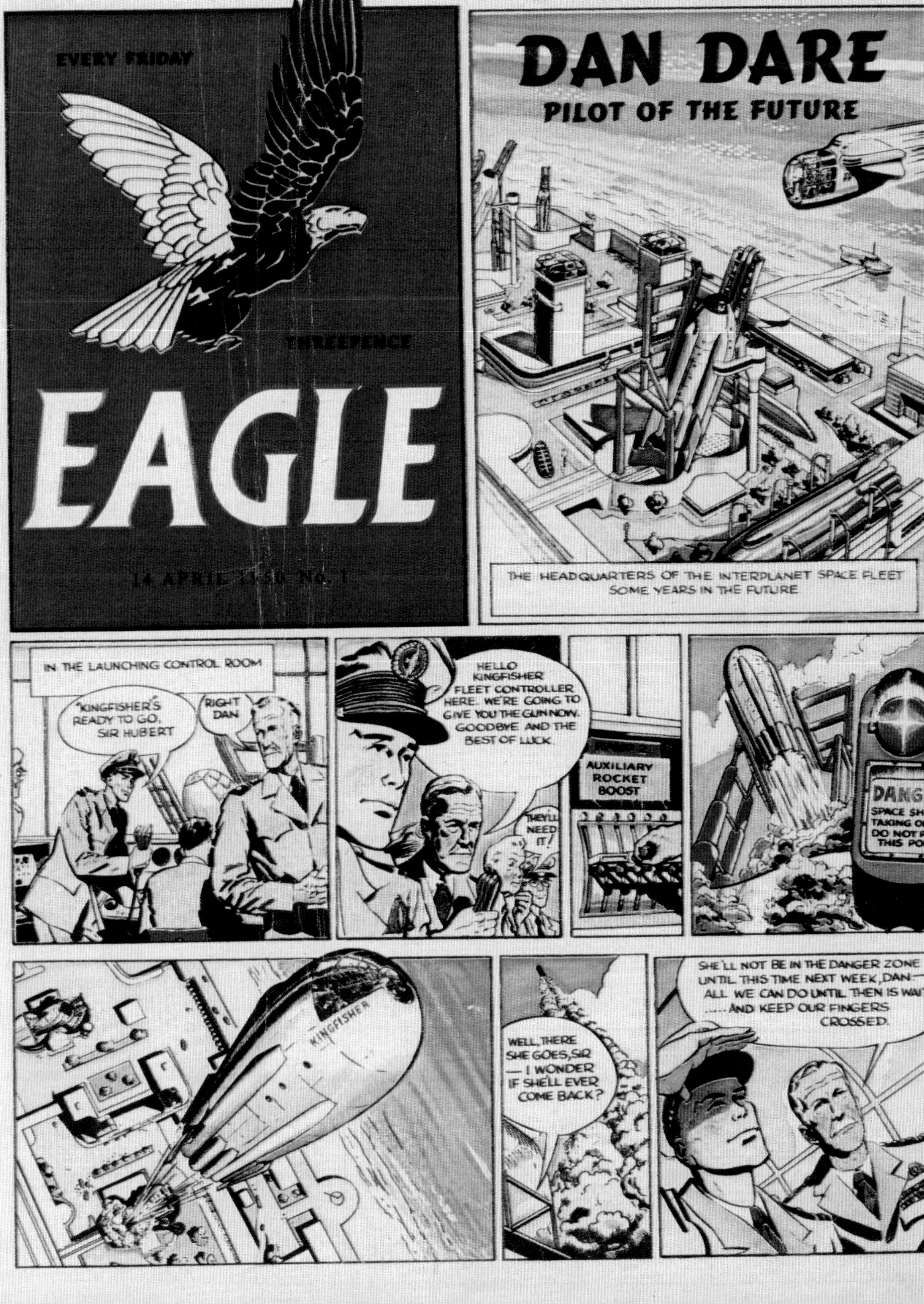
EVERY FRIDAY
THREEPENCE
EAGLE
14 APRIL 1950 No. 1
DAN DARE
PILOT OF THE FUTURE
THE HEADQUARTERS OF THE INTERPLANET SPACE FLEET SOME YEARS IN THE FUTURE
IN THE LAUNCHING CONTROL ROOM
"KINGFISHER'S READY TO GO, SIR HUBERT
RIGHT DAN
HELLO KINGFISHER FLEET CONTROLLER HERE. WE'RE GOING TO GIVE YOU THE GUN NOW. GOODBYE AND THE BEST OF LUCK.
AUXILIARY ROCKET BOOST
THEY'LL NEED IT!
DANGE
SPACE SHIP
TAKING OFF
DO NOT PAS
THIS POINT
KINGFISHER
WELL, THERE SHE GOES, SIR — I WONDER IF SHE'LL EVER COME BACK?
SHE'LL NOT BE IN THE DANGER ZONE UNTIL THIS TIME NEXT WEEK, DAN— ALL WE CAN DO UNTIL THEN IS WAIT .....AND KEEP OUR FINGERS CROSSED.

EAGLE 14 April 1950

THE NEW GAS TURBINE-ELECTRIC LOCOM

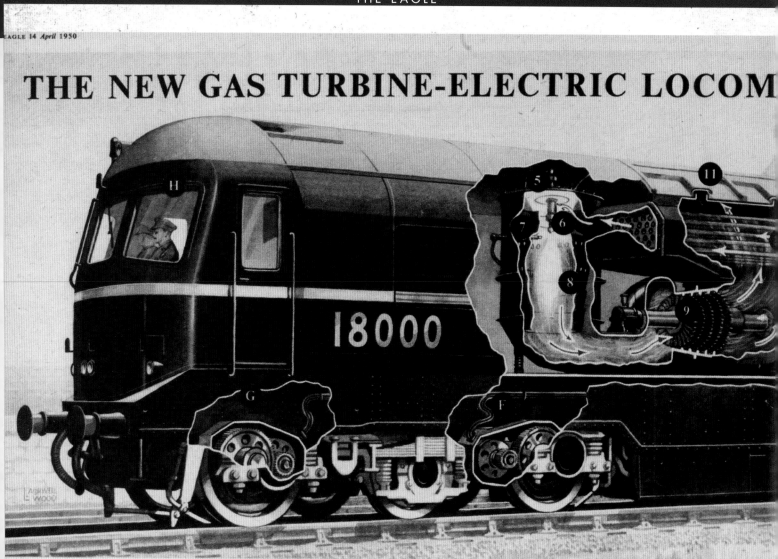

THE CUTAWAYS

The cutaway quickly became one of the first pages that young boys, and their dads, turned to when *Eagle* hit the mat. Detailed drawings in vibrant colours exposed the inner workings of anything the imagination could desire. Trains, planes, boats and automobiles were staples but there really was no limit to what could be opened up to the cutaway's glare. The subjects chosen covered processes from oil production to ice-cream making, buildings such as the 1951 dome at the Festival of Britain, and vast projects including the London Underground and the imagined 'Avenue of the Future'. Several artists, or draughtsmen, really, were used but the most well known is L. Ashwell Wood. Whilst saying he is the most well known, very little is actually known about him. A quick search on the internet merely brings up references to work on *Eagle* and other comics of the time. One *Eagle*

TIVE

EAGLE 14 April 1950

A new-comer to British Railways that will run on the Western Region Section
Length 70 ft. Weight 117 tons.

KEY TO CYCLE OF OPERATIONS

1. Air entry from grill at side of locomotive. 2. Turbine air compressor. 3. Compressed air pipe to pre-heater. 4. Compressed air passes through pipes of pre-heater which are heated by exhaust gases. 5. Oil fuel spray nozzle. 6. Air and fuel are mixed and fired in combustion chamber. 7. Igniter for starting up. 8. Flame tube. 9. Gas turbine, driven by expanding hot gases, drives the air compressor and generator through main shaft. 10. Hot exhaust gases passing upwards between tubes of pre-heater. 11. Exhaust gases to atmosphere. A. Reduction gears driving generator. B. Generator which produces electric power for driving the motors. C. Electric cables to motors. D.E.F.G. Electric motors and reduction gears driving the four main axles. H.H. Driver's control car each end.

18000

reader's father was lucky enough to meet Mr Wood. In a letter to the comic he explains that his father, a coalman, was delivering to an old lady and carried the coal into the front room. Who should he find on entering but none other than L. Ashwell Wood at his easel preparing another wonder of the cutaway world.

Harris Tweed, EXTRA SPECIAL AGENT

Harris Tweed

Harris Tweed was the product of John Ryan's vivid imagination. He is best remembered now as the creator of Captain Pugwash, the character that went on to feature in the popular show of the same name for children on the BBC. In fact 'Pugwash' first saw the light of day in the very first issue of *Eagle*, but his voyage on the high seas only lasted until Issue 19. The general consensus is that Marcus Morris felt it was aimed at too young an audience, but, not wanting to lose Ryan's input totally, he was encouraged to find another outlet for his bold style and slightly off-beat sense of humour. Three weeks before *Pugwash* walked the plank *'Harris Tweed, Extra Special Agent'* appeared.

READERS' LETTERS

(A prize of 5/- is paid for each letter published)

I THINK Fox hunting is a very cruel sport and surely if people must hunt foxes they could shoot them instead of letting the dogs tear them to pieces. – Janice Allen, 9 Trurorean Terrace, Truro, Cornwall.

I AGREE with the reader who mentioned the way people treat coloured folk and cannot understand why, after admiring a coloured sportsman on the field, white people should refuse them a meal in a restaurant. We are told in the Bible all men are our brothers. – Peter Berridge (11), 39 Elmcroft Ave., Edmonton, London N.9.

WHEN I was in Egypt last year I visited a Museum; inside were Egyptian Mummies in cases and very old ornaments. In one case was some ancient jewellery – over a thousand years old – and in another, old carved knives and forks. – Moya Spencer (9), "Green Shutters", Barbrook, Nr. Lynton, Devon.

OUR SCOUT troop recently adopted a 13-year-old leper scout; we collected £5, the cost of a year's treatment and shall receive reports of his progress every six months. – Keith Wright, 17 Wynchcombe Ave., Penn.

I HAVE never walked except on crutches since I was born. I have a private teacher who comes to teach me every day. I have lots of hobbies. A few weeks ago in EAGLE in Readers' Letters someone asked if anyone had as many pen friends as she had. Well I have 189 pen friends all over England and other countries. – Anne Strettle, Fulwood, Preston.

EAGLE CLUB
AND EDITOR'S PAGE

The Editor's Office
EAGLE
43 Shoe Lane, London, E.C.4

WE have had a great many requests from readers that we should start a Pen Pals Group. We have now decided to do this and we invite any of you who would like to make full use of it. Anyone who is interested in having a pen pal should write to 'Pen Pals', 4 New Street Square, London, E.C.4, giving his full name, address and age and a note about the kind of hobbies and pastimes that he is interested in and the type of people to whom he wishes to write. Please put this information on a sheet of paper and then moisten one corner of a 2½d. stamp and attach it to the paper. Enclose also an envelope addressed to yourself (unstamped). It is important that you should not forget the 2½d. stamp because we cannot possibly run the pen pals group if we have to provide stamps for everybody.

HERE are the answers to the competitions in Issue 8.

1. In the *Shapes* competition, the sender of the first correct solution opened was Patricia Tomlinson, Wishanger, Willingdon, Sussex.

2. *Cartoons Wanted*. We had a big entry to choose from in this competition and some of the drawings sent were most entertaining and skilfully drawn. The winning cartoon for the title 'A Black Look' was submitted by

D. Agg, 4 Radford Road, Lewes, Sussex, and we are reproducing his entry.

We are awarding a second prize to Frank Coulson, 22a Wellesley Road, East Croydon. The winning entry for 'A Brown Jumper' was Catherine Worth, 98 Polefield Hall Road, Prestwich, whose entry was delightfully simple and most amusing.

3. *The Noises They Make*: the first correct solution opened was submitted by Ian Barclay, 13 Maryfield Crescent, Leslie, Fife, Scotland, and the answers were:– Warble; Drone; Chirp; Squeak; Quaver; Pip; Chant; Cry; Yelp; Boom.

4. *To Make You Think*: Unfortunately there was a misprint in this competition which made the problem impossible to solve in round figures. The most ingenious attempt at a satisfactory solution, however, was made by John Woodruff, Police Station, Poulton-le-Fylde, Lancashire, and we are sending the prize to him. The problem should have read '3 sons were left £34 in their father's will.' Borrowing £2 and adding this to the £34 equals £36; of this, one half, to the eldest son, amounts to £18; one-third, to the second son, amounts to £12; and one-ninth, to the third son, amounts to £4 – total £34. The executor was then able to return the £2 borrowed.

5. *Do You Know*: The first correct solution opened was submitted by Elizabeth Watson, 30 Kirtleton Avenue, Weymouth, Dorset, and the answers were: Duck Billed Platypus; Guinea Pig; Penguin; Bat; Stickleback; Whale.

6. *Nine 'Ands' In A Row*: No competitor submitted the correct entry for this competition.

You remember that in Issue 5 we had a Test Selection Competition. No one submitted a list of the England team corresponding to the one selected officially. Even by eliminating Compton and regarding Bedser as twelfth man, no one got nearer than eight correct points. We have, therefore, decided not to award a prize for this competition. The prize money will be used to buy special prizes for another cricket competition which we shall be announcing shortly.

Yours sincerely,

THE EDITOR

SPORTING PERSONALITIES

J. A. PALMER-TOMKINSON

HERE ARE SOME OF HIS MAJOR WINS:
1936. The International Academic Ski-ing Championship.
1937. The Great Slilom in Switzerland
1938. The Tempo Trophy.
1039. (With his sister) The British Ski Championship at Wengen.
1947. The Anglo-Swiss University Downhill Race.
1948. The Duke of Kent's Cup.
1950. The Davos Parsenon – in 15·45 seconds – a great performance for a racer of thirty-four.

AS YOU CAN SEE, HIS STYLE IS BOTH VIGOROUS AND GRACEFUL, AND HE IS A MASTER OF DIFFICULT TURNS. SUCH PERFECTION IN THIS SPORT CAN BE ACHIEVED ONLY BY RIGOROUS SELF-DISCIPLINE AND UNREMITTING PRACTICE.

PALMER-TOMKINSON, A BASINGSTOKE FARMER, IS A WORTHY CAPTAIN OF THE BRITISH SKI-TEAM, WITH A WONDERFUL LIST OF INDIVIDUAL SUCCESSES TO HIS CREDIT.
IN 1948, AT WENGEN WERE, HE RAN HIS SKI-STICK POINT INTO HIS THIGH DURING A PRACTICE RUN, AND HAD TO BE TAKEN TO HOSPITAL ON AN IMPROVISED AMBULANCE.

(Above) Sometimes, the *Eagle* did get it wrong. (Left) James competed as a skier at the Winter Olympics either side of the Second World War. His son Charles Anthony Palmer-Tomkinson competed as a skier in the Winter Games of 1964. Charles's daughter Tara Palmer-Tomkinson was runner-up in the 2002 series of *I'm a Celebrity Get Me Out of Here*; no skiing was involved.

FOURPENCE

EVERY FRIDAY

EAGLE

29 SEPTEMBER 1950 No. 25

AS DAN DARE AND HIS COMPANIONS STRUGGLE THROUGH THE WILDS OF VENUS, THE WORLD'S GREATEST NEWSPAPER HIGHLIGHTS THE SUSPENSE AND FAMINE-THREAT BACK ON EARTH

DAILY WORLD POST

No. 17,777   ONE PENNY EUROPE : TEN CENTS PANAMERICA : FOUR ANNAS ASIA : ONE SUT PANAFRICA

PUBLISHED SIMULTANEOUSLY IN LONDON, NEW YORK, SAN FRANCISCO, TOKIO, DELHI, BAKU, ROME, BULAWAYO, SYDNEY AND MARSVILLE

FINAL LISE EDITION   MONDAY 20 SEPTEMBER 1995   THE HULTON PAPER   LONDON

VETERAN SPACEMAN IN MISSING EXPEDITION

SIR HUBERT GUEST, K.C.B., O.U.N., 65-year-old controller of the International Space Fleet, who accompanied the Space Expedition to find food on Venus. Sir Hubert, knighted in 1980 for his lifetime of service with the Fleet, was in the first ship to land on Mars in 1965. He has made over a hundred space flights.

STILL NO NEWS FROM VENUS

RADIO SILENCE BLANKETS DARE'S ROCKETS AS "RANGER" RETURNS TO EARTH

Space Station XI, Monday, 3 a.m.

SPACESHIP "Ranger" landed here an hour ago minus the three Rocket Ships which it carried to within 3,000 miles of Venus in the latest attempt to reach the mystery planet and find food to banish the threat of starvation from Earth.

Tired and worried-looking Captain Hunter, of the "Ranger", boarded a Helicar to the United Nations World Government Headquarters at New York. Thirty minutes later the following bulletin was issued from U.N.W.G.:–

COMMENT

DARE'S ROCKET THEORY JUSTIFIED ?

There seem to be grounds for cautious optimism in the 'partial success' reported in the Government bulletin. The fact that the Rocket Ships built to Colonel Dare's specification did succeed in penetrating the mysterious Ray-screen which has taken such a terrible toll of previous attempts, is the first piece of good news which has come from the planet.

The sad fact that through a radio blunder this brave and brilliant officer and his equally courageous companions may have lost their lives must not be allowed to diminish the importance of their achievement for mankind.

"The Prime Minister regrets to announce that there is as yet no definite information of the success or otherwise of the Rocket Ship expedition to Venus.

In view of the partial success achieved in getting through the Rayfield, a further expedition will be fitted out with Rocket Ships.

The fate of the members of the present expedition is problematic. The *Ranger* will return to orbit the planet in case any kind of signal is sent out by survivors."

Captain Hunter arriving in New York

TENSION MOUNTS IN FAMINE TROUBLE SPOTS

PEKIN, SUNDAY (*delayed*). Central and Southern China is in an explosive condition tonight according to messages reaching here from Canton, Hong Kong and Shanghai. The Teleview communications system has broken down, presumably owing to deliberate interference and messages are being transmitted by radio. Rioting is reported from many provinces as a result of the complete collapse of the food rationing arrangements. Ration cards have not been honoured for over two weeks in some cities.

SENATOR DEMANDS VITAMINEAT PROBE

World Senator Hartwell of North England has called for a U.N. Congressional enquiry into the activities of Vitamineats Inc., the giant International Company which makes and markets the well known Vitamineat Food Substitute Tablets. Charging the Company with using inferior ingredients and making excessive profits, the Senator also hinted that the sabotage of food supply arrangements may be charged against the combine.

Mr. Lucius K. Kettlewell, Chairman and Managing Director of the Company, commented last night, "the Senator had better be careful."

Read

EAGLE
(Incorporating 'Lilliput')
EVERY FRIDAY   4d.

MRS. DIGBY SAYS "HE'S ALIVE ALL RIGHT"

Mrs. Digby and family at their Wigan home

OTHER NEWS

MASS CHANNEL SWIM BY EGYPTIANS

An entire company of the Egyptian Army entered the water at Cap Gris Nez yesterday evening to swim the Channel in formation.

SUCCESS IN EAST AFRICA— PEANUT ARRIVES IN LONDON

There was a touching ceremony at the Strachey Memorial in London yesterday when a whole unblemished peanut was handed to the Minister of Food by a delegation representing equally the native tribes in the groundnut area and the survivors of the Strachey scheme.

WIGAN, Monday.
Interviewed in her Westbank St. home this afternoon, Mrs. Digby, wife of the only "Other Rank" member of the expedition, seemed very confident of her husband's safety. "He'll be all right," she said, when our reporter spoke to her in the parlour of this typically Lancashire home. "Albert's been in plenty of tight spots before with Colonel Dare."

Although 'Dan Dare' is set in the future, the values of the characters are very much of the time in which it is was created. Of course, the main aim of the strip was to excite and intrigue the readers, but this did not mean that they could not be educated along the way. Here we see Sondar, not long after he has first met Dan, showing off his knowledge of Earth customs, and maybe even informing a few readers of something they never previously understood.

You can take a space traveller a gazillion miles from home but he never forgets the simple joy of a home cooked Sunday roast. At a time when very few, if any, of the readers were able to get their hands on roast pheasant, the food fantasies of the crew were probably mirrored in the stomachs of the readers.

AMAZIN
FLYING AND

The Junction at Camden Town, London, wher
crossover junctions. Trains pass under or over
allowing traffic at peak

L ASHWELL
WOOD

THE TUBE

EAGLE 13 *October 1950*

UNDERGROUND
ROSSOVER JUNCTIONS

rthern Underground railway lines meet is a wonderful example of flying and
er without conflicting tracks in either direction in an ingenious layout, thus
o reach a maximum frequency of 110 trains an hour.

KEY TO NUMBERS

1. Camden High Street
2. Drains and street mains
3. Camden Town Station
4. Booking hall
5. Escalator
6. Motors driving escalator steps
7. Subways to platforms
8. Northbound platform to Highgate
9. Southbound platform from Highgate to Moorgate or Charing Cross
10. Southbound platform from Edgware to Moorgate or Charing Cross
11. Northbound platform to Edgware
12. Flyover tunnel
13 and 14. Crossover tunnels
15. Subway between tunnels
16. Burrowing tunnels
17 and 18. Flying junctions
19. Southbound tunnel to Moorgate
20. Northbound tunnel from Moorgate
21. Southbound tunnel to Charing Cross
22. Northbound tunnel from Charing Cross

JUNCTION

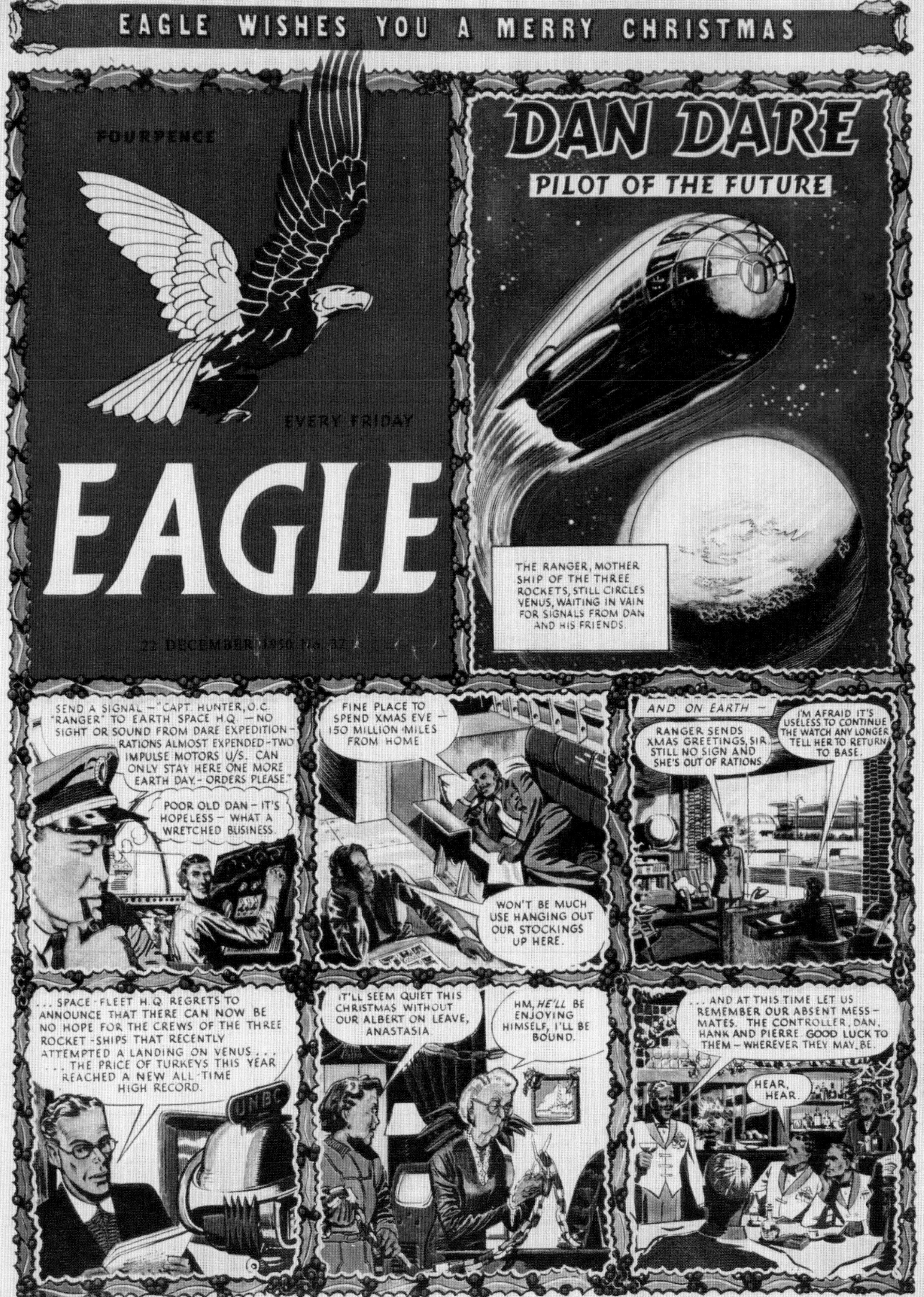
EAGLE WISHES YOU A MERRY CHRISTMAS
FOURPENCE
EVERY FRIDAY
EAGLE
22 DECEMBER 1950 No. 37
DAN DARE
PILOT OF THE FUTURE
THE RANGER, MOTHER SHIP OF THE THREE ROCKETS, STILL CIRCLES VENUS, WAITING IN VAIN FOR SIGNALS FROM DAN AND HIS FRIENDS.
SEND A SIGNAL – "CAPT. HUNTER, O.C. "RANGER" TO EARTH SPACE H.Q. – NO SIGHT OR SOUND FROM DARE EXPEDITION – RATIONS ALMOST EXPENDED – TWO IMPULSE MOTORS U/S. CAN ONLY STAY HERE ONE MORE EARTH DAY. – ORDERS PLEASE."
POOR OLD DAN – IT'S HOPELESS – WHAT A WRETCHED BUSINESS.
FINE PLACE TO SPEND XMAS EVE – 150 MILLION MILES FROM HOME.
WON'T BE MUCH USE HANGING OUT OUR STOCKINGS UP HERE.
AND ON EARTH –
RANGER SENDS XMAS GREETINGS, SIR. STILL NO SIGN AND SHE'S OUT OF RATIONS.
I'M AFRAID IT'S USELESS TO CONTINUE THE WATCH ANY LONGER. TELL HER TO RETURN TO BASE.
. . . SPACE-FLEET H.Q. REGRETS TO ANNOUNCE THAT THERE CAN NOW BE NO HOPE FOR THE CREWS OF THE THREE ROCKET-SHIPS THAT RECENTLY ATTEMPTED A LANDING ON VENUS . . . . . . THE PRICE OF TURKEYS THIS YEAR REACHED A NEW ALL-TIME HIGH RECORD.
UNBC
IT'LL SEEM QUIET THIS CHRISTMAS WITHOUT OUR ALBERT ON LEAVE, ANASTASIA.
HM, HE'LL BE ENJOYING HIMSELF, I'LL BE BOUND.
. . . AND AT THIS TIME LET US REMEMBER OUR ABSENT MESS-MATES. THE CONTROLLER, DAN, HANK AND PIERRE. GOOD LUCK TO THEM – WHEREVER THEY MAY BE.
HEAR, HEAR.

EAGLE CLUB NEWS

A Grand Christmas Present

A great many of you may be wondering what to give as Christmas presents to your brothers, sisters, cousins, friends.

We have got a suggestion for something which would make a really fine Christmas present, and it is one that lasts all the year round. Why not give your friends EAGLE or GIRL every week? We will see it is posted regularly to whatever address you give us, and we will let you have a special Christmas card for you to send off personally to your friends, letting them know that they will be receiving the paper every week during 1952. We think you can be sure that any one would be very glad to get a present like this.

All you have to do is to send a cheque or postal order made out to "Hulton Press Ltd." for 26/- if you want EAGLE or GIRL to be sent every week for one year: 13/- if you only want it to last for 6 months, and 6/6d if you want it to last for 3 months.

Send your cheque or postal order to The Editor, EAGLE, 43 Shoe Lane, London E.C.4, giving your name and address, and the name and address of the person to whom you wish the paper sent.

Eagle Carol Service

(See Editor's Letter)

Please send me .... admission (state number) tickets for the EAGLE Carol Service to be held at 3.30 p.m. on Saturday, 22nd December in Central London. I enclose stamped addressed envelope.

Your Name ....

Address ....

Readers' Letters

(A prize of 5/- is given for each letter published)

THANK YOU for the lovely service in St Paul's Cathedral on Saturday, December 22nd. I was very pleased to see so many people there and I am sure they enjoyed it as much as I did. I was also pleased to find so many of my favourite carols included. I thought the Christmas trees were very pretty outside the Cathedral and inside. – Judith Nuttall, 7 Red Cottages, Broadwater, Stevenage, Herts.

* * *

NOT VERY long ago I learned to drive a tractor. I can now drive it perfectly along the road and I can change all the gears for going round corners and through gates. – Peter Ewing (11), 3 New Houses, Papigoe, By Wick, Caithness.

EAGLE 25 January 1952

EAGLE CLUB NEWS
SALVO OF FUN AT STREATHAM

Balloon blowing takes some doing after such a big tea!

"Stick 'em up!" says cowboy Charles Chilton.

The Editor and the Mayor of Streatham stand up to a bit of friendly heckling.

The Mayor, with the Mayoress looking on, gets down to a friendly chat.

READERS' LETTERS

(A prize of 5/- is paid for each letter published)

READERS who go to church often will notice that every week the people and the Vicar say or sing the same prayers. Do you think that God gets tired of the same prayers every week? – Neil Upton, 52 Tennis Court Drive, Humberstone, Leicester.

[No, I'm sure He doesn't. I think He would prefer a lot more people to do it. It's because the words are the same and well-known, that we can all join together in the prayers. – Ed.]

ALL MALTESE readers are eagerly following "The Great Adventurer" as the story is now nearing the time when Paul will be shipwrecked on the rocks of Malta. This event is written in letters of gold in the history of Malta – we are all very proud of it. – Joe Camilleri, 101 Vinc. Bugeja Street, Hamrun, Malta G.C.

[This incident is shown in this week's issue. – Ed.]

MOST EAGLERS will know what a Dunce is, but I wonder how many will know what a Dunce was originally. The first Dunces were followers of Duns Scotus, a churchman opposed to the Renaissance. – M. Gough, Vicarage Lane, Swanmore, Southampton.

I AM a Chinese boy studying in an English School, and your magazine is very popular in my class. Everybody takes great interest in reading it and I like to read it also, for it deals with so many useful things. – Lew Chin Woon, 774 North Bridge Road, Singapore 7.

DO EAGLERS know that a clerk was once buried in the Bank of England? This man was an eight-foot giant whose name was Jenkins – he wanted to be buried there so that his body could not be taken by body-snatchers and sold, as a predecessor had been. – Pamela Thompson (15), 30 Ronald Drive, Denton Burn, Newcastle-on-Tyne 5.

I HAVE a set of jugs which belonged to my great, great, great, great auntie – she had them in 1786. – Maldwyn Rowland, 31 Brynhyford Terrace, Waunllwyd, Ebbw Vale, Mon.

From the Editor

EAGLE, 4 New St Square, London EC4

21 December, 1951

ON this, your second Christmas as EAGLE readers, my staff and I want to send you our warmest greetings for a very Merry Christmas. May all of you enjoy a very happy time and have the good fortune to receive the Christmas present you most want.

Amidst all our Christmas fun and exchange of presents, I want you to remember especially the real spirit of Christmas, which we sometimes tend to forget. Christmas Day is the birthday of Jesus Christ, and we give each other presents in remembrance of the gifts brought to Him by the Wise Men from the East. But we have rather wandered away from the original idea of present-giving at Christmas time. Long ago, it was the poor and needy who were given presents and this is something, amid our exchange of gifts with our friends, which we should remember. I asked you a few weeks ago to try to spare a toy in nice condition for the children in your nearest hospital or orphanage. If you have done this, then you are helping to rekindle the true Spirit of Christmas and soon you will find others following your good example.

ON our back page, this week and next, we try to present to you the Christmas story as it might have appeared to someone living on the spot at the time. Among the shepherds on the hill side at Bethlehem, there was almost certain to have been a boy helping his father to tend the sheep and run errands. Our back page tells how the tremendous events of the first Christmas appeared to this boy, and how the birth of the baby Jesus affected his life and that of his family.

OUR Carol Service takes place in St Paul's Cathedral tomorrow, Saturday afternoon. Will you please note that we have had to change the time of the Service from 3.30 to 2.30 p.m. Tell as many of your friends as possible about this change. St Paul's, known and loved throughout the British Empire, is yours for that afternoon, and it is up to you, representing the youth of Britain, to fill it to overflowing. I want to hear your Christmas praises ring round the Cathedral in no uncertain manner. So come, all of you who can. If you haven't got an admission ticket, never mind – we can fit you in somehow. Your parents can come with you if they want to.

I WOULD like to thank you all for the good wishes and Christmas Cards which have already reached my staff and me. It is our wish that through these pages of EAGLE we shall continue to give you as much happiness as we possibly can.

Yours sincerely,

Marcus Morris

Wherever Dan and the crew happened to be at Christmas, and whatever year it was, they always remembered to send a festive greeting back-in-time to the Fifties. The front covers of the late December issues were always decorated in some way to celebrate the time of year, and the crew always took time out from saving the universe to think of home.

EAGLE-BRITAIN'S NATIONAL STRIP CARTOON WEEKLY

The front cover of Issue 48 of Volume 1 (9 March 1951) highlights the sheer exuberance of the comic's artwork to a fantastic degree. It also, maybe, refers to the fighting that was raging in the East in 1951. The Korean War was close to reaching its first anniversary and was turning out to be the biggest global conflict since the end of hostilities in 1945. Was the *Eagle* trying to use this cover to convey images and iconography from this conflict?

DAN DARE
PILOT OF THE FUTURE

THE SHADOW OF WAR LOOMS OVER THE PLANET VENUS AS THE TREENS, SCIENTIFIC AUTOMATONS, PREPARE TO ATTACK THE THERONS FOR "INTERFERING" WITH THE TREEN PLAN TO TAKE OVER THE EARTH

FOR THE FIRST TIME IN CENTURIES THE TREENS SWITCH OFF THEIR RAY BARRIER OVER THE FLAME – BELT WHICH DIVIDES THE PLANET BETWEEN THE TREENS IN THE NORTH AND THE THERONS IN THE SOUTH.

HIGH FLYING TREEN RECONNAISSANCE TELEVIEW PLANES STREAK THROUGH THE STRATOSPHERE TOWARDS THE BORDER.

THROW SWITCH TWO ON NUMBER THREE – DOUBLE BANK CONDENSERS AND LINK RECTIFIERS FOR SECOND POWER STEP-UP. BRING IN MOTORS FOUR & FIVE.

IN MEKONTA, THE TREEN CAPITAL WHERE MANY WAR MACHINES ARE BEING SET TO WORK, THE TELEZERO BEAM PROJECTORS BEGIN TO BUILD UP POWER TO STRIKE AT THERON CITIES.

TELEZEROS THREE AND SEVEN WILL REACH FIRST SHORT RANGE OPERATIONAL POWER LEVEL IN ONE TAMIT. WE SHALL THEN BOOST CONTINUALLY UNTIL WE REACH MAXIMUM RANGE. THE REFLECTOR SPACE – CRAFT HAVE BEEN ALERTED TO TAKE OFF AS SOON AS WE RECEIVE THE ORDER.

THE TINY MEKON, RUTHLESS LORD OF THE TREENS, REVIEWS THE PROGRESS OF HIS PLANS

GOOD – HAS THE MOBILISATION OF THE ATLANTINE SERFS COMMENCED?

YES, O MEKON. MILITARY PARTIES ARE OUT COLLECTING THEM IN THE RESERVATIONS

THE HELPLESS ATLANTINES — DESCENDANTS OF HUMAN SLAVES CAPTURED CENTURIES AGO, ARE ROUNDED UP TO ACT AS CANNON FODDER FOR THEIR INHUMAN MASTERS

ADVICE ON YOUR PETS

Keeping Goldfish

By Professor Cameron

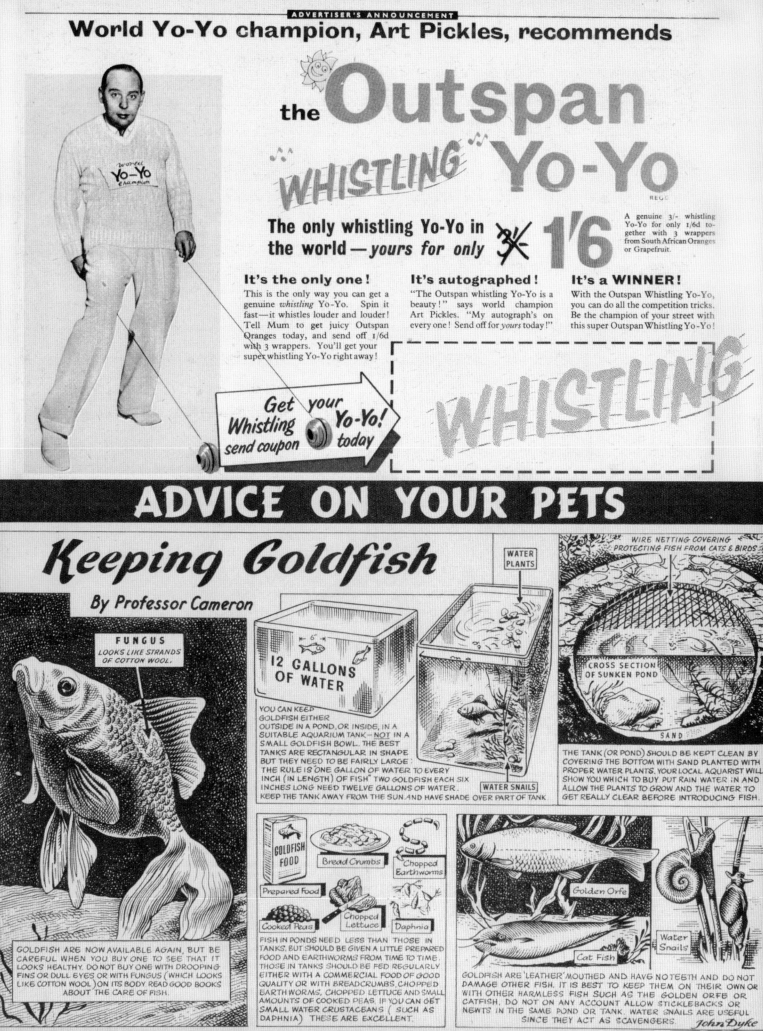

FUNGUS LOOKS LIKE STRANDS OF COTTON WOOL.

12 GALLONS OF WATER

WATER PLANTS

WATER SNAILS

YOU CAN KEEP GOLDFISH EITHER OUTSIDE IN A POND, OR INSIDE, IN A SUITABLE AQUARIUM TANK—NOT IN A SMALL GOLDFISH BOWL. THE BEST TANKS ARE RECTANGULAR IN SHAPE BUT THEY NEED TO BE FAIRLY LARGE: THE RULE IS ONE GALLON OF WATER TO EVERY INCH (IN LENGTH) OF FISH. TWO GOLDFISH EACH SIX INCHES LONG NEED TWELVE GALLONS OF WATER. KEEP THE TANK AWAY FROM THE SUN AND HAVE SHADE OVER PART OF TANK.

WIRE NETTING COVERING PROTECTING FISH FROM CATS & BIRDS

CROSS SECTION OF SUNKEN POND

SAND

THE TANK (OR POND) SHOULD BE KEPT CLEAN BY COVERING THE BOTTOM WITH SAND PLANTED WITH PROPER WATER PLANTS. YOUR LOCAL AQUARIST WILL SHOW YOU WHICH TO BUY. PUT RAIN WATER IN AND ALLOW THE PLANTS TO GROW AND THE WATER TO GET REALLY CLEAR BEFORE INTRODUCING FISH.

GOLDFISH ARE NOW AVAILABLE AGAIN, BUT BE CAREFUL WHEN YOU BUY ONE TO SEE THAT IT LOOKS HEALTHY. DO NOT BUY ONE WITH DROOPING FINS OR DULL EYES OR WITH FUNGUS (WHICH LOOKS LIKE COTTON WOOL) ON ITS BODY. READ GOOD BOOKS ABOUT THE CARE OF FISH.

GOLDFISH FOOD

Bread Crumbs

Chopped Earthworms

Prepared Food

Chopped Lettuce

Daphnia

Cooked Peas

FISH IN PONDS NEED LESS THAN THOSE IN TANKS, BUT SHOULD BE GIVEN A LITTLE PREPARED FOOD AND EARTHWORMS FROM TIME TO TIME. THOSE IN TANKS SHOULD BE FED REGULARLY EITHER WITH A COMMERCIAL FOOD OF GOOD QUALITY OR WITH BREADCRUMBS, CHOPPED EARTHWORMS, CHOPPED LETTUCE AND SMALL AMOUNTS OF COOKED PEAS. IF YOU CAN GET SMALL WATER CRUSTACEANS (SUCH AS DAPHNIA) THESE ARE EXCELLENT.

Golden Orfe

Water Snails

Cat Fish

GOLDFISH ARE 'LEATHER' MOUTHED AND HAVE NO TEETH AND DO NOT DAMAGE OTHER FISH. IT IS BEST TO KEEP THEM ON THEIR OWN OR WITH OTHER HARMLESS FISH SUCH AS THE GOLDEN ORFE OR CATFISH. DO NOT ON ANY ACCOUNT ALLOW STICKLEBACKS OR NEWTS IN THE SAME POND OR TANK. WATER SNAILS ARE USEFUL SINCE THEY ACT AS SCAVENGERS.

John Dyke

A LOCOMOTIVE DEPOT AT WORK

THE RAIL

EAGLE 16 March 1951

...is is an ideal layout for a Motive Power Depot, as it is correctly called, of the "...hrough road" type, that is, the tracks run parallel through the engine shed thus ...king up less space than the roundhouse type where the tracks radiate from a central ...ntable.

...these sheds the locomotive receives every attention necessary to keeping it in ...ning order. The numbered stages show the series of operations from the time the ...omotive backs in from its last journey until it is ready again for the next. The types ...locomotives shown are the new standard ones of British Railways in three colour ...emes.

KEY TO SEQUENCE OF OPERATIONS

(1) Acceptance road from main line. Fireman 'phones "On shed". (2) At the coaling tower. (3) Re-filling tender with water. (4) At the ash dropping pits. The ashes are taken in a hopper and hoisted to a discharge tower. (5) On the vacuum-operated turntable. (6) Engine now backs to inspection pits. (7) Enter shed – fitters take over. (8) Steam hydrants are used for smoke box cleaning and boiler washing. (9) Cleaning, lighting up and steam raising. (10) Exit shed, new crew take over and check water, coal, oil, etc., and vacuum brakes. (11) Fireman 'phones "Off shed" and engine is ready to enter main line to terminus. (12) Main line express out of terminus.

KEY TO OTHER NUMBERS

(13) Drivers' notice board for instructions. (14) Loco. superintendent's office. (15) Canteen and rest room. (16) Boiler house. (17) Empty trucks from coaling tower. (18) Full trucks for coaling tower move down slope by gravity and are hoisted to top of tower and emptied into a huge bunker. (19) Ash hopper discharge tower. (20) Ash trucks. (21) Running repair shops. (22) Engine having wheels dropped. (23) Floodlights for night operations. (23) Staff allotments.

DEPOT

HOW *EAGLE* IS PRODUCED

The complete story from a tree to your home

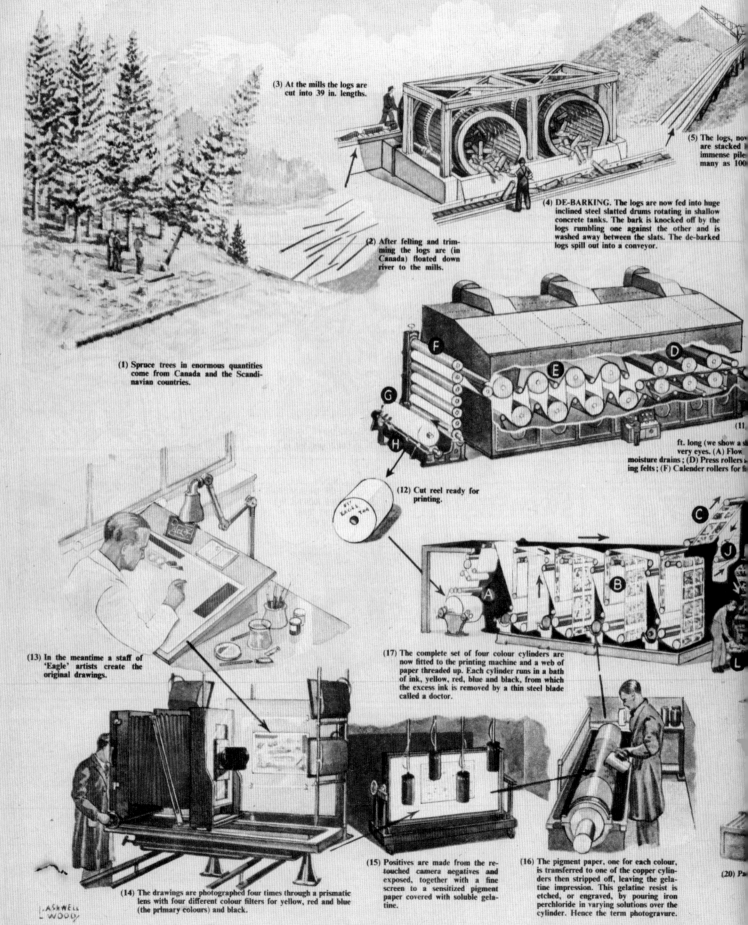

(3) At the mills the logs are cut into 39 in. lengths.

(5) The logs, now are stacked immense pile many as 100

(4) DE-BARKING. The logs are now fed into huge inclined steel slatted drums rotating in shallow concrete tanks. The bark is knocked off by the logs rumbling one against the other and is washed away between the slats. The de-barked logs spill out into a conveyor.

(2) After felling and trimming the logs are (in Canada) floated down river to the mills.

(1) Spruce trees in enormous quantities come from Canada and the Scandinavian countries.

(11

ft. long (we show a s very eyes. (A) Flow moisture drains; (D) Press rollers ing felts; (F) Calender rollers for fi

(12) Cut reel ready for printing.

(13) In the meantime a staff of 'Eagle' artists create the original drawings.

(17) The complete set of four colour cylinders are now fitted to the printing machine and a web of paper threaded up. Each cylinder runs in a bath of ink, yellow, red, blue and black, from which the excess ink is removed by a thin steel blade called a doctor.

(14) The drawings are photographed four times through a prismatic lens with four different colour filters for yellow, red and blue (the primary colours) and black.

(15) Positives are made from the retouched camera negatives and exposed, together with a fine screen to a sensitized pigment paper covered with soluble gelatine.

(16) The pigment paper, one for each colour, is transferred to one of the copper cylinders then stripped off, leaving the gelatine impression. This gelatine resist is etched, or engraved, by pouring iron perchloride in varying solutions over the cylinder. Hence the term photogravure.

(20) Pa

L. ASHWELL WOOD

PAPER MAKING

This is the story of *Eagle*. How many of you realise that your favourite magazine started life in a forest in far away Canada?

This sequence of pictures depicts the huge organisation and planning necessary to place a copy in your hands.

The first stages of the breaking down of the wood into fibres is done in two ways, one wholly mechanical, as shown here, and the other chiefly chemical. The mechanical pulp contributes 80 per cent of the mass of finished paper but as the structure of the fibres is not strong, the remaining 20 per cent consists of chemical pulp of larger fibres which bind the others together.

The chemical pulp comes from similar wood but is boiled or digested by steam into which is added a solution of sulphur dioxide and bisulphate of calcium. After washing, the chemical pulp, known as "half-stuff", is mixed with the mechanical pulp.

The pulp is imported into this country and now has to be transformed into paper, the simplified principle of which, is passing water containing the pulp over a fine sieve or screen, when the water runs away and a thin layer of pulp is left behind. This layer, when removed from the screen, dried and glazed, is the finished sheet of paper. This finished paper 25 ft. wide comes out of the huge machines at the rate of 1,400 feet a minute.

PRINTING

This is done by a rotary photogravure process which is the most up-to-date in the country and the wonderful machine which prints it is shown in simplified form.

The basic principle of the photogravure process is its use of an engraved or indented surface from which the paper receives its impression, the cylinders being flooded with ink and scraped by a thin steel blade, termed a doctor blade, so that the surface is cleaned again and the ink left only in the engraved portions to make contact with the printing paper and so produce the image as you see it.

All the colours of the original drawings must be reproduced by four colours and their combinations, so that four cylinders are produced which will print yellow, red, blue and black respectively. The superimposition of these coloured printed images will reproduce the colours and tones (you learn at school that yellow and blue make green, etc.) seen in your copy of *Eagle*.

DISTRIBUTION

The distribution of the magazine is a system unto itself, involving careful marketing, finance and transport. At last you get it from your local shop and there is *Eagle* ready for your pleasure.

(7) BEATING. Here the pulp is circulated and is further disintegrated by bruising to produce ends to the fibres. (A) At this stage chemical sulphite pulp known as "half-stuff" is also beaten into the mixture; (B) Roller with blunt knives; (C) Concrete hill; (D) Water supply.

(6) GRINDING INTO PULP. The logs are next conveyed to batteries of voracious grinders each driven by a 2,000 h.p. motor. (A) Operators slide the logs into the feed pockets; (B) Water supply; (C) Sandstone grinder roll; (D) Toothed pressure lead forcing logs against grinder. (E) Oil pressure piston cylinders. (F) Steaming ground pulp; more water is added and the pulp, after screening, is pumped to the beaters. This is called mechanical pulp.

(8) The pulp is again screened and filtered and pressed into sheets like blotting paper for export to the British Isles.

(9) A continuous stream of freight ships bring the wood pulp to our shores.

... MACHINE. The liquid pulp (like porridge), is pumped ... of a Fourdrinier paper machine. These machines are 360 ... for convenience). Here the pulp turns to paper before your ... (B) Web of wet pulp; (C) Wire screen through which the ... (E) Main paper drying cylinders semi-encircled by dry-... "the paper; (G) Finished roll of paper; (H) Roll cutters.

(10) The imported pulp is shredded and fed to another beater; here is added a liquid proportion of china clay to improve the surface and resin as a size to prevent ink spread.

(18) ROTARY PHOTOGRAVURE PRINTING MACHINE. (A) Paper reel; (B) First colour printing, one side only; (C) Paper passes to the other end for colour printing on reverse side; (D) Ink scraper or doctor blade; (E) Printing cylinder and ink reservoir; (F) Impression cylinder holding paper against printing cylinder; (G) Second colour printing on reverse side; (H) Webb is now split by a cutter into page width and parts company on its way to the folder; (I) In the meantime, the black and white section is being printed on one side at the back of this machine and passes right over to the left to be printed on the other; (J) The black printing returns and is split; (K) The four split webs come together and are cut and folded into 8 sheets; (L) Delivery of copies.

Copies ready for despatch.

(21) Labelling and despatch.

(22) By road or express train to wholesaler.

(23) Wholesaler to retailer.

(24) Retail shop.

(25) EAGLERS

First Birthday!

EAGLE is one year old

MARCUS MORRIS, *Editor.*

FRANK HAMPSON, *creator and artist of 'Dan Dare'.* 32-year-old Lancashire born. Worked on EAGLE when it was first thought of. Hobby – playing with three-year-old son Peter.

ELLEN VINCENT, *Editorial Assistant.* Worked with advertising firm. Hobby – Music.

CHARLES GREEN, *Editorial Assistant.* Makes model ships and railways. Hobby – Amateur dramatics.

ERIC BEMROSE, *head of the firm who print* EAGLE. Hobbies – Photography and Radio.

"TELL them how the thing started," suggested someone.

"What *thing?*" asked the Editor coldly.

"EAGLE, of course – tell them how it began."

"And all that's happened since – up till now," put in someone else.

"Not all, I hope," commented the staff cynic. "There are some things best forgotten."

"Like the time you put in a wrong instalment of a strip, for example?" suggested my neighbour callously. "Though I will say this for you – nobody noticed, which just goes to show."

We were all together in the Editor's room at what we are pleased to call an Editorial Conference. That simply means that the editorial staff were scattered around the room in positions of varying inelegance, perched on the arms of chairs and the edges of tables – and arguing about what special features to put in the birthday issue.

Various suggestions had been put forward. An editorial suggester usually starts off full of enthusiasm and ends up rather lamely – withered by the glare of half a dozen pairs of critical eyes.

But this suggestion seemed to hit the nail on the head – at least the Editor thought so, and his decision is always final.

"Yes, I think that's a good idea," he said, "and we could put in photographs of you all – if the paper will stand it."

So that's how this story came to be written. We weren't at all sure whether you (our readers) would *want* to know how EAGLE started – still less what we all looked like. But we decided to risk it.

"Of course, it really all started in the bath – the idea of EAGLE I mean," went on the Editor. "But we'd better miss that part out – and how Hampson and I worked on the idea at home for nine months and then touted it round London, getting turned down by one publisher after another. Better start from when Hulton Press took it up, and decided to publish. Now who's going to write the story?"

The Editor looked round the room. We shuffled uneasily in our chairs.

"Better make it a combined effort," he said, in a determined voice. "All put down your impressions – and then we'll sort them out."

IT was towards the end of 1949 when EAGLE really got going – six months before the first issue came out. While the Editor and the staff contacted artists and writers, sorted out material, planned features and then scrapped them, and gradually battered the paper into shape, others carried out complicated research into what boys liked most to read, how much pocket money they got, and what they spent it on.

Others planned the advertising campaigns to launch the paper. Others again planned schemes for giving the paper publicity among those who were (we hoped) going to read it.

Some suggestions were more hare-brained than others. The Editor, one bright spark suggested, should parachute into Hyde Park dressed up as an eagle. Then someone thought of letting off 200,000 balloons in various parts of the country – until the thought of the time and puff required to blow up that many balloons put it out of court.

At last we decided on the *Hunt the Eagle* plan. Cars with giant effigies of golden eagles on them were engaged to tour the country. Inside the cars,

loudspeakers announced "EAGLE is coming". Gift vouchers were hidden everywhere – the finder could claim a free copy at the nearest newsagent. And that nearly started a riot! We heard of one gang who gathered a handful of vouchers, collected their free copies from the shops, and then sold them at the street corner.

So the first number went off – and, back in the office, we held our breaths.

Then came the avalanche. Orders poured in from newsagents all over the country. EAGLE was selling like hot cakes.

But we needed more than a good start. We needed paper too. And of paper there seemed to be less and less every week – at a higher and

EAGLE *gets around – in fact, all over the world. Some of our keenest readers are the children of Tombstone, Arizona.*

Many thousands of letters reach us week by week. Here is the Editor and his secretary looking through some of them.

higher price. We had to take two bitter decisions. We must limit the size to sixteen pages, and that meant putting lots of ideas in cold storage. And EAGLE would have to go up to 4d. But our readers went on buying it in spite of that, in ever increasing numbers.

Meanwhile the rapid success of EAGLE Club almost overwhelmed us. Over 60,000 joined in the first week – and sixty thousand is a lot of letters to have about the place. An emergency staff worked all hours to get out the badges and membership cards – and each week the numbers increased.

That's how we began meeting some of our readers – at the trips and parties and prize-winning expeditions we arranged for Club members. That was the best part of all – meeting our readers.

The MUG's Badge took on too – though some people didn't understand the name at first. "A

special badge for those who are especially helpful to others – that's the idea," we explained. "We call them MUGS because that's what the spivs call people who help others. So we'll turn the tables on the spivs by being proud of the title."

Some got the wrong idea about how to win a MUG's badge. They thought the only way was to rescue someone from drowning. "Bill spends all his time by the canal waiting for someone to fall in," one father wrote. We hurriedly explained some of the thousand other ways of earning a MUG's badge. And now the idea seems to have caught on.

Then there are the letters – hundreds of them every week – from readers, giving their views and

An EAGLE reader takes a tumble while winter sporting in North Italy. The rest of the party tell him what he did wrong.

EAGLE *readers inspect the latest Minic toys. A visit to this London toy factory was one of the outings organized recently by EAGLE Club.*

criticisms and preferences. They are very frank and very helpful, and we keep a careful record of them all. We built up a staff of experts to answer the questions we received. "Please explain shortly Einstein's theory of relativity," one boy wrote. "Can you get me two tickets for the Cup-final?" asked another. (We couldn't!)

Then we started a *Hobbies Advice Bureau* and a *Pen Pals Scheme* – and that brought in thousands more letters.

How does it all work? And who does the work? As well as our Editorial staff, we have our staff of full-time artists – some of whom you see here. Then we have many other artists and writers and ideas men working for us.

Here's how it usually goes. The script-writer sends in his script for a strip-cartoon – *Riders of the Range*, for example (in this case Charles Chilton). This goes off to the artist who draws it in rough pencil form, back it comes for editorial

ROSEMARY GARLAND, *Editorial Assistant*, writes children's books. Expert on lighthouses. Hobby – Painting pictures.

JAMES HEMMING, *Editorial Consultant.* Author of five books. Went round the world lecturing in 1949. Hobby – Tennis.

CHAD VARAH, *Editorial Consultant.* Reports on all manuscripts. Escaped after arrest by Nazis in 1934. Hobby – Photography.

RUARI MCLEAN, *Editorial Consultant*, expert typographer. Ex-submarine Officer. Hobby – Driving an Austin 7.

PHYLLIS WASEY, *Secretary.* Has been with EAGLE since the first issue came out. Hobbies – Swimming and Cycling.

JOHN RYAN, *artist and creator of 'Harris Tweed'.* Teaches art at big Public School. Hobby – Collecting Roman coins.

ASHWELL WOOD, *Centre-spread artist.* Trained engineer, one-time draughtsman in aircraft company. Hobby – Cricket.

JACK DANIEL, *'Riders of the Range' artist.* Was a newspaper cartoonist. Ex-Desert Rat. Hobbies – Sculpture and Squash.

NORMAN WILLIAMS, *'Great Adventurer' artist.* Trained in Sheffield. Was a newspaper strip-cartoonist. Hobby – Stamp Collecting.

STROM GOULD. *'P.C. 49' artist.* Has 'panned' for gold, caught sharks and snakes. Hobby – Collecting New Guinea carvings.

HAROLD JOHNS, *Assistant artist on 'Dan Dare'.* Born in Devon, trained at Southport School of Art. Hobby – Photography.

Here are Miss Peabody, Sir Hubert and Digby posing in EAGLE studio for artist Frank Hampson in a dramatic scene from DAN DARE.

approval; back to the artist to do the finished artwork. Then when the balloons are lettered, the page is ready – some time in advance, we hope, of press day. Similarly the great number of stories sent in to us are vetted by one of our Readers, approved or rejected – and if approved, sent to an artist to be illustrated.

At last all the material is ready and up it goes to Liverpool by train in a special sealed satchel. A week later we get back a pasted-up "dummy" of the issue for our corrections and alterations. And so the issue goes to press, and the copies roll off the machine, 12,000 an hour, 200 a minute, 3½ a second. Our centre-spread this week shows how it is done.

And meanwhile our EAGLE Club staff are busy arranging the holidays and outings, and despatching the Club badges, the MUG's badges, the articles of one kind or another that EAGLE Club produce.

It's a busy life and it never stops.

How about the future? Well, we've got plenty of ideas and plans – but it would rather spoil things to tell you about them now. Our aim is "Bigger and Better" – and we hope to make use of many of the ideas you have sent in to us.

Meanwhile, thank you for all your letters, encouraging and congratulating us. Although its our birthday, not yours, we still want to wish you – and ourselves – "Many happy returns" of EAGLE birthdays.

JOHN RUSSELL, *Club Staff.* In charge of outside activities. Served in the Navy. Hobbies – Squash and Swimming.

DAN DARE, *Colonel,* Chief Pilot of International Inter-planet Space Fleet. Hobby – Jet Cricket.

When EAGLE was first started, we sent out cars bearing these huge golden eagles to all the most important towns in the country, to announce "EAGLE is coming".

A FLYING WING JET AIR-LINER

FLYING

THE FUTURE

Our artist's impression of a flying wing aircraft is based on scientific data and is quite within the realms of possibility. In fact an American 8 jet-propelled bomber — the Northropp YB-49 — is already built but still on the secret list. In the air-liner the whole of the cabin and cargo space is pressurized for high altitude flying at high speeds.

Eight super-jet engines give adequate power. New type combined elevator-aileron controls counteract the tendency to a nose-down movement when the take-off and landing flaps are used. An aircraft of this type would fly non-stop by night to America or India with sleeping passengers.

KEY TO NUMBERS

(1) Rudder and fin (port and starboard). (2) Side-slip indicator. (3) Exhaust vents for de-icing warm air. (4) Corrector for horizontal trim. (5) Aileron - elevator controller. (6) Trim tab. (7) Hydraulic operating gear. (8) Main spar. (9) Outer fuel tanks. (10) De-icing pipe from engines and air corrugations in leading edge of wing. (11) Air intakes to jet engines. (12) Four port super-jet engines. (13) Port undercarriage (retracted). (14) Inner fuel tanks. (15) Passengers' observation windows. (16) Lounge. (17) Galley and pantry. (18) Radio operator and navigator. (19) Captain and first officer. (20) Flight engineer. (21) Dining room. (22) Four starboard superjet engines. (23) Starboard undercarriage (retracted). (24) Two berth cabins. (25) Skylights and emergency exits. (26) Gentlemen's dressing room and toilet. (27) Ladies' dressing room and toilet. (28) Main entrance under wing. (29) Mails. (30) Freight. (31) Slotted flaps to assist take-off and landing. (32) Double skin of pressurized wing.

WING

DAN DARE
THE RED MOON MYSTERY

BE STILL, WILLY!

Dan and Co's plan to lure the Red Moon away from Earth with a chlorophyll light has succeeded and now, having met the Treen Fleet, they are transferring to Sondar's ship to watch the Treens attack the asteroid with their projectors.

DAN DARE

THE RED MOON MYSTERY

EAGLE CHRONICLERS

HERE are some more notes for *our* Chronicle of the *imaginary* town of Hulton Pressborough. Remember, these notes are only *examples* of the sort of things you should be looking for to include in your *real* chronicle of the district or place in which you live.

A.10. The Hulton Pressborough district is rich in dialect words and sayings not commonly encountered elsewhere. They are especially to be found among the older inhabitants of the surrounding villages. The following is a list of some of these sayings, with their more generally known equivalents. The last two seem to be most rarely used in modern times, but they were remembered by Mr William Longfurrow, an 81-year-old retired farm-worker of Great Ravenscroft, who recalls hearing them as a boy.

Local saying	Equivalent meaning
Don't pick your flowers and expect a showy garden.	You can't have your cake and eat it.
Open mind – shut mouth.	Wise men keep still tongues in their heads.
A crumb o' comfort's worth an oven full of dreams.	A bird in the hand's worth two in the bush.
Kind words often granite soften.	A soft answer turneth away wrath.
Rust, and you'll eat crust, Wear, and you'll better fare.	It's better to wear out than to rust out. (Through laziness).
Half-aquartern's still bread.	Half a loaf is better than no bread.

AND: EAGLE CHRONICLERS
A JOB FOR EVERYONE

WE feel that EAGLE and its readers should play their full part in the Festival of Britain this year. We are, therefore, launching on a nation-wide scale, a brand new scheme to enable *you* to play *your* part, and we hope that all of you will join in. Our EAGLE *Chroniclers Scheme* is something which can last for a very long time, and which can be of real benefit to future generations.

This is how it works:—

How is it that you know that King Alfred burnt the cakes, and that Lady Godiva saved Coventry from excessive taxation? It is only because someone at the time who lived near where these incidents happened took the trouble to write them down, and their records have been passed on to us. But thousands of similar events, which would have been of great interest to us, have been lost because there was no one to chronicle them.

During this Festival of Britain year especially, a great deal of local history may be made. Need the record of all this be lost, or can we EAGLE readers help in chronicling it for the future?

Forming a Group

We suggest that *Eaglers* in the same school or the same district should form a group, and together plan to produce a Chronicle of their own town or district or village. They should invite some one older (perhaps their headmaster or headmistress) to act as Editor-in-Chief, and give advice.

Then each member of the Group, who would be known as EAGLE Chroniclers, should be entrusted with one particular part of the Chronicle. Here are some of the subjects into which it could be divided:—

1. Brief historical notes on your District, including local Notables and Folk Lore.
2. Interesting Architecture of the District
3. Local Government activities.
4. Plans of your District (with details of population, rates, roads, transport, etc.).
5. Social Life of District (Youth Organizations, Institutes, Literary Societies, etc.).
6. Local Flora and Fauna.
7. Local Art (drawings of beauty spots, etc.)
8. Local Sport (1951 records, teams, etc.)
9. Festival Activities of the District. Notable visitors, etc.

These subjects could easily be divided up into smaller sections, or you may be able to think of many more subjects to deal with. Every section could be illustrated with photographs and drawings.

Twelve Prizes

When you have collected all the material together, you should then hand it over to the one in your school or district who is the best "pen-man", who could write it out neatly. EAGLE will give a prize to the 12 groups who produce the best Chronicle.

This scheme of EAGLE Chroniclers is something in which almost everyone can take part, because it does not matter how big your group is. All you have to do in the first place is to call a meeting of EAGLERS you know and make your plans.

When you have formed your group, the one of you who is appointed as Chairman should write in to me telling me what district you are going to cover. We will give you all the advice and help we can. Later on we shall make arrangements for all the Chronicles produced to be judged to find the 12 prize-winners. We shall, of course, give you plenty of time to make your Chronicle and shall not start the judging until the autumn.

READERS LETTERS

(A prize of 5/- is paid for each letter published)

TWO SUMMERS ago my brother found a baby crow that had fallen out of its nest, brought it home, fed it on milk and glucose and kept it warm in a box with straw and a hot water bottle. He grew to be a very large bird – we never caged him and he flew about all day and slept in a large tree. He always tapped on the window for meals and liked to be fed by hand. He was very naughty and as soon as clothes were pegged on the line he flew down and pulled out the pegs. He became so cheeky that my brother put him in a box and took him up to the heath. As the crow circled the sky my brother said "We will never see him again – he has lost faith in us because we put him in a box" – and we never did! – Robert West (9), 117 Mayplace Road East, Branhurst, Kent.

MY HOBBY is searching the countryside and collecting all manner of country-grown[?], pressing them in a thick book and th[?] fastening them in a scrap book and labell[?] them. – Raymond, 11 Newthorpe Ro[?] Norton, Doncaster, Yorks.

MY GRANDMOTHER has an orange which [is?] 35 years old. She gave it to my grandfath[er?] when he went over to France in 1916 duri[ng?] the first World War. He carried it in [his?] pocket until 1919 when he returned to En[g-]land. It is now inedible, and of course ve[ry?] hard. – H. W. Burningham, 48 Thurs[?] Road S.E.9.

I HAVE tried many times to understand [?] journeys of St Paul when reading my Bib[le?] but failed. Now, thanks to EAGLE, his journe[ys?] and adventures are being explained to me i[n a?] way I can understand. – John Winter, [?] Kirkpatrick Road, Mile Cross, Norwich.

READERS' LETTERS
(A prize of 5/- is paid for each letter published)

I WAS most interested in your illustration of the "Vanguard," as I was lucky enough to spend an afternoon on board her when she was anchored in Portland Harbour. We were not allowed to visit all the parts you illustrated, but the afternoon included a visit to the Admiral's Bridge. – Patricia Mason, 80 Woodfield Road, Birmingham 12.

I WONDER if any other family has a Nature Club? We have; it is called the Secrets of Nature Club, and all of us – Daddy, Mummy and six children – belong. It is run on strictly business-like lines; we pay weekly subscriptions which help to pay for outings or new equipment, have a small library to which we hope to add as it pays for itself (½d. a day p[er?] book), keep a log book of all outings, an[d?] hold meetings to discuss the Club's progres[s?] – Mary Ward, 46 Brighton Road, Bristol.

A FEW weeks ago in EAGLE there wer[e?] picture strips of Ray playing cricket, in th[e?] article "Cricket with the Masters". I foun[d?] an old book, cut out the strip pictures one [at?] a time, and stuck them on the corner of eac[h?] page, making sure they were in the righ[t?] order. When this was done, all I had to d[o?] was to flick the pages of the book, and [I?] could see Ray actually playing cricket. – Arthur Gilbert, 21 Nearcroft Road, Roy[?] Oak Est, Wythenshawe, Manchester.

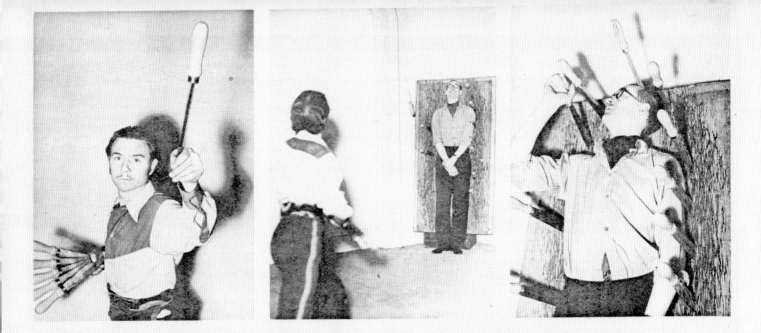

I BECOME A KNIFE-THROWER'S TARGET

by MACDONALD HASTINGS, *Eagle Special Investigator*

WITHOUT wasting any precious time, I asked the knife-thrower if he ever missed. Thoughtfully, he tested the steel point of one of his wicked-looking weapons on the tip of his finger.

"It's like this," he said. "I'm not going to pretend to you, Mr Hastings, that I'm anything that I'm not. No man is infallible. That's right, isn't it? And what I always say is that a man who never makes a mistake, if you get my meaning, never makes anything."

"That's Hal Denver all over," said the girl who usually stands at the business end of the Sensational Denver's Knife-Throwing performance. "Modest, that's him."

"What I'm anxious to learn," I said, "is what he's got to be modest about. You ought to know, if anybody does."

"Tell him," said the knife-thrower. "Go on, I haven't got any secrets. Tell him about the time when I pinned you by your hair to the board."

"Was it an accident?" I enquired feelingly.

"I'll say it was an accident," said the girl. "When I pulled out the knife, it took half my hair with it."

"Still, you've got a lot of hair," I said hopefully. "Not like me."

"Yes," said the knife-thrower, "but, apart from her curls, my partner doesn't take up much room. She's built the way I like my targets to be, on the small side. When she stands up against the board, there's plenty of space to miss all around her."

"What are you looking at me for?" I said.

"Can't help it. Ever since I saw you, I've been thinking to myself: 'He's a very big man. When we put him up against the board, he'll fairly well cover it'."

"Have you ever thought up any way of overcoming the difficulty?"

"Nothing much we *can* do about it, is there? You'll just have to squash up and make yourself as small as you can. My partner'll show you what to do."

The girl smiled encouragingly. I smiled wanly back.

"You'd better take your coat and waistcoat off," she said. "A little while ago, Hal threw a knife which went right through the sleeve of a man's coat, and his shirt as well."

"Did he do it on purpose?" I said.

"Of course he didn't do it on purpose."

Slowly – as slowly as I could anyway – I stripped off my jacket and loosened my collar and tie. I wished, as I've wished so often before, that I had the courage to tell the knife-thrower to go away and practise on somebody else. But the Editor had sent a photographer to get the pictorial record of my impending execution. Hal Denver was already bracing up his shirtsleeves with elastic bands and arranging his weapons of torture in patterns on the floor. And his partner was gently backing me up against the board.

LOOKING desperately for an excuse to delay the fatal moment, I noticed that the top of the board came below my head.

"It's no use," I said triumphantly. "I'm too tall."

For a moment the knife-thrower was baffled. He'd got to admit that I had presented him with an unexpected snag.

"The best part of the act," he explained in a worried voice, "is when I throw two hatchets which land on either side of your head."

"Hatchets?!"

"Sure. That's the climax."

"When he throws the hatchet at me," said his partner, "he aims straight at the middle of my forehead. As the hatchet spins through the air, I duck and it hits the board where my head ought to be."

"Tell him about last week – remember? – when I threw a bit low," said the knife-thrower.

"Don't," I said.

"Oh, it's all right," said the girl. "He didn't hit me with the blade. It was just the handle that got me on the back of the neck. But it did make me feel funny."

"Funny! It sounds very serious to me."

"You're quite right," said the knife-thrower. "It *is* serious."

I felt that I couldn't agree more.

While they were talking, Hal Denver and his partner, were man-handling the heavy board, pitted and scarred with knife slashes. With devilish ingenuity, they were raising it

another foot from the ground by balancing the board on the top of the property box used to carry the tools of the knife-throwing trade.

"O.K." said Hal.

Stepping back from the board, he gathered up a bunch of long knives, like a hand of cards and, selecting one, crouched down and flourished it at me in the air.

"Hold your arms in," said his partner. "You want to make yourself as insignificant as you can. Lean your head back and, whatever you do, DON'T MOVE."

I felt like a specimen beetle pinned to a collector's tray. With hypnotised attention, I watched the knife-thrower working himself up for his task.

After several preliminary scares, he was dissatisfied with the set-up. He told me to relax while he produced an enormous tape-measure and carefully measured out the ground.

"Just an extra precaution," he said. "I'm not going to pretend, Mr Hastings, that I don't feel a bit nervous myself working on you. You know what I mean. I usually throw my knives at a particular point of the board. No offence meant, but, with you, you sort of get in the way."

"As it's me, couldn't you shorten the distance at which you throw the knives?"

"That'd be a certain short cut to trouble. I only throw at one distance, eighteen feet exactly, and no mistakes."

"Or else . . ." echoed the girl.

"That's how they bill us on the halls," said the knife-thrower proudly. "The Sensational Denvers. No mistakes, or else . . . Sounds good, doesn't it?"

I tried to agree.

"All right. One to be ready, two to be steady . . . and a few knives just to get us both used to it."

Hal, who was wearing a sort of Spanish outfit with bell-bottomed trousers and a short bolero jacket, tossed back the black locks of hair off his nose, spread his legs, crouched down on one knee, and, holding one of his long knives by the tip of the blade, sighted me carefully.

"Aim to miss, that's the secret," he said.

I agreed heartily.

"What part of me are you going to start on?"

"Always begin at the legs, and work upwards."

"I'm glad it's legs first."

"Doesn't follow," said the girl. "Hal's last partner had to have five stitches in her leg once."

"That's right," said the knife-thrower. "Cut her about dreadfully."

As he spoke, the knife left his hand. I

watched the flash of it and heard it hiss as it span through the air. Then there was a sullen thump close to my legs which made the board I was leaning on vibrate against my back.

A moment later, another knife and then another, cut through the air and landed trembling in the wood round my thighs and waist. Three more followed, the last one landing neatly within six inches of my ear.

"I threw wide that time so you wouldn't get the wind-up," said the knife-thrower. "Now we'll give you the whole dozen, six up one side, six up the other."

AS he explained, he wrenched the knives out of the wood. The blades were about eleven inches long, the handles another six inches. They were very heavy, and the point sunk deep through the wood of the three inch thick board.

I asked Hal if it was possible to get knives like them.

"I wouldn't know," he said. "This set belonged to an old fellow who worked in my father's circus. When I was a boy it used to be my job to clean the rust off them. I got to throwing them myself and, one day, when the old fellow was ill, I went on and did the act. I've done it ever since, with these same knives."

"How long have you been a knife-thrower?"

"About sixteen years."

"Do you ever practise?"

"Not unless I meet someone like you. It isn't easy to get targets in this business, you know. And throwing at playing cards, the way they do in story-books, teaches you nothing. You've got to work on the real thing, as you might say."

I shall never forget the swish of those hatchets

Getting my own back!

ADVICE ON YOUR PETS

TRAINING YOUR FOX-TERRIER PUPPY
by Professor Cameron

GAIN YOUR PUPPY'S CONFIDENCE BY HOLDING HIM FIRMLY AND COMFORTABLY SUPPORT HIS WEIGHT AND REMEMBER IN ALL TRAINING THAT A FEW WORDS OF PRAISE AND ENCOURAGEMENT ARE QUITE AS IMPORTANT AS SCOLDING.

GROWING PUP'S TIME TABLE (ROUGH GUIDE ONLY)

7 AM Let out.
8·30 AM Light Meal.
9 AM Morning Walk.
12·30 PM Meal.
3 PM Afternoon Walk.
6 PM Evening Meal.
7 PM Let out and So to bed.

REGULARITY IS THE MOST IMPORTANT THING IN TRAINING. GIVE MEALS AND EXERCISE REGULARLY AS POSSIBLE AND SEE THAT YOUR PUP GOES TO BED AT ABOUT THE SAME TIME EACH NIGHT. DON'T BE TOO RIGID, BUT REGULAR HABITS LEARNED IN PUPPY-HOOD WILL MAKE LIFE MUCH EASIER FOR BOTH OF YOU.

YOUR COMMANDS SHOULD BE FEW AND SIMPLE, BUT THEY **MUST** BE OBEYED: NEVER 'PLAY' AT HITTING A DOG – A HALF-HEARTED PAT IS WORSE THAN USELESS. ON THE RARE OCCASIONS WHEN CHASTISEMENT IS NECESSARY IT–

– SHOULD BE FOR A REASON WELL UNDER-STOOD BY THE PUPPY DON'T HIT HIM OR SCOLD HIM AFTER HE HAS COME BACK TO YOU OR DECIDED AT LAST TO OBEY.

BE FIRM BUT SENSIBLE ABOUT "HOUSE TRAINING." SCOLD FOR ANY MESSES MADE IN THE HOUSE, BUT BE SURE TO LET YOUR PUP OUT FREQUENTLY– AND SHOW HIM WHERE TO GO IN THE GARDEN. WHEN OUT ON WALKS TRAIN HIM TO USE THE GUTTER– THIS IS QUITE EASY WITH PATIENCE, AND IT HELPS TO AVOID THE NASTY NUISANCE OF FOULED PAVEMENTS.

EXERCISE SHOULD BE REGULAR AND IS BEST PROVIDED BY TWO GOOD WALKS A DAY. WHEN YOUR PUP WANTS TO "LET OFF STEAM" HE CAN LEARN TO RETRIEVE A RUBBER BALL BUT **DON'T** TIRE HIM OUT AND **NEVER** THROW STONES, WHICH WHEN SWALLOWED CAN CAUSE OBSTRUCTION THAT MAY BE FATAL.

John Dyke

MOST DOGS TAKE READILY TO CAR-TRAVEL, BUT HELP YOUR PUP TO BE A WELL-BEHAVED PASSENGER BY LIFTING HIM PROPERLY INTO THE CAR AND SEEING THAT HE IS COMFORTABLE WHILST TRAVELLING. IF YOUR PUP IS ONE OF THE UNFORTUNATE SUFFERERS FROM "CAR SICKNESS" YOUR VET. CAN SUPPLY TABLETS BEFOREHAND, PREVENTING TROUBLE ON THE JOURNEY. WRITE TO PROFESSOR CAMERON % 'EAGLE' IF YOU HAVE ANY QUESTIONS OR PROBLEMS.

Your first EAGLE Annual!

Great New Strips, Stories, Articles

HERE'S DAN DARE!

HERE'S P.C. 49!

HERE'S HARRIS TWEED!

Here are *all* your Eagle favourites!

176 Pages! Sixteen full-colour pages of strips! Thrilling stories! The latest Science inventions! Real-life adventures, exciting hobbies. All new and all complete. Order your Eagle Annual where you get your Eagle—and order it NOW!

Now ready! – only 8/6

The Adventures of P.C.49

PC49 was created for radio by Alan Stranks and told stories in the everyday life of Police Constable Archibald Berkeley-Willoughby. As well as being broadcast over the airwaves and getting picked up by *Eagle*, there were two films made featuring the popular PC. In the first, snappily titled 'The Adventures of P.C. 49: Investigating the Case of the Guardian Angel', our hero was played by Hugh Latimer. He had a long career as a jobbing actor. In 1957 Latimer appeared in an episode of *Dixon of Dock Green*, in 1972 he showed up in *New Scotland Yard*, and in 1980 he saw how times had changed when he was cast in *Juliet Bravo*.

The Adventures of P.C.49

FROM THE FAMOUS RADIO series by ALAN STRANKS

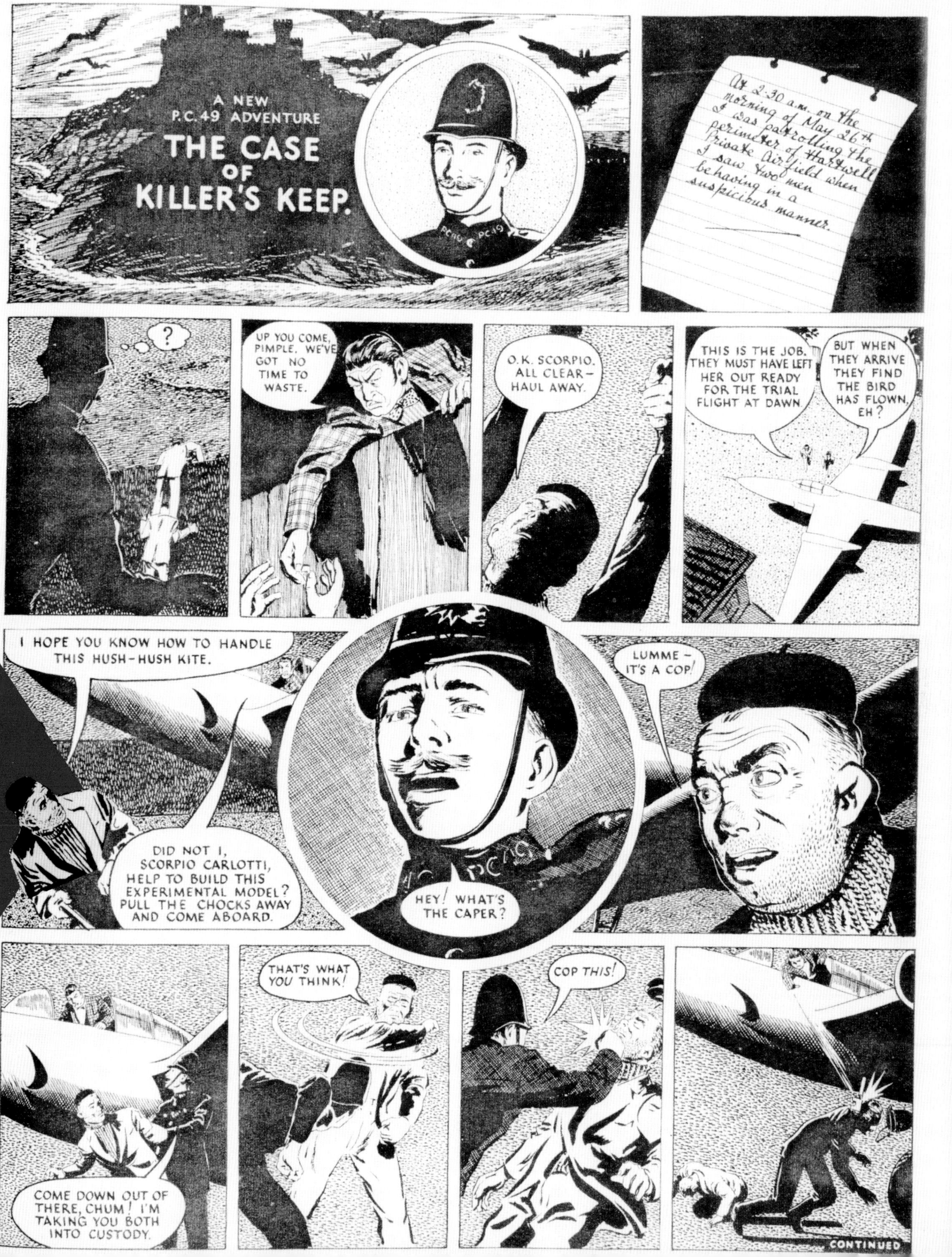
A NEW P.C.49 ADVENTURE
THE CASE OF KILLER'S KEEP.
At 2:30 a.m. on the morning of May 26th I was patrolling the perimeter of Hartwell Private Airfield when I saw two men behaving in a suspicious manner.
?
UP YOU COME, PIMPLE. WE'VE GOT NO TIME TO WASTE.
O.K. SCORPIO. ALL CLEAR—HAUL AWAY.
THIS IS THE JOB. THEY MUST HAVE LEFT HER OUT READY FOR THE TRIAL FLIGHT AT DAWN.
BUT WHEN THEY ARRIVE THEY FIND THE BIRD HAS FLOWN, EH?
I HOPE YOU KNOW HOW TO HANDLE THIS HUSH-HUSH KITE.
DID NOT I, SCORPIO CARLOTTI, HELP TO BUILD THIS EXPERIMENTAL MODEL? PULL THE CHOCKS AWAY AND COME ABOARD.
HEY! WHAT'S THE CAPER?
LUMME—IT'S A COP!
COME DOWN OUT OF THERE, CHUM! I'M TAKING YOU BOTH INTO CUSTODY.
THAT'S WHAT YOU THINK!
COP THIS!
CONTINUED

EAGLE-BRITAIN'S NATIONAL STRIP CARTOON WEEKLY

Travelling the universe, saving the world and the human race, time and again Dan Dare and his crew always fall back on home comforts. In this penultimate instalment of 'the Venus story', the team are desperate for the basics of life, and maybe their choices tell the reader a little about each one. Sir Hubert desires a bath; Dan, food; Professor Peabody (the only regular young female character), clothes; and good old Digby, sleep. The central panel, signed by Frank Hampson himself, shows the crew tucking in to a Theron feast.

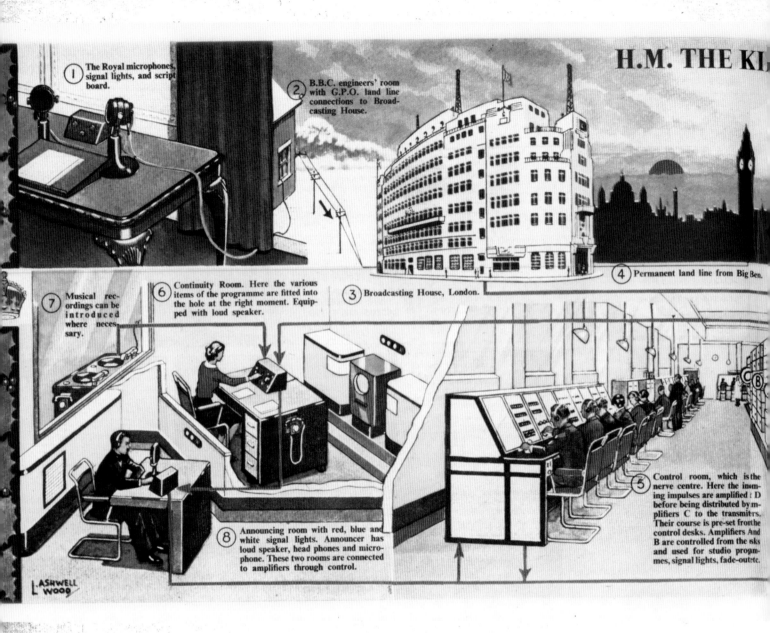

1. The Royal microphones, signal lights, and script board.

2. B.B.C. engineers' room with G.P.O. land line connections to Broadcasting House.

H.M. THE KI...

3. Broadcasting House, London.

4. Permanent land line from Big Ben.

5. Control room, which is the nerve centre. Here the incoming impulses are amplified t D before being distributed by amplifiers C to the transmitrs. Their course is pre-set frothe control desks. Amplifiers And B are controlled from the sks and used for studio propmmes, signal lights, fade-outtc.

6. Continuity Room. Here the various items of the programme are fitted into the hole at the right moment. Equipped with loud speaker.

7. Musical recordings can be introduced where necessary.

8. Announcing room with red, blue and white signal lights. Announcer has loud speaker, head phones and microphone. These two rooms are connected to amplifiers through control.

L. ASHWELL WOOD

THE KING

S CHRISTMAS BROADCAST

ON Christmas Day, subject to circumstances, the King speaks to his loyal subjects throughout the world.

In this special EAGLE feature we endeavour to show, in a very simplified manner, what happens when His Majesty speaks and how you receive it on your set almost simultaneously.

Should the King speak from Sandringham, his voice will impinge on the moving coil microphones and be transformed into electrical impulses of audio frequency. Two microphones are used as a precaution.

These impulses are conveyed to Broadcasting House over G.P.O. land lines.

Here the incoming microphone impulses are amplified (or boosted up) and distributed instantaneously to all the B.B.C. Transmitting Stations, and also by G.P.O. land wire.

Here, again, the microphone impulses are further amplified and superimposed on a strong carrier wave current, generated at the station by the transmitter.

This modulated current is fed to the aerial wire from some of which it is radiated to the British Isles and from the others to the four corners of the Empire, to be reconverted into sound by millions of radio receivers.

The waves travel through the ether with the same velocity as that with which light is transmitted from the sun. This velocity is 186,000 miles per second, so that His Majesty's voice travels once round the earth in one-seventh of a second.

CANADA AND NEWFOUNDLAND

ALL EMPIRE SHIPS AT SEA

Amplified microphone current being borne along on transmitted carrier wave.

PACIFIC ISLANDS AND THE FAR EAST

SOUTH AFRICA

AUSTRALIA AND NEW ZEALAND

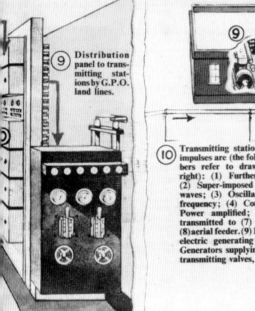

(9) Distribution panel to transmitting stations by G.P.O. land lines.

(10) Transmitting station. Here the impulses are (the following numbers refer to drawing on the right): (1) Further amplified; (2) Super-imposed on carrier waves; (3) Oscillated to high frequency; (4) Controlled; (5) Power amplified; (6) Finally transmitted to (7) feeders and (8) aerial feeder. (9) In the Diesel-electric generating plant; (10) Generators supplying current to transmitting valves, etc.

(12) And so to everybody in the British Isles and the Empire overseas.

S P E A K S

PILOT OF THE FUTURE

DAN DARE

Large of head, and therefore enormous of brain, The Mekon was Dan Dare's most enduring enemy. Intelligent beyond the wildest imaginings of Man he had an ego to match the size of his dome and, of course, like all the best villains, it was this that enabled him to be defeated. Floating around on what looks like a Subbuteo base, The Mekon ruled the Treens with an iron will. Dan came up against him on many occasions and, although he was always defeated in the end, he always came back for more, the ultimate recidivist.

The occasional use of real photographs in the 'Dan Dare' stories added to its allure. It brought a sense of reality to the adventures that had never been seen before. From the reader's point of view, it meant that these people were real, they must be, there's a photograph of Sir Hubert. It's actually Frank Hampson's dad, but don't tell anyone.

DAN DARE
PILOT OF THE FUTURE

THE MEKON, LORD OF THE TREENS, SUMMONS THE THREE CAPTIVES TO HIS PRESENCE.

THEY SHOULD DECEIVE THE EARTH ALL RIGHT AND BEING ARCHAIC SINGLE PLANE PHOTO-GRAPHS THEY WON'T GIVE ANYTHING AWAY ABOUT OUR TECHNICAL SUPERIORITY.

MM—QUITE A TOUCHING SPECTACLE OF KINDLY TREENS OVERFLOWING WITH GOODNESS TO THEIR LITTLE HUMAN FRIENDS

Left to right: Mr. H. Berkeley Hollyer; Mrs Grimes; Alderman F. J. March, Father of the Torquay Council; and John Grimes, Mug of the Year, taking tea during the EAGLE holiday that John spent with his mother at Torquay.

LOOK OUT FOR THESE EAGLE CARS!

Watch out for the Humber cars with the dummy gold Eagles on their roofs! Watch out for them wherever you go! They are handing out free leaflets which give you advance news of the next exciting Dan Dare adventure. These leaflets also include special EAGLE coupons which we hope you will fill up and take round to your newsagent. We are sending out this fleet of cars all over Britain in order to remind you to make sure you're in at the *start* of the new Dan Dare serial: and also to remind you that there is only one certain way of getting EAGLE every week – and that is by placing an order with your newsagent. There are, by the way, a few more copies of EAGLE available now; and so, if until now you have had to borrow or share with a friend, now's the time to get your own copy while the chance is still there.

READERS' LETTERS

(A prize of 5/- is paid for each letter published)

I RECENTLY polished my EAGLE badge and was surprised how dirty it had become over the past year. After I had finished it was shining like a new pin. Don't you think it would be a good idea if all *Eaglers* polished their badges fairly regularly and kept them clean and smart? – Alexander Parkinson, Thomlea, 14 Seafield Road, Aberdeen.

WE LIVE at the foot of a snow-capped mountain, the highest mountain in Africa. They say that at the top is a leopard embedded in ice. No one knows how long it has been there or how it ever reached the snow line – climbers say they have really seen it. – Peter Guy, Box 97, Moshi, Tanganyika.

I FIND it very interesting to walk round a ploughed field looking for things that have come to the surface in ploughing. Yesterday I found a whelk shell, and a lot of oyster shells. As I live 70 miles from the sea can these be relics of the time when the sea covered this part of England? – Christopher Knowles, 1 Woodside Road, Burton Joycee.

HE'S WON A BIKE

Michael Lager (10) of Westbury, Norwich, is the proud winner of Bike-a-Week Competition No. 11. Michael is looking forward to lots of summer cycling.

Readers' Letters

I WONDER how many *Eaglers* know that at the top of Big Ben above the clock faces is a bright light known as the Ayrton Light or Clock Tower Lantern. At sunset the Speaker of the House of Commons presses a switch near his chair, and the lantern lights up. It is to tell Londoners that Parliament is at work – it often burns far into the night until the House adjourns. – Ernest Brown, 107 Ringstead Crescent, Sandgate, Sheffield 10.

IN THE cricket match between Nether Wallop and Picrust Parva you have shown four stumps for the wicket. Is this a mistake? – Edwin Vale, 5 Arbroath Road, S.E.9.

(*Originally, two stumps were used – later a third was introduced in order to speed up the game. Many people consider that cricket today is still inclined to be rather slow, causing matches to be drawn, so we assume that a fourth wicket will be introduced by 1996.* – Ed.).

Readers' Letters

(5/- is paid for each letter published)

I AM twelve years old and have lived in twenty-eight different houses. Can any reader beat that? – V. Kilner, 46 Clock-House Road, Beckenham, Kent.

• • •

I THINK it is a deplorable hobby for boys to throw messages inside bottles into the sea. When they reach the shore they invariably break, and can thus cause many accidents. – David Irving, "Park House", Rayleigh Road, Hutton, Essex.

• • •

THE MIDDLE stump in cricket first came in 1775. A match was being played between Hambledon and Kent. Hambledon wanted 14 runs to win when the last man came to the crease. A player named "Lumpy" Steven was bowling fast, underhand lobs. Three times the ball passed under the bail and between the stumps – the law was "If ye wicket is bowled down it is out" – so there came the middle stump. – *Eagler* 127037, 64 Kimbolton Road, Bedford.

• • •

UP NORTH here are some exceedingly strange place-names, such as Quaking Houses, Pity Me, Johnny Dab, Shiny Row, Windy Nook and Windy Ridge – neither of the latter are very much more windy than any other place. There are als Philadelphia, New York, Washington, Hollywood and Quebec. These are only a few of the queer and cosmopolitan names of this district. – Michael Shields, 27 Valley View, Primrose, Jarrow, Co. Durham.

GREAT NEWS FOR GIRLS!

Now you're to have your OWN colour weekly — Sister paper to Eagle . . . .

Girl

Black Beauty – everyone's favourite animal story

Kitty Hawke – daring girl pilot

MISS BERRY? SHE COULDN'T HAVE STOLEN THE CUPS! THERE'S SOMETHING FISHY GOING ON!

AND IT'S UP TO US TO FIND OUT WHAT IT IS!

The Mystery at Pine Ridge – Exciting school story

Ann Mullion and the Silver Sabot – thrilling story of smugglers

YOU MEAN YOU SPOTTED THE TRAP?

OF COURSE! I KNOW YOU NEVER PRINT YOUR CAPITALS AND YOU'VE NEVER SIGNED ANYTHING BUT 'BILL' IN A LETTER TO ME.

The Adventures of Penny Wise, Private Detective

It was not very long before Hulton Press and Marcus Morris realised that they may have tapped into a goldmine. With letters being received regularly complaining about readers' sisters poring over their copies of *Eagle* it did not take too much of a leap of faith to come up with *Girl*. In the autumn of 1951, *Girl* was launched. It was very much the sister paper of *Eagle*, and there were many activities that were advertised in both. In early 1953 a little brother, *Robin*, came along and was followed just a year later by the last in the family, *Swift*.

Grand COMPETITION
2,000 Prizes!
Win a
REAL LIVE ADVENTURE
which you choose yourself
BICYCLES
RADIOS
CAMERAS
etc., etc.

Watch out for full details in the first issue of GIRL

20 large pages, 12 of them in full colour, every Friday

Look out for the first issue of GIRL on Friday, November 2nd

4½d

"GIRL" may be difficult to find, so to make sure of your copy, fill in this coupon and give it to your newsagent right away!

WESSEX FIREWORKS — *the best in the world*

EVER SEEN A FLYING SAUCER?

Flying Saucers are in the news! A man in America even claims to have spoken to Flying Saucer visitors from Venus! Maybe you've never seen a Flying Saucer but there's a big thrill in store for you when you see and hear the spectacular WESSEX 'Flying Saucer' whizzing through the air!

WHO WAS ST. CATHERINE?

St. Catherine of Alexandria, Christian martyr and patron saint of wheelwrights and mechanics, according to legend tried to make Emperor Maximinus give up his worship of false gods. As punishment he ordered her to be broken on the wheel, but by a miracle the wheel shattered at her touch. The famous WESSEX assorted-coloured paper Pin-wheels are the finest 'Catherine Wheels' ever made. They're real beauties!

WHY SARUM SCARUM?

Salisbury, the City of New Sarum,—the home of WESSEX fireworks—had its origins in Old Sarum, an important Roman site and later home of the kings of Wessex. Its famous Cathedral built between 1220 and 1266 has the highest spire in Europe measuring 404-ft. William Pitt, Prime Minister of England, was born in the Parish of Old Sarum and was its member of Parliament in the 18th century. This is where the exciting WESSEX Sarum Scarum gets its name!

WHAT COLOUR IS A CHAMELEON?

The colour of a Chameleon, a small lizard, depends on its surroundings. It has the remarkable power of changing colour to match them. The WESSEX 'Chameleon Floodlight' pierces the night sky with a magnificent intensity of three colours changing quite magically just like the amazing lizard.

MOUNT EVEREST – WHY THE NAME?

Mount Everest, the highest mountain in the world, 29,002-ft. is named after Sir George Everest, Surveyor General in India from 1830 to 1843. In commemoration of the British team's recent triumph over Everest, WESSEX present their spectacular rocket EVEREST CLIMBER — the 'tops' in firework thrills! You must see it in action!

WHERE DOES AN AIR BOMB BANG?

An Air Bomb actually explodes in the air, not after hitting the ground, as most bombs do. The WESSEX AIR BOMB is of course perfectly safe, but like a real air bomb it throws out shells which burst high in the air with a really satisfying detonation and flash of lightning.

GREECE TO LONDON—ON FOOT!

The makers of Wessex Fireworks provided the pyrotechnics for the Olympic torch, relayed from the ancient stadium in Greece to the modern Wembley Stadium in London. 1,688 torches were used and the athletes covered about 2,000 miles on foot in fourteen days.

WESSEX TO THE RESCUE!

Marine Distress Signals made by WESSEX are used at sea in times of emergency. By day they emit a vivid orange cloud of smoke and by night intensely bright red flares suspended on Parachutes that can be seen at great distances.

WHAT IS THE WYVERN?

The 'Wyvern' is a legendary animal (an heraldic monster) with the forepart of a winged dragon and the hind part of a serpent or a lizard. It was once the Royal Crest of the old Kingdom of Wessex (remember Alfred), but is now the trade mark of the makers of Wessex Fireworks

A SPECTACULAR NEW FIREWORK!

The new Wessex 'Sonic Fireball' offers you something new and unusual in fireworks magic. It's a supersonic thrill. Don't miss this splendiferous attraction.

WESSEX ON LAND, SEA, AND IN THE AIR

Among the many things made by WESSEX have been Smoke Screens to cover movements of troops, tanks and ships, Tear Gas Bombs, Insecticidal Bombs to destroy malarial mosquitoes, and even coloured Smoke Markers to be dropped from helicopters when locating whales in the Antarctic.

I BECOME A LIVING FIREWORK

By MACDONALD HASTINGS, EAGLE Special Investigator

I EXPECTED him to wear a cloak and a conspirator's hat, but, although he didn't dress the part, Mr Brock was as businesslike as Guy Fawkes on November the Fifth.

"We'll wait until it's quite dark," he said ominously. And he peered out of the window of his office as suspiciously as if he had a cask of gunpowder under each arm.

I'd have felt much better about it if the plan had been to blow up somebody else. But that wasn't the idea at all. Yes, you've guessed it. The plot was to make a firework out of me.

Mr Brock, in dark whispers with the editor, had arranged an assignment for me at his works at Hemel Hempstead. So when everybody else had gone home, when the owls were hooting and the witches were warming-up their broomsticks, I stumbled through the gloom into Mr Brock's cellar. Well, it wasn't quite a cellar. It was one of a series of isolated sheds. But, as I waved my torch to light my way, the beam lit on notices warning me at my peril to leave all "smoking materials" at the gate. Sitting on barrels of gunpowder is Mr Brock's business.

He assured me that it was quite safe. These days the manufacture of fireworks is so carefully regulated that accidents scarcely ever happen. But what Mr Brock had planned for *me* scarcely ever happens either.

We marched off, like an execution squad, with a man pushing a herse-like barrow in front of us. It was a moonless night with a high wind, and Mr Brock had to guide my faltering footsteps over the fields.

"We're going to the trial ground," he shouted in my ear. "It's the place where we try out our new ideas."

So that was it.

"Will it hurt?" I asked.

"What hurt?"

"When you light me up?"

"Good heavens no. In the old days at the Crystal Palace we used to put on a show like you every week."

"But the Crystal Palace was burnt down," I said.

"Not by us," replied Mr Brock, firmly.

We had come to a place which, in the light of our electric torches, reminded me of a battlefield in the war. It was littered with the burnt-out remains of explosives. There was a sort of wire enclosure, studded about with posts, and the ground had been churned into sour and blackened mud.

"This'll do, Woodie," said Mr Brock.

The shadowy figure of the man in charge of the barrow came to a halt. Using my torch, I looked to see what he'd got aboard.

"This is a living piece," said Mr Brock, "which we call the boxers. It's one of our best effects and it ought to make a good picture. Woodie will show you what to do."

"Is Woodie in this?" I asked.

"Woodie's the other boxer," said Mr Brock.

My heart warmed to Woodie. At any rate, he stood as good a chance of being blown up as I did.

"What's it like?" I whispered.

"O.K." said Woodie hoarsely. "All you

have to look out for is the bang-pop-bang when you're lit up."

I said I could quite believe that.

"Never you mind," said Woodie comfortingly. "When you've been in this business as long as I have you won't feel really well unless you've got a burn or two. Anyhow you'll be all right in this."

Woodie dragged off the barrow something that looked like a divers suit, with a square headpiece and a rectangular window in front.

"Asbestos," he said.

I took off my coat and jacket and, sitting on the barrow, hauled on the gear. When the headpiece was attached, I was so isolated from the others that they had to give me a tap to attract my attention.

The next phase was that Mr Brock hooked on to my shoulder a life-size cut-out of a man mounted on wood. After that, he strapped another device on my arm.

Through my window, I could see that the outer side of the frame was outlined in paper-tubing, mounted on rows of cylinders about the size of a cigarette.

As I stood there in my suit, with the gear weighing down on my shoulder, Mr Brock tapped my headpiece to remind me to move very carefully. At the same time, he worked busily with a pair of scissors, splitting up the paper tubes, pocketing the ends together, and joining them up into a continuous line from my top to my toe.

I know now that the paper tubes are what are called quick match. The cylinders on which they are mounted are small fireworks named la:ces. What Mr Brock was doing was joining up the tubes of quick match to fire the priming in the lances, and to make sure that I burned properly from head to toe.

While Mr Brock was dealing with me, Syd was also being serviced. At last, we were both moved rather stiffly into position.

"Are you ready?" shouted Mr Brock through the asbestos suit.

I WASN'T ready – who would be? – but, if I'd raised any objection from the inside of my armour, nobody would have heard me. So I just stood there, holding up my arms, as Mr Brock had instructed me, in a boxing position. Heaven knows, at that moment nobody could have felt less in a fighting mood than I.

I didn't see Mr Brock strike the match. All I can tell you is that, a moment later, I found out what it feels like to be inside an explosion. Woodie said I was to look out for the bang-pop-bang. That was a memorable understatement.

Inside my suit, the whole world was suddenly eclipsed in a blinding fiery burst of hiccups. Woodie was blowing up too. We were both popping and crackling like a couple of chickens roasting on a spit.

It didn't last long. As the quick match fired the lancework, we both settled into a warm glow. Much too warm. After a moment or two, I felt very hot. By the time we'd burnt out, I'd decided that there must be a crack or two in my asbestos suit.

When they got me out, I was smelling like

milk that's boiled over. My face was blackened with powder and, sure enough, I'd baptised myself as a pyrotechnist by collecting a burn on my arm.

But Mr Brock made it better by saying that I had now qualified as a firework type. If I liked, he said, I could come as an apprentice and help his people in the burning of one of their big displays. So, of course, I went.

As a preliminary, Mr Brock gave me a first lesson in the business. For example, he told me that real operators never talk of letting off fireworks. The old hands say: When do we burn?

Next, I found out that burning a firework display is a very different matter from touching off a few squibs or catherine wheels. It's an art, of which Mr Alan St Hill Brock is certainly the greatest master in the world. For six generations, his family have made fireworks. And, in that time, fireworks have developed from mere showers of flame-coloured sparks and fire, to the complicated devices and colour effects which you can see in a display today.

Up to the beginning of the last century, all fireworks were flame-coloured. Then the manufacturers introduced Chlorate of Potash. Chlorate of Potash, mixed with various metal salts, is the method by which fireworks are now tinted in colour. Chlorate of Potash is dangerous stuff, improperly used, but it's the secret of the red, yellow, green and blue stars which burst out of Roman Candles, Shells and Rockets today. The discovery of the uses of magnesium, and later aluminium, have also played a big part. In fact, you can say that, although the Chinese used saltpetre, charcoal, and sulphur to make the first fireworks a thousand years ago, fireworks as we know them have been perfected only in the past hundred and fifty years.

You can't compare the sort of fireworks that come out of a box at home with the

enormous shells, rockets, set-pieces and revolving devices which are burnt at a big display. On one occasion, a former Mr Brock actually let off a revolving wheel which was fifty feet in diameter. When it was fired, the effect spread more than a hundred feet.

I didn't let off a firework myself as big as that. But I didn't do badly. Mr Brock put me in charge of some enormous frames of rockets. They were joined together with quickmatch, so that a touch set off three, five, or twenty at a time.

I was given a pocketful of "port-fires" to light my flights of rockets. My job was to let them off, when I got a shout from the chief operator in charge of the display.

Letting off a single rocket is good fun. But, when you set off five rockets at a time, they go off like a sock in the jaw. There's a roar and a bang, and if you're not careful, you sit down on your backside in surprise.

But, although firing flights of rockets is exciting, they're nothing to the big shells. Shells are fired out of mortars like small iron cannon sunk in the ground. The effect they give in the air is like a mushroom of sparks. And, if you are near them on the ground when they go off, the rush of the explosion as they lift is something quite terrific.

When we fired our display, I almost fell flat on my face when the first shell went off behind me. Afterwards, I got wise.

Whenever our chief operator (Mr Harry Austin) said: "Right, Harold," to his other assistant, I knew that was the moment to expect a big shell. And I ducked.

They didn't ask me to be a living firework again. But I burnt two holes in an old suit firing flights of rockets. So, one way and another, Mr Brock has no reason to be ashamed of me as his assistant. I've learned how to burn, and I've burnt.

The end

Mr Brock put me in charge of some enormous frames of rockets

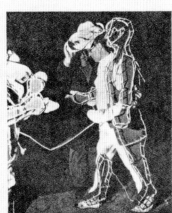
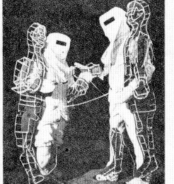
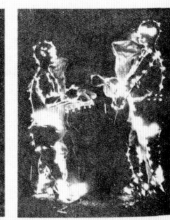

The plot was to make a living firework out of me

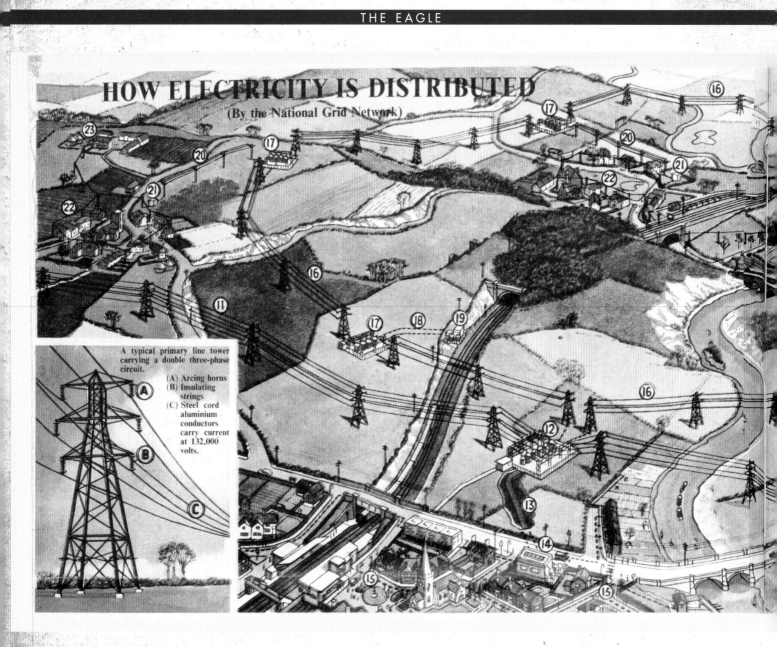

HOW ELECTRICITY IS DISTRIBUTED
(By the National Grid Network)

A typical primary line tower carrying a double three-phase circuit.

(A) Arcing horns
(B) Insulating strings
(C) Steel cord aluminium conductors carry current at 132,000 volts.

ELECTR

We have seen, in last week's EAGLE, how electricity is generated at 11,000 volts. Here we show how this current is stepped up in pressure, and made available to city, town, village and isolated farm in every part of Great Britain. A National network of transmission lines link the main power stations with local undertakings. There are nearly 3,000 miles of primary transmission lines altogether, carrying 132,000 volts.

Main Grid Rooms are in touch by private telephone with all the power stations in their area, and with each other, so that power can be switched from one to another in case of failure. The supply of each section can be increased, diminished, or cut off according to the requirements of the load.

KEY TO NETWORK

(1) Main power station. (2) Boiler house. (3) Turbo-generating room. (4) 11,000 volt current from turbo-alternators is stepped up to 66,000 volts by transformers. (5) Switch house. (6) Cable tunnels. (7) Power house control room distributing the current in various ways. (8) 66,000 volt underground feeder cables to city sub-stations. (9) 66,000 volt underground cables to transformers. (10) Primary step-up transformer station. Here the current is stepped up to 132,000 volts for primary transmission lines. (11-11) Primary transmission lines carrying 132,000 volts and connected up to other main power stations throughout the country. (12) Primary step-down transformer station. Here the current is stepped down to 66,000 volts for secondary transmission lines. (13) 66,000 volts underground cables to town sub-station. (14) Town sub-station. Here the current is stepped

down again to 400 or 250 volts for town supply. (15) 250 volt underground cables for house to house distribution. (16-16) Secondary transmission lines carrying 66,000 volts round sections of the countryside. (17-17) Secondary step-down transformer stations. Here the current is further reduced to 11,000 volts for rural transmission. (18) 11,000 volt underground cables to electric railways. (19) Transformer stations for railway. (20-20) 11,000 volt lines for rural transmission. (21-21) Local transformers again reduce the current to 250 volts for village supply. (22-22) 250 volts transmission lines. (23) 250 volt supply to farm. (24) 250 volt supply to country hotel. (25) 250 volt supply to quarry. (26) 11,000 volt supply to factory. (27) 250 volt underground cables to houses from factory transformers. It will be noticed that the whole system is interchangeable. Should the main power station fail or be overloaded the supply can be maintained from other main power stations or vice versa.

ICITY

PICTURE REVIEW OF EAGLE'S SECOND YEAR

Dan Dare Recording. At Star Sound Studios in London, Frank Hampson, with son Peter, explains to *Eaglers* how the machine works. This was the first recording of Dan Dare.

What has EAGLE been doing in the past year – since our first birthday? Bringing you happiness and interest, we hope, and a strong sense of comradeship between our readers all over the British Isles – and beyond.

Below we look back on some of our second year activities in pictures and hope you will enjoy them.

Visit to the T.T. Races at the Isle of Man. The Editor and competition winners are photographed before they take their seats in the plane to fly them over to the Isle of Man.

Chat with an Engine Driver. Which is better – to be a passenger or the driver? Here you see the driver and fireman exchanging views with EAGLE readers at Waterloo.

Mug of the Year for 1951. EAGLE sent John Grimes, last year's No. 1 MUG, to Torquay with his mother for a summer holiday. Here you see John with Mr Hollyer and Mr March of Torquay Corporation.

The Daily Splash! On your mark . . . ready . . . and into the swimming pool was just part of the fun at our holiday camp at Little Canada, Isle of Wight, last summer.

Sampling the soup. Seeing round hotel kitchens can be a hungry business and when the cook says, "Try this, son," *Eaglers* are apt to form a quick queue! It tasted good, too!

See that up there? Cadet W. P. Embleton of the Canadian Pacific *Beaverdell* shows an EAGLE party round the vessel at London Docks.

After Dinner. A good time for quiet reading or for exploring the "log cabin" at our Holiday Camp at Little Canada, Isle of Wight.

On the way to Lords. England's cricketers, Denis Compton, Godfrey Evans and Alec Bedser stopped to have a friendly chat with *Eaglers* before the Test last June.

Film Premiere of *Tom Brown's Schooldays*. John Howard Davies, who played Tom Brown and who is also an EAGLE club member, chats to other *Eaglers* before they see the film premiere at the Gaumont Theatre, Haymarket.

Iceland Visit. Sponsored by EAGLE, Richard Lawrence and Michael Keen went with the British Schools Exploring Society's Expedition to Iceland. Their parents and an EAGLE representative greet them on their return to London.

Christmas Carols at St Paul's. What better end to the year of 1951? St Paul's was filled to overflowing by EAGLE readers and their parents. Our collection was given to the Children's Society and Dr Barnardo's Homes.

Trip in a Helicopter. One of the high spots of our past year was a helicopter trip between Birmingham and London for prizewinners. *Eagler* Terence Ball finds the dashboard pretty exciting, especially with an interested pilot there to explain it all clearly.

A quiet corner. Robin Holloway's father was exhibiting at the Festival Exhibition of the Royal Society of British Arts. Half way round, Tony thought a rest was indicated so he settled to read his EAGLE.

EAGLE—BRITAIN'S NATIONAL STRIP CARTOON WEEKLY

H.M.S. EAGLE

THE NEW WONDER AIRCRAFT CARRIER OF THE ROYAL NAVY

It is fitting that in the second birthday number of EAGLE we introduce the first and exclusive drawing of Britain's latest and largest aircraft carrier, with some of her crew spelling out her name on the flight deck.

H.M.S. Eagle has a displacement of 45,000 tons and the four sets of steam turbines give her a speed of 31½ knots. She is 803 ft. 9 ins. long and 112 ft. 9 ins. wide. The enormous area of flight deck is equivalent to over two acres.

The great hangars can accommodate over 100 aircraft. This space could stow 263 double-deck buses. The full crew is 2,750 men.

Armament consists of 16-4.5 in. high-angle dual-purpose guns and 60-40 m.m. Bofors anti-aircraft guns. The ship has the first operational squadron of jet aircraft to go into service with the Navy-Supermarine Attackers of 800 Squadron.

H.M.S. Eagle is indeed a fine ship. *In another issue of EAGLE we shall show one of the Attackers.*

HMS

KEY TO ABOVE DECKS

(1-1) Aircraft catapults. (2-2) Forward 4.5 in. guns. (3) Forward aircraft lift. (4-4) Multiple 40 m.m. anti-aircraft guns. (5) 5 ton mobile crane. (6) Flight control bridge. (7) Navigating bridge. (8) Fire control director towers. (9-9) Radar gun control apparatus. (10) Tripod mast with radar navigating scanner. (11) New type funnel. (12) Funnel uptakes from boiler room. (13) Single 40 m.m. guns. (14) Aircraft safety barriers lowered (six in all). (15) Aircraft safety barrier raised. (16) Single 40 m.m. guns. (17-17) Gunnery directors. (18) Multiple 40 m.m. anti-aircraft guns. (19) Fire control director towers. (20) Aerial masts. These are lowered outboard when flying is in progress. (21) Life saving Carley floats. (22) Flight deck centre line, marked off every 20 feet. (23) Supermarine Attacker jet aircraft parked on flight deck. (24) Aircraft and boat crane. (25) After aircraft lift (lowered). (26-26) After 4.5 in. guns. (27) Arrester wires (16 in all), to assist in pulling up landing aircraft, engage them with a hook on the tail. (28) Round down landing lights.

KEY TO BELOW DECKS

(29) After upper hangar. (30) After lower hangar. (31) Twin balanced rudders (port side). (32) Port propellers. (33) After port engine room. (34) Forward port engine room. (35) Ward room. (36) Officers' baths. (37) Torpedo room. (38) After boiler room. (39) Oil fuel tanks. (40) Forward boiler room. (41) Auxiliary machinery. (42) Aero-engine room. (43) Bakery. (44) Forward lower hangar. (45) Forward upper hangar. (46) Crew space and wash places.

THERE IS A SPECIAL MESSAGE FOR READERS ABOUT H.M.S. EAGLE ON PAGE 11

EAGLE

Flight to Adventure!

CHEERIO, EAGLERS! I'M OFF TO CANADA FOR THRILLS AND SPILLS AS ...

... EAGLE SPECIAL INVESTIGATOR!

Headline News! EAGLE has sent its own Special Investigator to Canada to provide *you* with first hand, thrilling accounts of adventure on that vast and varied Continent. Macdonald Hastings is going to drive a loco through the Rockies, pan for gold, visit a logging camp, travel by dog team to the remote posts of the Royal Canadian Mounted Police. He will also take a good look at the cockpit of a BOAC stratocruiser during his flight to Canada.

Thrills in plenty are in store for you during the following weeks. See that you're 'in' on EAGLE Special Investigator's Canadian adventures – they're going to be talked about by all the boys in Britain who read EAGLE. Be sure you don't miss them! Order your EAGLE now!

YIPPEE!

MACDONALD HASTINGS, Our Special Investigator, rides the range.

YIPPEE!

Our Special Investigator takes off to Adventure!

I FLY THE ATLANTIC

On the Flight Deck of a B.O.A.C. Stratocruiser
by MACDONALD HASTINGS

In the 20 June 1952 issue Macdonald Hastings began a report on one of his greatest early adventures. Travelling 15,000 miles in just 15 days, the self-styled *Eagle* Special Investigator (ESI) had been set a major task by his editor. His 1,000 mile-a-day journey would see him riding with cowboys, investigating with the Mounties, racing a dog-team in the frozen north and travelling through the Rocky Mountains on the Canadian Pacific Railway. Squeezed in between all of this, he had to go logging, and mining for gold.

Such a trip was an expensive outlay for the *Eagle*, but they made sure they got their money's worth out of it by spreading Hastings' reports over 16 weeks. The final instalment came on the 19 September, with Macdonald being hunted by a Grizzly Bear. When it was all over he needed, in his words, 'a stiff double milkshake'.

From the

Editor

EAGLE, 4 New St Square, London EC4

14 *March*, 1952

BECAUSE EAGLE goes to press a few weeks before it reaches your newsagent, it was not possible for us to pay tribute in these pages to His Majesty King George VI at the time of his death. I feel, however, that you would not want me to let the passing of our beloved King go by without my talking to you about him.

King George VI stood for all the ideals which I hope are the aims of each one of you. Here was a man who, although afflicted with ill-health, strove to overcome his handicaps so completely that he became one of the most sincerely loved monarchs of our history. Here was a man, good, kind, courageous – and who, for all his Crown of State, was imbued with the humility of the truly great, thus endearing himself to the old and young, the rich and poor, the strong and the weak. May we all learn from his gracious example.

As head of a great Empire our young Queen Elizabeth has a heavy and arduous task before her. The devotion of the youth of the country can be a great help to her and I am sure all of you will serve her with wholehearted loyalty.

CONGRATULATIONS to the following on winning the MUG's Badge: Twelve-year-old *Noel Spreadbury* of 16 Bells Orchard, Wareham, Dorset,

has received high recommendations from both home and school for his sound common sense and quickness to be of service whenever he can. He was going to dinner with two or three of his school friends when a nasty accident occurred involving an old lady who was badly hurt. Noel had never seen a bad accident before; nevertheless he was in action at once and the speed with which he got through to the police and the help he gave to the old lady, assisted by Georgina Barnes, another pupil, marks him out as a true MUG.

Yours sincerely,

Marcus Morris

SECONDARIES

PRIMARIES

A BIRD'S FLIGHT DEPENDS MAINLY ON ITS PRIMARY AND SECONDARY FEATHERS. IF THESE QUILL FEATHERS, AS THEY ARE CALLED, BECOME DAMAGED, THE ABILITY TO FLY IS LESSENED, AND MAY EVEN BE LOST UNTIL THE DAMAGE IS REPAIRED.

THE BARBS ON EACH SIDE OF THE QUILL ARE BOUND TOGETHER BY A SERIES OF HOOKS WORKING IN A WAY SIMILAR TO A ZIP FASTENER. A RUFFLED FEATHER CAN BE RESTORED TO SHAPE BY A SLIDING PRESSURE OF THE FOREFINGER AND THUMB ALONG THE BARBS, MOVING FROM THE QUILL OUTWARDS. A BIRD PREENS ITS QUILL FEATHERS IN THE SAME MANNER, ITS BEAK TAKING THE PLACE OF THE FOREFINGER AND THUMB.

BARBS

QUILL

QUILL

BARB

PROXIMA

DISTAL

BARB

A DIAGRAM OF THE HOOKS OR BARBULES (NOT TO SCALE). THE CLAWS OF THE DISTAL BARBULES HOOK ON TO THE RACKS FORMED BY THE PROXIMAL BARBULES. THE HOOKS ARE MINUTE, LIKE FINE HAIRS, PACKED CLOSE TOGETHER, KNITTING THE BARBS INTO A FLEXIBLE, WIND-PROOF SURFACE. IN THE PICTURE A SPACE HAS BEEN LEFT BETWEEN THE BARBULES, AND THEIR SHAPE SIMPLIFIED IN ORDER TO SHOW THEIR ARRANGEMENT AND THE METHOD OF WORKING.

ONE DRY SPRING, A HOUSE MARTIN, SEEKING MATERIAL FOR ITS NEST, BECAME ENTRAPPED IN THE MUD OF A HALF DRY POND. WHEN RESCUED, ITS PLUMAGE WAS COVERED WITH THICK SLIME.

TOLD AND DRAWN BY BACKHOUSE

TO PREVENT IT CAKING ON THE PLUMAGE, THE SLIME WAS RINSED OFF. THE MARTIN, ITS PLUMAGE SOAKING AND BEDRAGGLED, AND UNABLE TO FLY, BEGAN PREENING ITSELF, USING A SLIDING ACTION TO RESTORE THE ALL IMPORTANT WING FEATHERS, NEARLY TYING KNOTS IN ITSELF TO REACH THE TIPS OF THE WING AND TAIL.

AFTER MANY STOPS FOR A REST, THE MARTIN TOOK OFF TO REJOIN ITS COMPANIONS, ITS PLUMAGE RESTORED TO SHAPE, THE BARBULES OF THE WING FEATHERS RE-HOOKED. NEXT TIME YOU SLIDE THE TAG OF A ZIP-FASTENER, REMEMBER THAT NATURE WORKED OUT THE IDEA FIRST.

Occasionally, *Eagle* would run a series which appeared to be based on one or two great ideas, but then expatiated on the subject matter for too long. 'Nature Invented It First' and 'Their Names Made Words' are two classic examples.

'Nature Invented It First' appears to be a fantastic concept when it compares the zip fastener with the barbs on the feather of a bird's wing, but when it compares a whale to a submarine, it's time to move on.

Similarly, 'Their Names Made Words' is quite marvellous when relating the story of the Earl of Sandwich and his bread meal which he created to avoid having to stop playing cards to eat. The creation of the Cardigan (thank you James Thomas Brudenell, 7th Earl of Cardigan) is also a treasure, as are the tales of Plimsoll, Macadam, Wellington, and … actually they're all really good.

THEIR NAMES MADE WORDS *Cardigan*

James Thomas Brudenell
7th Earl of Cardigan (1797-1868)

THE 7th EARL OF CARDIGAN LIVED AT A TIME WHEN COMMISSIONS IN THE ARMY COULD BE BOUGHT. HE WAS AMBITIOUS AND WEALTHY AND BOUGHT HIS WAY STEADILY UP UNTIL, IN 1832, HE PURCHASED THE COMMAND OF THE 15th HUSSARS, AS HE WANTED TO WEAR THEIR SPLENDID UNIFORM.

HIS BROTHER OFFICERS HATED HIM FOR BUYING HIS WAY OVER THEIR HEADS, AND HIS FIERCE TEMPER DID NOT MAKE THINGS ANY EASIER. IN 1840 HE WOUNDED ONE OF HIS OFFICERS IN A DUEL ON WIMBLEDON COMMON. DUELLING WAS ILLEGAL SO LORD CARDIGAN WAS ARRESTED AND TRIED IN THE HOUSE OF LORDS HE WAS FOUND "NOT GUILTY" ON A TECHNICAL POINT.

IN 1854 THE CRIMEAN WAR WITH RUSSIA BROKE OUT AND LORD CARDIGAN WENT OUT WITH THE ARMY IN COMMAND OF A CAVALRY BRIGADE.

AT THE BATTLE OF BALACLAVA ON OCTOBER 25th, 1854, A MISUNDERSTOOD ORDER LED TO THE FAMOUS CHARGE OF THE LIGHT BRIGADE IN WHICH LORD CARDIGAN, GALLOPING IN FRONT OF HIS MEN, LED THEM IN THE ILL-FATED ATTACK ON THE HEAVILY-DEFENDED RUSSIAN BATTERIES.

WINTER IN THE CRIMEA WAS SO HARD AND BITTER THAT IT WAS SAID THE RUSSIANS HAD TWO EXTRA GENERALS FIGHTING FOR THEM — GENERALS JANUARY AND FEBRUARY. OUR TROOPS SUFFERED SEVERELY FROM THE COLD AND WRAPPED THEMSELVES IN EVERY BIT OF CLOTHING THEY COULD FIND. ON THEIR HEADS THEY WORE WHAT BECAME KNOWN AS "BALACLAVA HELMETS"— STILL IN USE TODAY.

LORD CARDIGAN INVENTED FOR HIS OWN USE AGAINST THE COLD WHAT HE DESCRIBED AS "A LONG WOOLLEN OVER-WAISTCOAT". OTHER OFFICERS COPIED HIM AND ORDERED WHAT THEY CALLED "CARDIGANS" AFTER HIM.

EAGLE 7 November 1952

THEIR NAMES MADE WORDS *Sandwich*

John Montagu
4th Earl of Sandwich (1718-1792)

JOHN MONTAGU SUCCEEDED HIS GRANDFATHER AS EARL OF SANDWICH IN 1729. HE WAS EDUCATED AT ETON AND CAMBRIDGE, AND TOOK HIS SEAT IN THE HOUSE OF LORDS IN 1739 AS A FOLLOWER OF THE POWERFUL DUKE OF BEDFORD.

THANKS TO THE INFLUENCE OF THE DUKE OF BEDFORD HE HELD MANY IMPORTANT AND WELL PAID POSTS, ALTHOUGH HE WAS INTERESTED IN NONE OF THEM. HE WAS FIRST LORD OF THE ADMIRALTY FROM 1771 TO 1782, WHILE THE AMERICAN WAR OF INDEPENDENCE WAS BEING FOUGHT, AND IT WAS PARTLY DUE TO HIS BAD ADMINISTRATION THAT BRITAIN LOST THE WAR.

NEVER BEFORE HAD THE ROYAL NAVY BEEN SO BADLY RUN. BRIBES WERE TAKEN, STORES STOLEN, SHIPS SENT TO WAR UNSEAWORTHY AND WITHOUT ENOUGH AMMUNITION, FOOD OR STORES. THE "ROYAL GEORGE" SANK IN STILL WATER AT SPITHEAD, WITH HEAVY LOSS OF LIFE, BECAUSE A GREAT PIECE OF HER BOTTOM FELL OUT.

HIS ONLY GOOD ACTION WAS HIS ENCOURAGEMENT OF CAPTAIN COOK IN HIS EXPLORATIONS. IN RETURN, WHEN COOK DISCOVERED SOME ISLANDS IN THE PACIFIC, HE CALLED THEM THE SANDWICH ISLANDS. (THEY ARE NOW CALLED HAWAII.)

CHART OF THE SANDWICH ISLANDS

LORD SANDWICH PREFERRED GAMBLING TO ANYTHING ELSE AND WOULD SPEND LONG HOURS AT THE CARD TABLE. ONE DAY, HE WAS SO BUSY PLAYING CARDS AT HIS CLUB THAT HE DID NOT WANT TO STOP FOR DINNER, SO HE TOLD THE WAITER TO BRING HIM A SLICE OF MEAT BETWEEN TWO SLICES OF BREAD.

Sandwiches
EGG & CRESS
HAM & TONGUE
CHEESE
SARDINE
TOMATO
CUCUMBER

OTHER MEN FOLLOWED SUIT AND TOLD THE WAITER TO BRING THEM A "SANDWICH". SO THE CUSTOM SPREAD UNTIL TODAY MORE "SANDWICHES" ARE EATEN THAN EVER BEFORE.

EAGLE 22 June 1956

THE ROUTEMASTER
THE WORLD'S MOST UP-TO-DATE BUS

The prototype of London's 'Bus of the future', the 64-seater *Routemaster*, has recently gone into public service.

The new bus, which is of revolutionary design, will be produced in quantity in about three years' time and will replace London's trolleybuses as they become worn out.

Between 1,600 and 1,700 of the new buses will be built, at an approximate cost of £8,000,000. The *Routemaster* is of chassis-less design, with the front and rear mechanical units carried on sub-frames which are attached to the body. The engine is an A.E.C. 9.6-litre Diesel, developing 125 h.p., and the radiator is mounted under the main floor. Gear selection is by electro-hydraulic valves operated by a lever on the steering column, thus providing only two foot-pedal controls, accelerator and brake.

Additional comfort for passengers is provided by the coil springs on the front wheels and very large hydraulic shock-absorbers on the rear sub-frame — the first bus in the world to have 'private car' independent springing.

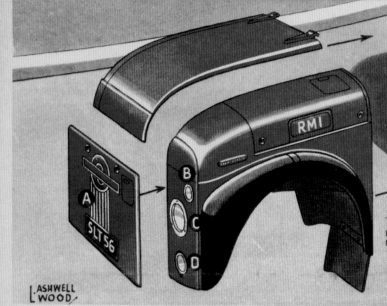

L. ASHWELL WOOD

The detachable parts of the front portions of the *Routemaster* make for easy maintenance.

(A) Air intake to radiator fan.
(B) Side-lights.
(C) Head-lights.
(D) Adjustable fog-light.

THE ROUT

EAGLE 22 June 1956

ROUTEMASTER

KEY TO PARTS

(1) Inlet to air-conditioning system. (2) New-type direction indicator. (3) Route-number panel. (4) Gear selection lever on steering column. (5) Hand-brake lever; rear wheels only. (6) Accelerator and foot-brake. (7) A.E.C. 9.6-litre Diesel engine. (8) Fuel injection pump. (9) Independent front coil springs. (10) Track rod from worm and nut steering gear. (11) Fluid flywheel transmission. (12) Radiator header tank. (13) Radiator with air intake on top, mounted under the floor. The fan and water-pump is at the forward end. (14) Front sub-frame member. (15) Point of attachment to body frame (either side). (16) Fuel tank; 25 gallons. (17) Universal joints of driving shaft. (18) Electrically-selected and hydraulically-operated, direct transmission four-speed gearbox. (19) Four-wheel, hydraulic foot-brake supply cylinders. (20) The entire central section is arranged under the floor. (21) Exhaust silencer. (22) Point of attachment to body frame (either side). (23) Rear sub-frame member. (24) Universal joints of driving shaft. (25) Spiral bevel final drive to back axle. (26) Rear sub-frame carrying back axle. (27) Offside hydraulic shock-absorber. (28) Nearside hydraulic shock-absorber. (29) The conductor has a special recess in which to stand, giving a clearer way for passengers getting on and off the bus.

1856 — 1956

The London General Omnibus Company was formed a hundred years ago. This interesting comparison shows the winning design in a contest for the best horse-bus when the company began operations.

It seated twelve passengers inside, six a side, facing each other (like 'trussed fowls', as a critic said) and room for ten more on the roof, sitting back to back. From 2-horse power to 125-horse power a hundred years later, London Transport's latest, the Routemaster, seats sixty-four passengers in well-upholstered comfort.

EMASTER

EAGLE 15 June 1956

THE GERMAN POCKET-BATT

The 10,000 ton German Pocket-Battleship *Admiral Graf Spee*, out-shot and out-manoeuvred by three British cruisers at the Battle of the River Plate in 1939, was one of three Pocket-Battleships serving in the German Navy during World War II. Ingenious in design, these ships were the first of such size to have electrically welded hulls, and to be propelled by Diesel engines. *Graf Spee's* engines gave her a remarkable speed of 26 knots !

KEY TO NUMBERS: (1) Quarter deck. (2) Rudder. (3) Starboard propeller. (4) Quadruple torpedo tubes. (5) Officers' quarters. (6) Ship's office. (7) Three 11-inch Krupp guns; maximum range, 30,000 yards. (8) After gun-turret. (9) Fresh-water tanks. (10) Torpedo room. (11) 11-inch magazine. (12) Operating theatre. (13) Sick bay. (14) 5.9-inch magazine. (15) Auxiliary machinery. (16) Gun trunk. (17) Engineers' mess. (18) After starboard 5.9-inch guns. (19) After twin 4.1-inch anti-aircraft guns. (20) After main director-tower and range-finder. (21) Reconnaissance seaplane. (22) Catapult. (23) Secondary armament director-tower. (24) Mainmast. (25) Engine exhaust vents. (26) Searchlight platform. (27) Admiral's barge. (28) Starboard twin 4.1-inch anti-aircraft guns. (29) After starboard M.A.N. Diesel engines. (30) Forward starboard M.A.N. Diesel engines. Altogether there are eight sets of these engines employed, developing some 54,000 h.p. It was reported, at the time, that the high speed produced by these Diesels resulted in a vibration so severe as to interfere with accurate shooting during the River Plate action. (31-31) Vulcan clutch. (32-32) Oil fuel tanks in double hull. (33) Starboard gear-box. (34) Torpedo bulge. (35) 5.9-inch magazine. (36) Petty Officers' mess. (37) Seamen's mess. (38) Fans. (39) Stores. (40) Forward starboard 5.9-inch guns. (41) Armourer. (42) Foremast. (43) Upper control top and range-finder. (44) Searchlight platform. (45) Control tower. (46) Conning tower and range-finder. (47) Forward gun-turret. These turrets are fitted with bomb-deflecting crowns. (48) Three 11-inch Krupp guns; maximum range, 30,000 yards. (49) Main ammunition trunk. (50) Magazines and handing rooms for 11-inch guns. (51) Compressors. (52) Seamen's mess. (53) Breakwater. (54) Capstan gear. (55) Pronounced chine. (56) Chain locker. (57) Paint store. (58) Bulbous bow to reduce wave resistance.

THE POCKET

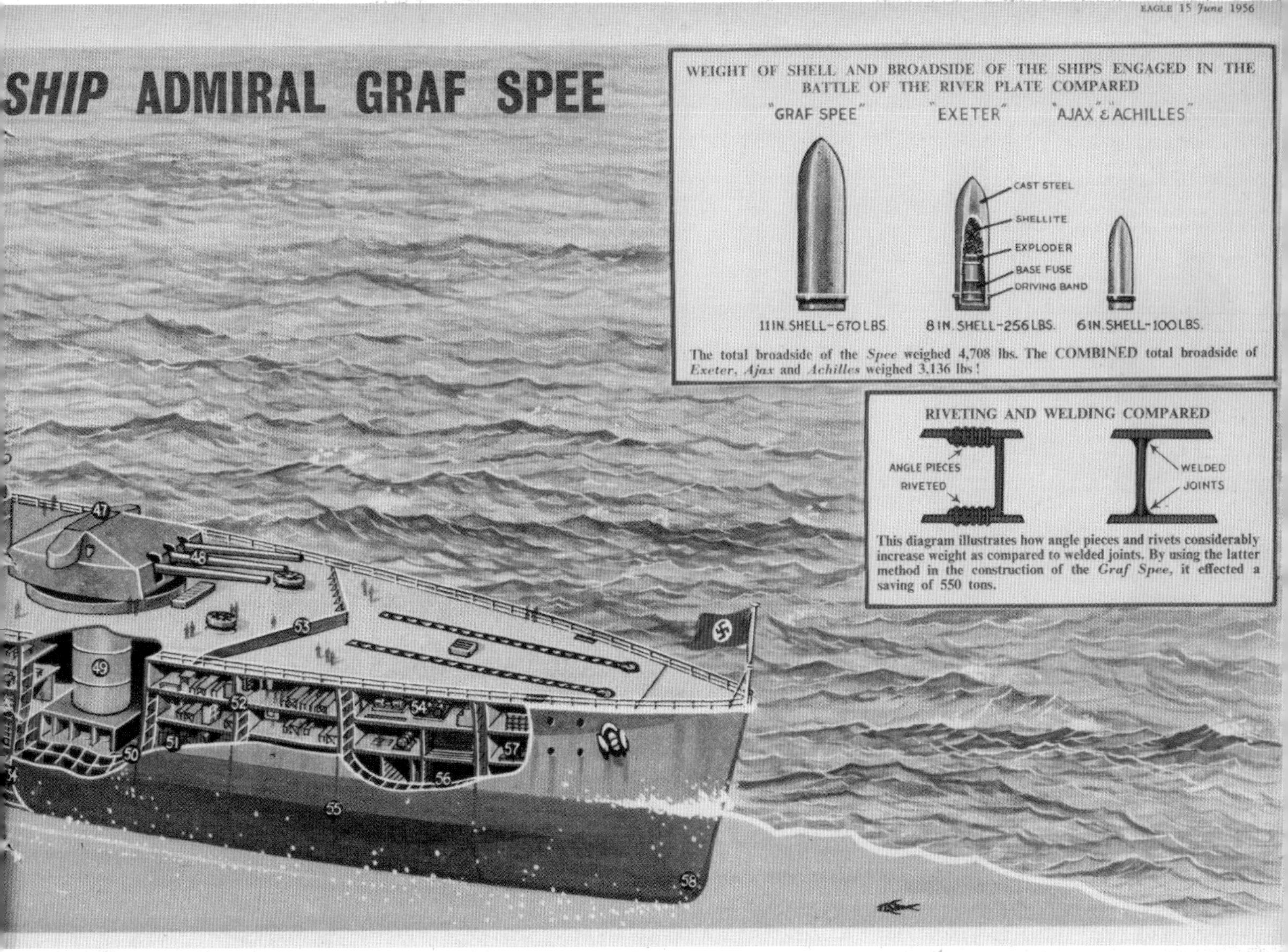
EAGLE 15 June 1956
SHIP ADMIRAL GRAF SPEE
WEIGHT OF SHELL AND BROADSIDE OF THE SHIPS ENGAGED IN THE BATTLE OF THE RIVER PLATE COMPARED
"GRAF SPEE"
"EXETER"
"AJAX" & "ACHILLES"
CAST STEEL
SHELLITE
EXPLODER
BASE FUSE
DRIVING BAND
11 IN. SHELL – 670 LBS.
8 IN. SHELL – 256 LBS.
6 IN. SHELL – 100 LBS.
The total broadside of the *Spee* weighed 4,708 lbs. The COMBINED total broadside of *Exeter, Ajax* and *Achilles* weighed 3,136 lbs!
RIVETING AND WELDING COMPARED
ANGLE PIECES
RIVETED
WELDED
JOINTS
This diagram illustrates how angle pieces and rivets considerably increase weight as compared to welded joints. By using the latter method in the construction of the *Graf Spee*, it effected a saving of 550 tons.
47
48
49
50
51
52
53
54
55
56
57
58

BATTLESHIP

EAGLE GALLERY OF FAMOUS SPORTSMEN

No. 36 FRED TRUEMAN (*Yorkshire and England*)

This 21-year-old ex-miner from Stainton, Yorkshire, who is at present serving in the R.A.F., made a sensational Test debut for England this season when he took four India wickets for 27 runs, three of them in eight balls without conceding a run. Already he is being called a second Larwood because, in short spells, he is the fastest bowler England has had since the "Nottingham Express" was in his prime. Fred, who is strongly-built, and also a hard-hitting batsman, made his first appearance in first-class cricket in 1949, and was selected for a Test trial in 1950. Last year he did the "hat trick" against Notts and gained his county cap. He is certainly a player to watch.

EAGLE GALLERY OF FAMOUS SPORTSMEN

No. 67 JOE DAVIS

Joe Davis, undefeated World Snooker champion for twenty years, is one of sport's greatest names. Recently, aged 51, Joe completed his 500th century, a feat that will probably never be equalled. To score a snooker century a player must 'pot' one of twenty-one balls in one of six pockets with every stroke, playing reds and colours in correct order until 100 has been scored.

Joe made his first century in 1927, his 500th in February of this year. Most of his hundreds were made with 'Old Faithful', the cue he bought for 7s 6d in 1929.

PETER MURPHY (*Birmingham City*) beats his man

Former Spurs player, PETER MURPHY, noted for his speed, craft and accurate marksmanship, has played a big part in Birmingham City's League and Cup success this season, and in the pictures he demonstrates a sleight-of-foot trick that had Tommy Briggs somewhat baffled. 'Got him this time!' Tommy thought to himself as he advanced to the tackle. He was almost certain that Peter would attempt to move the ball outside him. Then he had a moment's doubt. A feint of Peter's foot, and the mere hint of a sway *inside* made Tommy start to shift his weight – just what Peter wanted. At once the quicksilver inside forward made an oblique turn and swept past him on the outside with the ball under close control. Simple? So it looks in the pictures. But in fact it all happened quick-as-a-wink, the result of Tommy's split-second's hesitation. And of course it is the result of years of practice on Peter's part.

RANDY TURPIN'S PET PUNCHES by W. BARRINGTON DALBY No 1

[*Pictures by Carl Sutton*]

Here you see Randy shadow-boxing, and in the pictures he is setting himself to throw that devastating left hook which has put many of his opponents down for the full count. Notice his beautiful balance and intense concentration as he looks for the opening.

He starts the punch – forward and upward – and then whips it over towards the jaw of his imaginary opponent. Notice particularly how Randy is turning his wrist at the last moment to make sure of landing with the knuckle part of the closed glove.

SPUNKY'S SPORTS QUIZ

What is the length of a Rugby pitch?

Answer. The laws state that the distance between goal-line and goal-line must not exceed 110 yards.

PROFESSOR BRITTAIN EXPLAINS: TIM

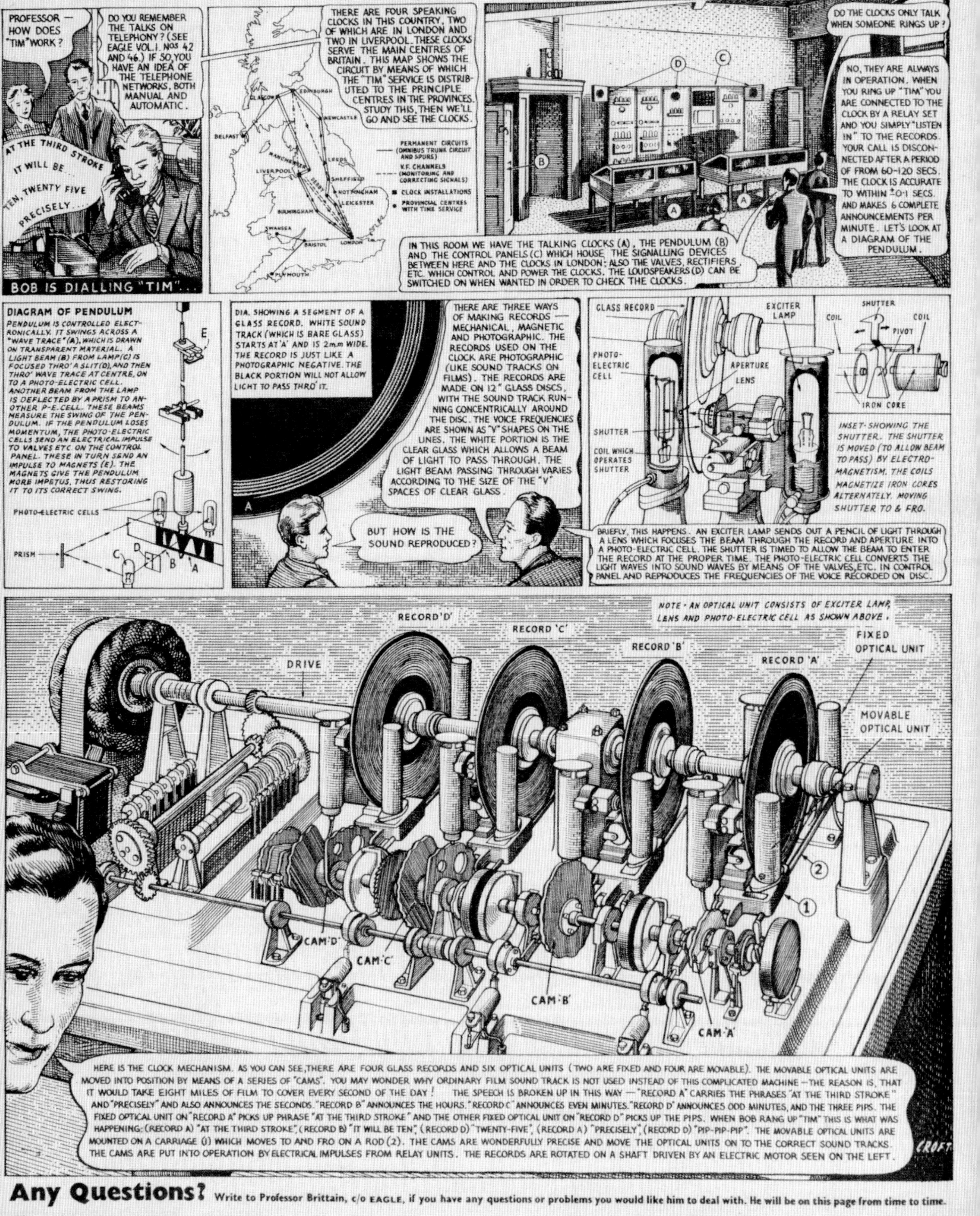
PROFESSOR — HOW DOES "TIM" WORK?
DO YOU REMEMBER THE TALKS ON TELEPHONY? (SEE EAGLE VOL.1. Nos 42 AND 46.) IF SO, YOU HAVE AN IDEA OF THE TELEPHONE NETWORKS, BOTH MANUAL AND AUTOMATIC.
AT THE THIRD STROKE IT WILL BE... TEN, TWENTY FIVE PRECISELY...
BOB IS DIALLING "TIM"...
THERE ARE FOUR SPEAKING CLOCKS IN THIS COUNTRY, TWO OF WHICH ARE IN LONDON AND TWO IN LIVERPOOL. THESE CLOCKS SERVE THE MAIN CENTRES OF BRITAIN. THIS MAP SHOWS THE CIRCUIT BY MEANS OF WHICH THE "TIM" SERVICE IS DISTRIBUTED TO THE PRINCIPLE CENTRES IN THE PROVINCES. STUDY THIS, THEN WE'LL GO AND SEE THE CLOCKS.
EDINBURGH
GLASGOW
NEWCASTLE
BELFAST
MANCHESTER
LEEDS
LIVERPOOL
SHEFFIELD
DERBY
NOTTINGHAM
LEICESTER
BIRMINGHAM
SWANSEA
BRISTOL
LONDON
PLYMOUTH
PERMANENT CIRCUITS (OMNIBUS TRUNK CIRCUIT AND SPURS)
V.F. CHANNELS (MONITORING AND CORRECTING SIGNALS)
CLOCK INSTALLATIONS
PROVINCIAL CENTRES WITH TIME SERVICE
DO THE CLOCKS ONLY TALK WHEN SOMEONE RINGS UP?
NO, THEY ARE ALWAYS IN OPERATION. WHEN YOU RING UP "TIM" YOU ARE CONNECTED TO THE CLOCK BY A RELAY SET AND YOU SIMPLY "LISTEN IN" TO THE RECORDS. YOUR CALL IS DISCONNECTED AFTER A PERIOD OF FROM 60-120 SECS. THE CLOCK IS ACCURATE TO WITHIN ±0·1 SECS. AND MAKES 6 COMPLETE ANNOUNCEMENTS PER MINUTE. LET'S LOOK AT A DIAGRAM OF THE PENDULUM.
IN THIS ROOM WE HAVE THE TALKING CLOCKS (A), THE PENDULUM (B) AND THE CONTROL PANELS (C) WHICH HOUSE THE SIGNALLING DEVICES BETWEEN HERE AND THE CLOCKS IN LONDON; ALSO THE VALVES, RECTIFIERS, ETC. WHICH CONTROL AND POWER THE CLOCKS. THE LOUDSPEAKERS (D) CAN BE SWITCHED ON WHEN WANTED IN ORDER TO CHECK THE CLOCKS.
DIAGRAM OF PENDULUM
PENDULUM IS CONTROLLED ELECTRONICALLY. IT SWINGS ACROSS A "WAVE TRACE" (A), WHICH IS DRAWN ON TRANSPARENT MATERIAL. A LIGHT BEAM (B) FROM LAMP (C) IS FOCUSED THRO' A SLIT (D), AND THEN THRO' WAVE TRACE AT CENTRE, ON TO A PHOTO-ELECTRIC CELL. ANOTHER BEAM FROM THE LAMP IS DEFLECTED BY A PRISM TO ANOTHER P-E. CELL. THESE BEAMS MEASURE THE SWING OF THE PENDULUM. IF THE PENDULUM LOSES MOMENTUM, THE PHOTO-ELECTRIC CELLS SEND AN ELECTRICAL IMPULSE TO VALVES ETC. ON THE CONTROL PANEL. THESE IN TURN SEND AN IMPULSE TO MAGNETS (E). THE MAGNETS GIVE THE PENDULUM MORE IMPETUS, THUS RESTORING IT TO ITS CORRECT SWING.
PHOTO-ELECTRIC CELLS
PRISM
DIA. SHOWING A SEGMENT OF A GLASS RECORD. WHITE SOUND TRACK (WHICH IS BARE GLASS) STARTS AT 'A' AND IS 2mm WIDE. THE RECORD IS JUST LIKE A PHOTOGRAPHIC NEGATIVE. THE BLACK PORTION WILL NOT ALLOW LIGHT TO PASS THRO' IT.
THERE ARE THREE WAYS OF MAKING RECORDS — MECHANICAL, MAGNETIC AND PHOTOGRAPHIC. THE RECORDS USED ON THE CLOCK ARE PHOTOGRAPHIC (LIKE SOUND TRACKS ON FILMS). THE RECORDS ARE MADE ON 12" GLASS DISCS, WITH THE SOUND TRACK RUNNING CONCENTRICALLY AROUND THE DISC. THE VOICE FREQUENCIES ARE SHOWN AS "V" SHAPES ON THE LINES. THE WHITE PORTION IS THE CLEAR GLASS WHICH ALLOWS A BEAM OF LIGHT TO PASS THROUGH. THE LIGHT BEAM PASSING THROUGH VARIES ACCORDING TO THE SIZE OF THE "V" SPACES OF CLEAR GLASS.
BUT HOW IS THE SOUND REPRODUCED?
GLASS RECORD
EXCITER LAMP
PHOTO-ELECTRIC CELL
APERTURE
LENS
SHUTTER
COIL WHICH OPERATES SHUTTER
SHUTTER
COIL
PIVOT
COIL
IRON CORE
INSET-SHOWING THE SHUTTER. THE SHUTTER IS MOVED (TO ALLOW BEAM TO PASS) BY ELECTRO-MAGNETISM. THE COILS MAGNETIZE IRON CORES ALTERNATELY. MOVING SHUTTER TO & FRO.
BRIEFLY, THIS HAPPENS. AN EXCITER LAMP SENDS OUT A PENCIL OF LIGHT THROUGH A LENS WHICH FOCUSES THE BEAM THROUGH THE RECORD AND APERTURE INTO A PHOTO-ELECTRIC CELL. THE SHUTTER IS TIMED TO ALLOW THE BEAM TO ENTER THE RECORD AT THE PROPER TIME. THE PHOTO-ELECTRIC CELL CONVERTS THE LIGHT WAVES INTO SOUND WAVES BY MEANS OF THE VALVES, ETC. IN CONTROL PANEL AND REPRODUCES THE FREQUENCIES OF THE VOICE RECORDED ON DISC.
NOTE · AN OPTICAL UNIT CONSISTS OF EXCITER LAMP, LENS AND PHOTO-ELECTRIC CELL AS SHOWN ABOVE.
RECORD 'D'
RECORD 'C'
RECORD 'B'
RECORD 'A'
FIXED OPTICAL UNIT
DRIVE
MOVABLE OPTICAL UNIT
CAM 'D'
CAM 'C'
CAM 'B'
CAM 'A'
HERE IS THE CLOCK MECHANISM. AS YOU CAN SEE, THERE ARE FOUR GLASS RECORDS AND SIX OPTICAL UNITS (TWO ARE FIXED AND FOUR ARE MOVABLE). THE MOVABLE OPTICAL UNITS ARE MOVED INTO POSITION BY MEANS OF A SERIES OF "CAMS". YOU MAY WONDER WHY ORDINARY FILM SOUND TRACK IS NOT USED INSTEAD OF THIS COMPLICATED MACHINE — THE REASON IS, THAT IT WOULD TAKE EIGHT MILES OF FILM TO COVER EVERY SECOND OF THE DAY! THE SPEECH IS BROKEN UP IN THIS WAY — "RECORD A" CARRIES THE PHRASES "AT THE THIRD STROKE" AND "PRECISELY" AND ALSO ANNOUNCES THE SECONDS. "RECORD B" ANNOUNCES THE HOURS. "RECORD C" ANNOUNCES EVEN MINUTES. "RECORD D" ANNOUNCES ODD MINUTES, AND THE THREE PIPS. THE FIXED OPTICAL UNIT ON "RECORD A" PICKS UP PHRASE "AT THE THIRD STROKE" AND THE OTHER FIXED OPTICAL UNIT ON "RECORD D" PICKS UP THE PIPS. WHEN BOB RANG UP "TIM" THIS IS WHAT WAS HAPPENING: (RECORD A) "AT THE THIRD STROKE", (RECORD B) "IT WILL BE TEN", (RECORD D) "TWENTY-FIVE", (RECORD A) "PRECISELY", (RECORD D) "PIP-PIP-PIP". THE MOVABLE OPTICAL UNITS ARE MOUNTED ON A CARRIAGE (1) WHICH MOVES TO AND FRO ON A ROD (2). THE CAMS ARE WONDERFULLY PRECISE AND MOVE THE OPTICAL UNITS ON TO THE CORRECT SOUND TRACKS. THE CAMS ARE PUT INTO OPERATION BY ELECTRICAL IMPULSES FROM RELAY UNITS. THE RECORDS ARE ROTATED ON A SHAFT DRIVEN BY AN ELECTRIC MOTOR SEEN ON THE LEFT.
CROFT

Any Questions? Write to Professor Brittain, c/o EAGLE, if you have any questions or problems you would like him to deal with. He will be on this page from time to time.

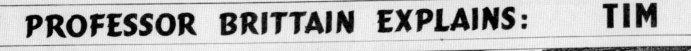

P.C.49 by ALAN STRANKS and JOHN WORSLEY THE CASE OF THE SPOTTED TOAD

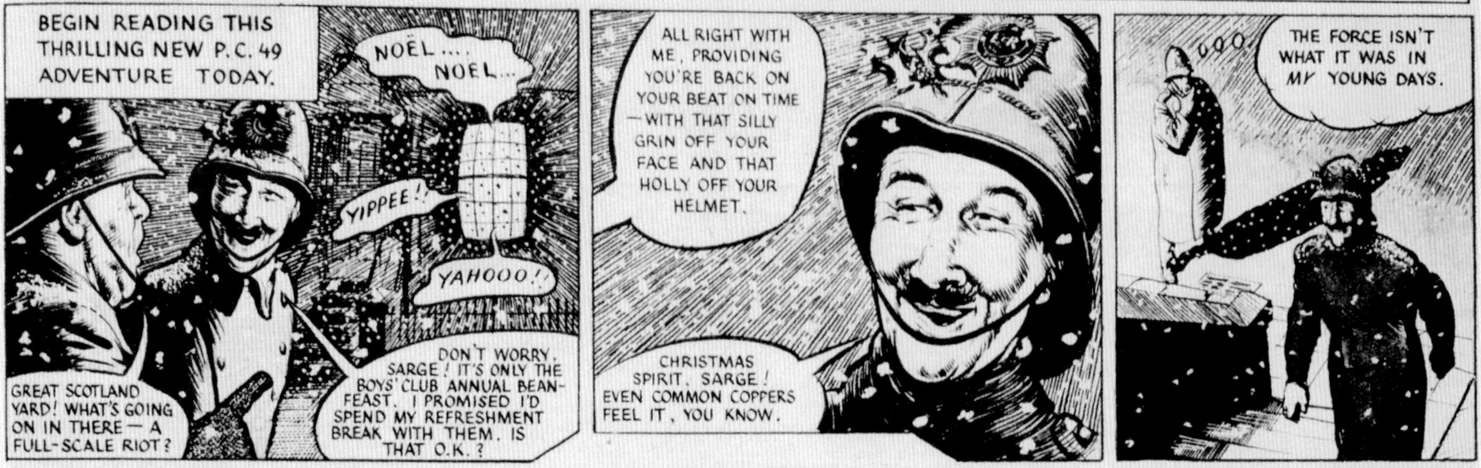

BEGIN READING THIS THRILLING NEW P.C. 49 ADVENTURE TODAY.
NOËL.... NOEL...
YIPPEE!
YAHOOO!
GREAT SCOTLAND YARD! WHAT'S GOING ON IN THERE — A FULL-SCALE RIOT?
DON'T WORRY, SARGE! IT'S ONLY THE BOYS' CLUB ANNUAL BEAN-FEAST. I PROMISED I'D SPEND MY REFRESHMENT BREAK WITH THEM. IS THAT O.K.?
ALL RIGHT WITH ME, PROVIDING YOU'RE BACK ON YOUR BEAT ON TIME — WITH THAT SILLY GRIN OFF YOUR FACE AND THAT HOLLY OFF YOUR HELMET.
CHRISTMAS SPIRIT, SARGE! EVEN COMMON COPPERS FEEL IT, YOU KNOW.
THE FORCE ISN'T WHAT IT WAS IN MY YOUNG DAYS.

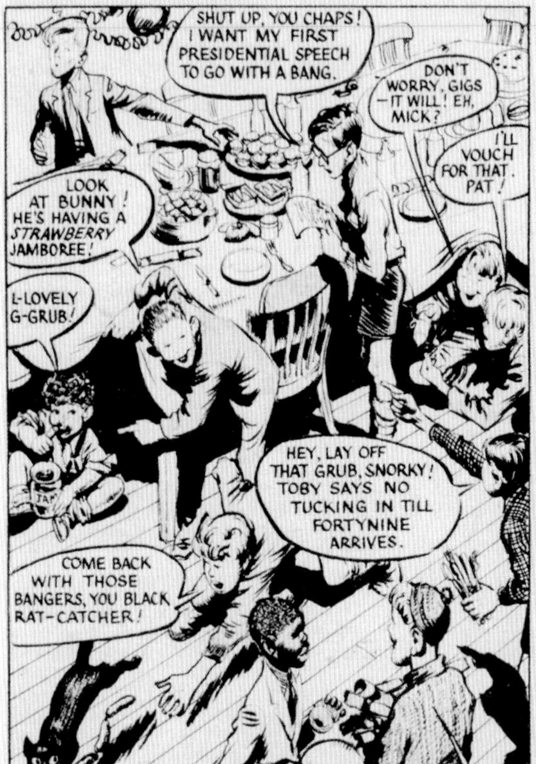

SHUT UP, YOU CHAPS! I WANT MY FIRST PRESIDENTIAL SPEECH TO GO WITH A BANG.
DON'T WORRY, GIGS — IT WILL! EH, MICK?
I'LL VOUCH FOR THAT, PAT!
LOOK AT BUNNY! HE'S HAVING A STRAWBERRY JAMBOREE!
L-LOVELY G-GRUB!
HEY, LAY OFF THAT GRUB, SNORKY! TOBY SAYS NO TUCKING IN TILL FORTYNINE ARRIVES.
COME BACK WITH THOSE BANGERS, YOU BLACK RAT-CATCHER!
WHEN WILL FORTYNINE ARRIVE, O TOBY?
ANY MINUTE NOW, TIKI OLD SCOUT!

P.C. 49'S CHRISTMAS PARTY

All the Gang had got together
For a wizard Christmas Treat.
Happy laughter shook each rafter at The Club!
Outside was bitter weather –
Driving snow and blinding sleet;
Inside was Bags of Cheer and Tons of Grub!

Sure, the MULLIGANS were present –
Och, they're Terrible those Twins!
And they're up to ev'ry mortal kind of trick.
But you can't tell who's the culprit,
For they're like as two new pins
And you might be blaming PAT instead of MICK.

There were TOBY, MONGATIKI,
SNORKY, GIGS and BUNNY, too,
With his funny little "physog" all a-shine,
Impatiently awaiting
For a certain Bloke in Blue –
Their Friend and Founder – P.C. FORTY-NINE.

When at last their Hero entered
How the Gang began to shout!
They nearly burst his eardrums with the din!
They drank his health thrice over
Till the Ginger Beer ran out,
Then ev'rybody started tucking in!

How they talked of the Adventures
They had shared in days gone past
And the perils they had faced beside their Chum.
The pile of grub diminished
And the moments flew too fast
While they dreamed of New Adventures yet to come.

All too soon the Party ended,
All too soon the grub was gone,
Then at last The Founder scrambled to his feet.
"Well, Cheerio!" he chortled,
"Time and Crime are marching on,
And it's time that I got marching on my beat!"

As he stood there, gaily waving
At the open Clubroom door
He little knew that just across the road
Two evil men were waiting
With a grudge against the Law
And so begins – "The Case of The Spotted Toad."

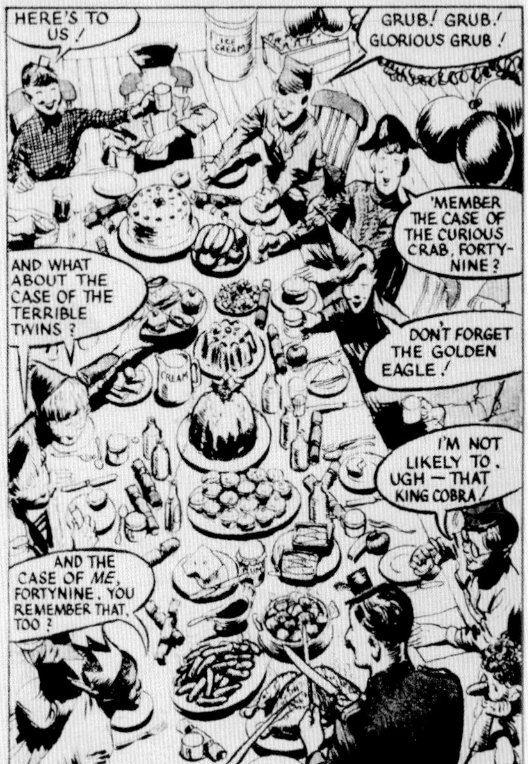

HERE'S TO US!
GRUB! GRUB! GLORIOUS GRUB!
'MEMBER THE CASE OF THE CURIOUS CRAB, FORTY-NINE?
AND WHAT ABOUT THE CASE OF THE TERRIBLE TWINS?
DON'T FORGET THE GOLDEN EAGLE!
I'M NOT LIKELY TO. UGH — THAT KING COBRA!
AND THE CASE OF ME, FORTYNINE, YOU REMEMBER THAT, TOO?
I REMEMBER 'EM ALL, CHUMS — AND THE GRAND PARTS YOU FELLOWS PLAYED. I WONDER WHAT THE NEXT ONE WILL BE?
C-CRIME MARCHES ON!

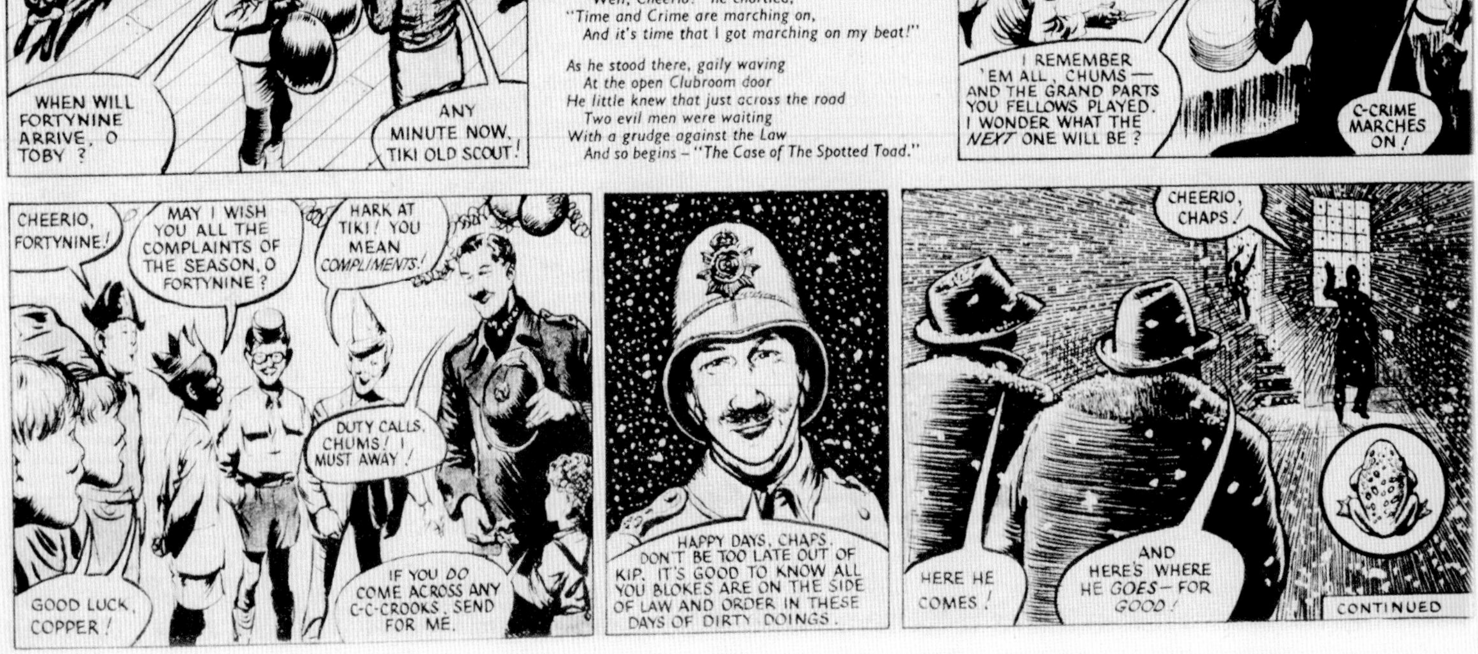

CHEERIO, FORTYNINE!
MAY I WISH YOU ALL THE COMPLAINTS OF THE SEASON, O FORTYNINE?
HARK AT TIKI! YOU MEAN COMPLIMENTS!
DUTY CALLS, CHUMS! I MUST AWAY!
GOOD LUCK, COPPER!
IF YOU DO COME ACROSS ANY C-C-CROOKS, SEND FOR ME.
HAPPY DAYS, CHAPS. DON'T BE TOO LATE OUT OF KIP. IT'S GOOD TO KNOW ALL YOU BLOKES ARE ON THE SIDE OF LAW AND ORDER IN THESE DAYS OF DIRTY DOINGS.
CHEERIO, CHAPS!
HERE HE COMES!
AND HERE'S WHERE HE GOES — FOR GOOD!
CONTINUED

A real rifle!

THE B.S.A. Cadet and Cadjet Major Air Rifles are the real thing. Strongly built, light and easy to handle, B.S.A. Air Rifles are perfect for target shooting or for killing vermin. Both models use inexpensive 'Pylarm' pellets.

THE CADET
is sufficiently powerful to kill rats and other vermin at up to 30 yards. Tops for target shooting too. Extra heavy trigger pull for safety in inexperienced hands.

THE CADET MAJOR
is larger and more powerful than the 'Cadet'. Fitted with a variable trigger and adjustable rear-sight, it has a range of 40 yards.

BSA
CADET & CADET MAJOR AIR RIFLES

Write for fully illustrated Leaflet and address of your nearest
stockist to B.S.A. GUNS LTD. 117, ARMOURY RD. BIRMINGHAM 11

BUILD REALISTIC MODELS with
BRICKPLAYER
Bricks & Mortar Building Kits

It enables you to build Fire Stations (see illustration), Houses, Garages, Railway Stations, Signal Boxes, or from your own imagination. All railway models will fit 'O' gauge scale. Buildings can be permanent, or dismantled by merely soaking in water and the bricks used again and again.

Brickplayer Kits at 28/6 and 52/6 are available from Good Toyshops, Hobby Shops and Departmental Stores.

If your dealer cannot supply, write for address of nearest stockist to :

J. W. SPEAR & SONS LTD. (Dept. E), ENFIELD, MIDDLESEX

EAGLE 13 *February* 1953

BRITISH CARS FOR EXPORT
THE VAUXHALL *VELOX*

Did you know that, on an average, 27,000 British-made cars are exported every month from this country? Their value is £9,000,000.

The new Vauxhall *Velox* is one of these cars and is of outstanding design. It is long, wide and handsome, which has a special appeal for buyers overseas. The model shown here is fitted with left-hand steering. The 2½ litre, 6-cylinder 'square' engine, rated at 23½ h.p. gives a maximum speed of 80 m.p.h. The gearbox is built as a unit with the engine, and acceleration is 0 to 50 m.p.h. through all the gears, using the steering column gear-change lever, in 14 seconds.

The Vauxhall *Wyvern* is a very similar car but has a smaller, 1½ litre engine.

KEY TO PARTS

(1) Cooling radiator and fan. (2) Water pump and thermostat. (3) Air cleaner for carburettor. (4) Zenith carburettor. (5) Overhead valves. (6) Two rear pistons of 6-cylinder 'square' engine, that is, an engine in which the diameter of the piston is equal to the piston stroke. (7) Exhaust pipe. (8) Dynamo for charging battery. (9) Front Lockheed hydraulic brake; two-leading-shoe type. (10) Independent coil-spring front suspension. (11) Worm and ball steering gear. (12) Steering column gear changing connections to gearbox. (13) Single plate clutch. (14) Gearbox with three forward speeds and one reverse; synchromesh on top and second speeds. (15) 12-volt battery for starting, lighting and coil ignition. (16) Ventilation and car heating unit. (17) Ducts to car interior and anti-mist for windscreen. (18) Front universal. (19) Hand-brake lever for mechanically operated rear brakes. (20) Steering column gear-change lever. (21) Push-button door openers. (22) Outside push-button door openers. (23) Propeller shaft to back axle. (24) Propeller shaft recess for allowing up and down movement of the back axle. (25) Upholstery of back seat. (26) Rear universal joint. (27) Hypoid (off-centre) spiral bevel back axle drive and differential casing. (28) Hydraulic brake leads. (29) Leading and trailing shoe type hydraulic rear brakes. (30) Telescopic shock absorbers fixed to rear springs. (31) Petrol tank (11 gallons). (32) Luggage boot. (33) Spare wheel. (34) Exhaust pipe.

L. ASHWELL WOOD

VAUXHA

EAGLE 13 *February* 1953

RADIATOR RECOGNITION

Diagram showing the piston and cylinder of a 'square' engine. The bore and stroke are the same.

LL VELOX

The life of a Universe-saving hero can be tough, so home comforts are always gratefully received. The Automatic Shaving Kit and the hi-tech shower were years ahead of their time. They still are. Occasionally some of the artwork excels even the amazing standards set by the studio, and it is easy to see why so many of the artists worked such long unsociable hours. It seems unnecessary to have such high levels of detail, but it was this specifically which made *Eagle*, and *Dan Dare* and the all-important front-page, stand head and shoulders above the opposition of the time.

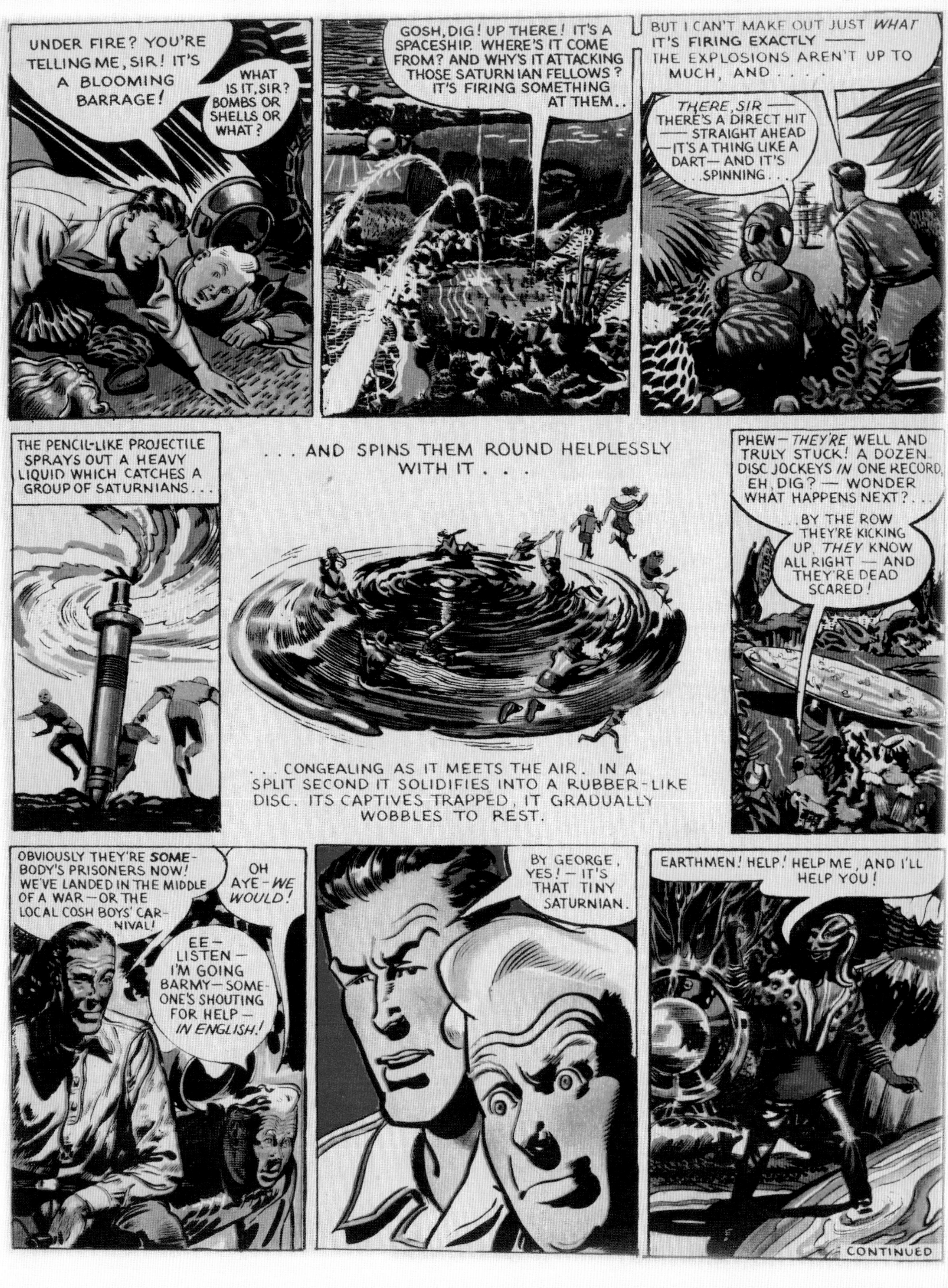
UNDER FIRE? YOU'RE TELLING ME, SIR! IT'S A BLOOMING BARRAGE!
WHAT IS IT, SIR? BOMBS OR SHELLS OR WHAT?
GOSH, DIG! UP THERE! IT'S A SPACESHIP. WHERE'S IT COME FROM? AND WHY'S IT ATTACKING THOSE SATURNIAN FELLOWS? IT'S FIRING SOMETHING AT THEM . .
BUT I CAN'T MAKE OUT JUST WHAT IT'S FIRING EXACTLY —— THE EXPLOSIONS AREN'T UP TO MUCH, AND . . . .
THERE, SIR — THERE'S A DIRECT HIT — STRAIGHT AHEAD — IT'S A THING LIKE A DART — AND IT'S . . SPINNING . . .
THE PENCIL-LIKE PROJECTILE SPRAYS OUT A HEAVY LIQUID WHICH CATCHES A GROUP OF SATURNIANS . . .
. . . AND SPINS THEM ROUND HELPLESSLY WITH IT . . .
. . . CONGEALING AS IT MEETS THE AIR. IN A SPLIT SECOND IT SOLIDIFIES INTO A RUBBER-LIKE DISC. ITS CAPTIVES TRAPPED, IT GRADUALLY WOBBLES TO REST.
PHEW — THEY'RE WELL AND TRULY STUCK! A DOZEN DISC JOCKEYS IN ONE RECORD, EH, DIG? — WONDER WHAT HAPPENS NEXT? . .
. . BY THE ROW THEY'RE KICKING UP, THEY KNOW ALL RIGHT — AND THEY'RE DEAD SCARED!
OBVIOUSLY THEY'RE SOMEBODY'S PRISONERS NOW! WE'VE LANDED IN THE MIDDLE OF A WAR — OR THE LOCAL COSH BOYS' CARNIVAL!
OH AYE — WE WOULD!
EE — LISTEN — I'M GOING BARMY — SOMEONE'S SHOUTING FOR HELP — IN ENGLISH!
BY GEORGE, YES! — IT'S THAT TINY SATURNIAN.
EARTHMEN! HELP! HELP ME, AND I'LL HELP YOU!
CONTINUED

GOOD NEWS for your younger brothers and sisters!

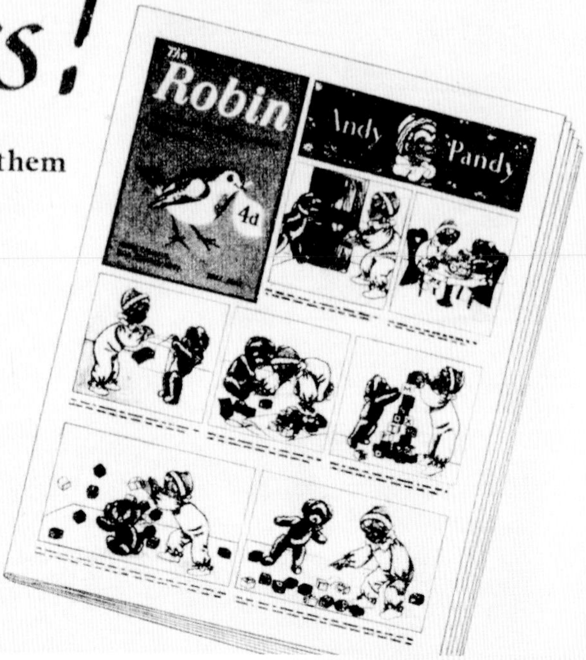
The
Robin
4d
Andy
Pandy

The Robin

— a strip cartoon paper **specially for them**

Every Monday 4d

Now boys and girls under 7 years old are going to have a paper of their very own . . . THE ROBIN ! Just like EAGLE and GIRL, it will have lots of colour, and be full of grand pictures and stories.

There'll be lots of new friends to meet in THE ROBIN's 12 big pages—and some already well known and loved. The popular BBC characters Andy Pandy . . . Tai-Lu . . . The Flowerpot Men *exciting things to cut out for scrapbooks, stories to read, and lots of puzzles and fun.*

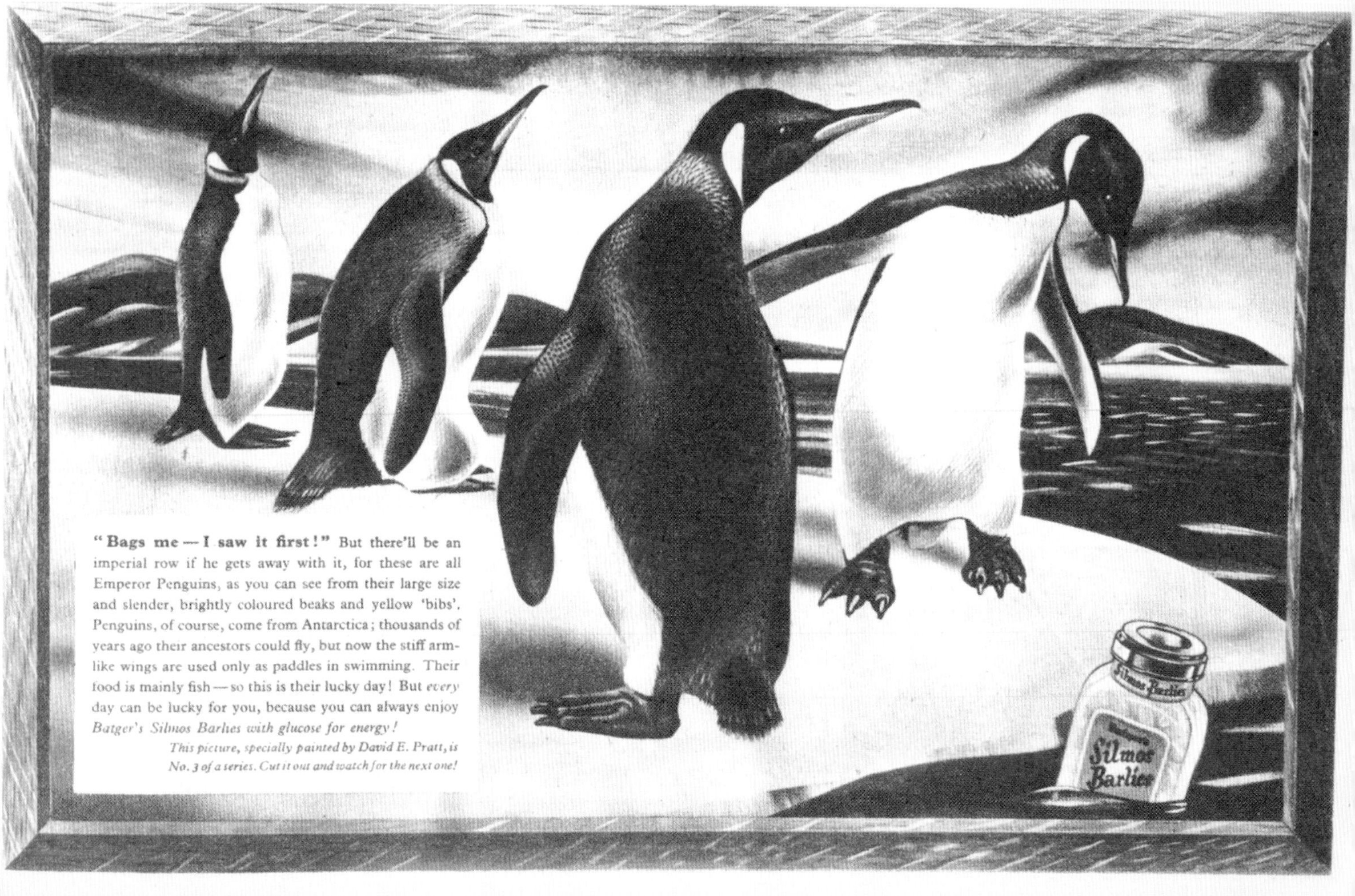
Silmos Barlies
Silmos
Barlies

"Bags me — I saw it first!" But there'll be an imperial row if he gets away with it, for these are all Emperor Penguins, as you can see from their large size and slender, brightly coloured beaks and yellow 'bibs'. Penguins, of course, come from Antarctica; thousands of years ago their ancestors could fly, but now the stiff arm-like wings are used only as paddles in swimming. Their food is mainly fish — so this is their lucky day! But *every* day can be lucky for you, because you can always enjoy *Batger's Silmos Barlies with glucose for energy!*

This picture, specially painted by David E. Pratt, is No. 3 of a series. Cut it out and watch for the next one!

PRIZEWINNERS AT THE CIRCUS

Two thousand EAGLE and GIRL prize-winners were taken to Bertram Mills Circus at Olympia, where they had a wonderful time. Horses, zebras, dogs, elephants, sea-lions and penguins all seemed set to give their best performance and appeared to enjoy the show every bit as much as the onlookers.

During the performance EAGLE readers were first amazed, then delighted, to find that the Mekon himself was performing in the ring.

At the end of the evening, Mr Bernard Mills asked two lucky members, sitting in certain seats, to come down into the ring where he presented them with seven tickets each for next year's Circus at Olympia.

The Auguste whispers a few friendly tips to the Mekon on circus ring procedure.

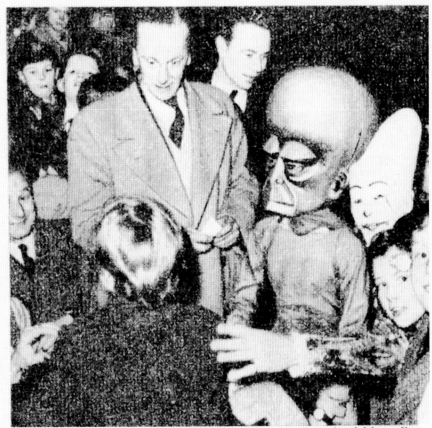

The Mekon at the Circus! But underneath that grim, green head it's really Paul, EAGLE's postboy!

WHODUNNIT?   Find the vital clue!

Alec, the office-boy, comes back from lunch to find the office ransacked and Miss Potts, the secretary, sitting tied in her chair.

Alec unties Miss Potts and phones the police. "What's happened?" he cries. Before Miss Potts can explain the police arrive.

Miss Potts tells the police inspector that two men held her up and tied her in the chair. Then they started to ransack the office before they found the week's takings.

The inspector seems to be satisfied – but Alec isn't. He tells the inspector something he's spotted which leads to Miss Potts' arrest. Can you spot what gave Miss Potts away?

The Leaf of Life

IN JAPAN there exists a plant which cannot be killed. Even when cut in half it will thrive without warmth or moisture. A leaf of it pressed between the pages of a book can throw out roots and grow. Such a plant was well named 'The Leaf of Life.' – *Ronald Webster, Camelon, Falkirk, Stirling.*

The Mekon's Here!

"HOW'S THIS for a scarer!" It won first prize in the local Coronation Carnival. – *H. Godsland, Easton, Nr. Stamford, Northamptonshire.*

CONKERS ...a game linking the Elizabethan eras

The game is as old as the country's horse-chestnut trees – it was mentioned by Shakespeare and played in the villages of Merrie England during the reign of Elizabeth I. Research has shown that the origins of the game are lost in the mists of antiquity; however, the experts say that it is quite likely that the game as we know it differs only slightly from the original game of Conqueror (hence the derivation 'Conkers') played by men in bygone times.

Text books of English folk-lore in the Central Reference Library, indicate that the recognized method of amassing victories, as in the case of a 'fiftyer' becoming a 'sixtyer' on beating a 'tenner', can be traced to the ancient superstitions of primitive warriors, who assumed that the virtues of a defeated enemy's weapon passed into their own when the battle was won.

During the reign of Good Queen Bess, Conkers was already established as a traditional game of English children. In a recent Television production of Shakespeare's *Merrie Wives of Windsor* – the boys in the play were shown playing Conkers. The picture shows a typical old-time game in progress.

Here is twelve-year-old Ian Lyons who recently defeated the pick of England's Conker players to become Television's National Champion. Ian's lapel proudly bears witness to his skill as a Konka player. Ian says, 'It's great fun and more interesting than ordinary Conkers – and most important of all – lets me play my favourite game all the year round!'

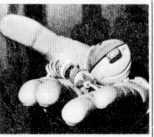

This shows the New Elizabethan Konka made of tough cellulose acetate – a material typical of this modern age. The counters and Eagle strung on the whipcord are for scoring, providing actual proof of the owner's prowess.

Here is Ian lining up for a 'strike'. The action is similar to the traditional version, with the difference that great accuracy is required, rather than brute force, to ensure a hit on the nose. Ian is not going to miss this one!

A successful strike! This remarkable strobos-copic action picture taken at 1/10,000 sec. exposure, shows the Konka's cap flying up the cord. Ian is 'keeping his eye on the ball' – a good tip for all would-be champions!

LANCASHIRE HOTPOT
by KENNETH WHEELER

To which Lancashire club will the honours go in this Coronation year Cup Final at Wembley? To famous Bolton Wanderers, six times finalists, three times Cup winners and unbeaten at Wembley; or to gallant Blackpool, three times finalists since the war, but never the winners? Will everybody's favourite, Stanley Matthews, at last capture that elusive winners' medal, or will Nat Lofthouse, the centre forward everyone admires, crown his triumphant season with this additional honour?

Let tomorrow's game decide the better team on the day, and whichever it proves to be you can rest assured that the Cup couldn't go to a finer set of sportsmen.

Now for messages from the rival managers and captains:

The Rival Managers

Bill Ridding, who was England's trainer in the World Cup series at Rio, took us into the Bolton dressing room and pointed to a notice hanging on the wall.

Teach me to win when I may, and, if I may not win, then, above all I pray, make me a good loser, we read.

'That is the spirit in which Bolton Wanderers will take the field at Wembley, as they do in all their games', said Bill Ridding. 'But the boys are playing well, they are fit and confident. What's more we've got a match-winner just as outstanding as Blackpool's Stanley Matthews; Nat Lofthouse.

'Perfect timing, balance and co-ordination are his to command as a result of long practice allied to natural ability. You'll note that he has scored in every round so far.

'I must admit to having a personal angle here. As a former centre forward, it was always my ambition to play on the winning side at Wembley, but injury ended my playing days at the age of 24. Now I can only achieve my ambition by remote control and through Nat.

'But football is a team game, and it is on Bolton's splendid harmony and team work this season that I base my confidence that Willie Moir, and not Harry Johnston, will be first up the steps after the match is over to receive the Cup'.

Next we asked for the views of Joe Smith, manager of Blackpool and former international inside forward who scored a winning goal in the first Cup Final ever played at Wembley.

'I've been fortunate enough to play in two Wembley Cup Finals', said Joe Smith, 'and each time I was on the winning side. Strangely enough, my team was Bolton Wanderers!

'There have always been friendly connections, as well as a strong rivalry, between Blackpool and Bolton, but there is no doubt which side I shall be on in this Final.

'Although unbeaten at Wembley as a Bolton player, I've twice seen the team I manage beaten there, and now I want to see Blackpool win the Cup for the first time in history.

'No manager could wish for a finer set of lads than I've got at Bloomfield Road. From star internationals like Stanley Matthews, Stan Mortensen and Harry Johnston – not forgetting Allan Brown – down to the youngest members of the staff – they give a loyalty and service to our club that is without equal.

'I feel that victory can be the only just reward for their fighting spirit'.

The Rival Captains

'I've been a Blackpool player since I was fifteen years old, and there's only one team for me!' said Harry Johnston, of Blackpool and England. 'Since I first became skipper I've had one great ambition – to lead the Tangerines to victory at Wembley. Twice I've come near to realizing that ambition; now I'm hoping that it will be a case of third time lucky.

'We have a particular incentive to win this time. We owe it to Allan Brown, who again misses the Final, because he broke his leg in scoring the winning goal in the sixth round at Highbury, and to Stanley Matthews, whose glittering career would be tragically incomplete without the reward of a winners' medal.

'Winning isn't going to be easy because the Trotters are a grand team, but that's the way we want it. We all love a good fight. We'll do our best, and if that's not good enough then there'll be no bitter feelings down Blackpool way.'

The final word goes to Willie Moir, of Bolton Wanderers and Scotland.

'They're cautious folk in Stoneywood, near Aberdeen, where I come from, so you can't expect me to risk a prophecy,' said Willie Moir, 'but this I will say: if we don't win the Cup it won't be for want of trying.

'I'm proud to have been given the honour of leading the Trotters this season, because they are the finest team I've ever known, in every sense. Like Harry Johnston I've been a footballer all my life, and my greatest ambition has always been to be on the winning side at Wembley.

'We can't both win, Harry, but I agree with you – let's make it a good fight, and may the better team win'.

England centre forward, NAT LOFTHOUSE, who could prove Bolton's match-winner.

Bootle born STAN HANSON is a fine, reliable goalie who joined Bolton in 1935. He is shown winning a duel with Everton's inside left in the Cup semi-final tie.

MALCOLM BARRASS, Bolton's international centre half, was born in Blackpool!

JOHNNY WHEELER (Bolton). He is wing half and deputy centre forward.

International Bolton forwards are HAROLD HASSALL (left) and BOBBY LANGTON (right).

TROTTERS' TRAINING MACHINE
With England trainer Bill Ridding as their manager the Bolton team are red-hot on training, and bad weather doesn't stop them. They have an indoor running track, and in the dressing room is this special cycling machine. As you move the pedals so the needle moves round the dial in front. Once round the dial represents a cycle ride of ½ mile.

Quicksilver STAN MORTENSEN is the Blackpool shooting-star who could, if he is fully fit, win the Cup for Blackpool. In the pictures on the right (taken by Carl Sutton) Stan is shown making one of his typical full-blooded drives at goal.

(Right) HARRY JOHNSTON, followed by Scottish international goalkeeper GEORGE FARM, leads the Blackpool team on to the field.
*
(Below). The sturdy Blackpool full-backs, EDDIE SHIMWELL (left) and TOM GARRETT (right).

Hard tackling HUGH KELLY is a hard-playing Scottish international wing half.

ERNIE TAYLOR, born in Sunderland, carves openings for the other Blackpool forwards.

Action plus! Speedy left-winger, BILL PERRY, is a South African. He played in the 1951 Final.

Inside, or centre forward JACKIE MUDIE is another from Scotland. He, too, played in the 1951 Final.

(Right). Making his third attempt to win the only football honour that has escaped him is EAGLE Readers' Favourite Footballer, STANLEY MATTHEWS. With Harry Johnston he shares the hope that it will be a case of third time lucky.

HARRY JOHNSTON, Blackpool Captain.

WILLIE MOIR, the Bolton Captain.

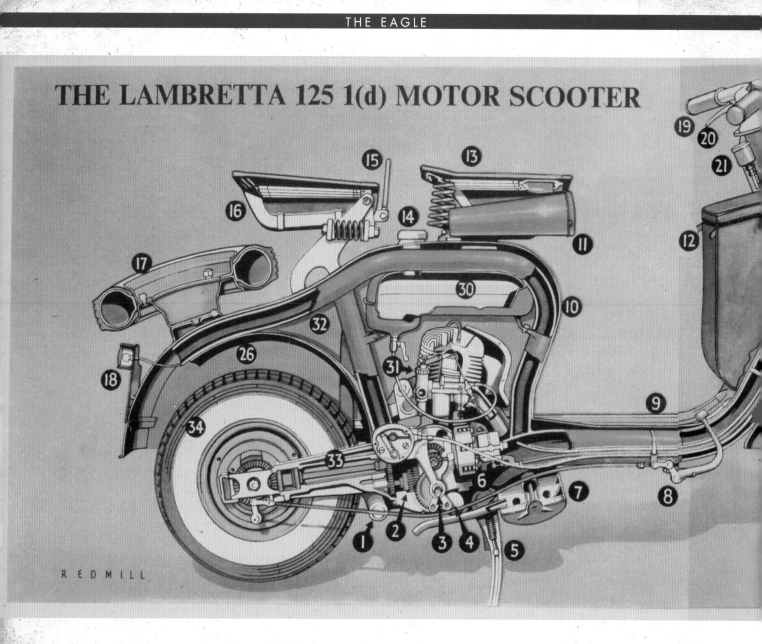

THE LAMBRETTA 125 1(d) MOTOR SCOOTER

REDMILL

THE COMPLETE

Motor scooters are not by any means a new type of vehicle. Many were produced after World War I, but they did not gain any great popularity. Today, however, they are firmly established, especially on the Continent. The Lambretta is Italian designed and built.

There are a number of reasons for their demand, notably economy. These small vehicles will do about 130-140 miles to the gallon, a pillion passenger can be carried in comfort and they are as weather proof as an open machine can be. A windscreen and luggage carrier can be fitted and the engine is fully enclosed and reliable.

Our sectional drawing is coloured to show up the machine's various characteristics, the standard colour of the scooter being greenish-grey as shown in the small drawing.

A sidecar for goods or passenger can be fitted.

ENGINE

Capacity: 123 cubic centimetres. Power: 5 h.p. Two-stroke single cylinder, air cooled. Engine, transmission and rear wheel together form a unit, which swings on a strong pivot incorporated in the frame, giving sturdiness and safety. Fan-cooled air directed around cylinder by cowl. Ignition and lighting by flywheel magneto. Unloaded weight: 187 lbs. Saddle height: 30 ins. Wheelbase: 50 ins.

KEY TO PARTS

(1) Torsion bar within transverse tube for rear-springing. (2) Gearbox; 3 speed. (3) Kickstart, not shown, is mounted here. (4) Engine pivot point. (5) Stand. (6) Multi-plate clutch. (7) Silencer. (8) Brake pedal with cable. (9) Footrest. This continues by the side of engine for pillion rider's use. (10) Sheet steel body-work. (11) Tool box. (12) Detachable bag. (13) Sprung saddle. (14) Filler cap. (15) Handle for use of pillion rider. (16) Saddle for pillion rider. (17) Spare wheel (extra). (18) Rear light. (19) Twist grip gear-change, combined with (20) Clutch lever. (21) Speedometer. (22) Combined light switch and horn button. (23) Front brake lever. (24) Headlamp. (25) Electric horn. (26-26) Metal panelling, easily detachable. The engine is entirely enclosed. (27) Tyres, 4 by 8 inches. (28) Front suspension by swinging arms and helical springs. (29) Brake arm and cable. Finned brake drums. (30) Fuel tank. Capacity: 1.3 galls. Reserve: ½ pint. Consumption: 140 m.p.g. Range: 190 miles. Lubrication: petroil 5%. (31) Carburettor incorporating a fuel filter. It is fitted on air filter which is not shown. (32) Frame of steel tube. (33) Shaft drive. (34) Wheels are made in two halves that can be taken apart. Therefore no tyre levers are required to fit a new tyre; interchangeable front and rear.

THE COMPLETE MACHINE

MACHINE

From the EDITOR
EAGLE 4 New St. Square, London, E.C.4.

1 May, 1953

NOTE the date – the first of May! And excitement is really beginning to run high with the Coronation only a month away.

London seems busier, bigger and more bustling than ever. Workmen are still hard at it, fixing stands on the Coronation route and putting up standards to hold decorations. The big stores are vying with one another for the most spectacular window displays to attract our overseas visitors.

Many people from distant lands have arrived already and almost any day you can spot a group of enquiring foreigners around a gesticulating Londoner as he tries, in the language of signs, to tell them which way to go for Trafalgar Square, Piccadilly, Buckingham Palace and so on. Everyone seems to end up looking slightly dazed and rather hazy about which direction to take, but finally smiles break out all round to show there is goodwill in plenty and that spirits are high.

You may like to know who have been appointed to carry the various standards in the Grand Procession in Westminster Abbey at the Coronation on June 2nd. The Union Standard will be carried by Captain J. L. M. Dymoke, the Standard of Wales by Lord Harlech, Ireland by Lord de L'Isle and Dudley, Scotland by Viscount Dudhope and England by the Earl of Derby. Following these will be the Royal Standard carried by Viscount Montgomery of Alamein.

CONGRATULATIONS to *Richard Marston* on winning the MUG's Badge. Nine-year-old Richard, living at 35 Church Road, Westbury - on - Trym, Bristol, had a pretty big responsibility to tackle recently. Just after the family had moved to a new house his father was posted to Egypt for two and a half years and his mother became very ill. No help was available for two days so Richard had to take over. He looked after his younger brother, aged three years, taking care of his mother, doing all the shopping, etc. – and all without any fuss. Even when his mother grew well again Richard still continued to do what he could to help her.

Yours sincerely,

Marcus Morris

Every boy can build with Meccano...

Brian Gulley of St. Saviours, Jersey, won a prize in the 1952/3 Meccano International model-building competition with this fine model of a galleon.

Meccano models grow stage by stage like their counterparts in real life. And Meccano outfits grow too, with accessory outfits and extra parts. In this way Meccano keeps pace year after year with boys' interests!

MECCANO
MADE IN ENGLAND BY MECCANO LTD.

Be a crack shot with a Diana AIR GUN

MILBRO ROLLER SKATES Sturdy and Speedy. Adjustable from 8½" to 10½". Get your Diana and Milbro Skates from your local sports dealer - if in difficulty please write direct to:-

There's no end to the fun you'll have with a Diana – it's the ideal Christmas or Birthday present. Diana Air Guns are so accurate and well-balanced that you can soon become a real marksman! And that's something to be proud of! There's a wonderful range available – from the No. 2 Air Pistol at 20/- to the powerful No. 27 Air Rifle £22 (22 calibre) at £8.16.8 And remember, when you buy Diana you buy the best!

Use Coleshman Wasted Slugs out-of-doors and Milbro Plastic Pellets for target practice indoors.

MILLARD BROTHERS LTD.
DIANA WORKS, CARFIN, MOTHERWELL, SCOTLAND

...and Home

MY FATHER is a chimney sweep. One day he had to go to a certain address. A lady opened the door to his knock and showed my father the room where the chimney had to be swept. There was a man at an easel, drawing. Who should it be but L. Ashwell-Wood, the man who draws for the centre-page of EAGLE. At that moment he was on a drawing for the EAGLE. – P. D. Ross, Willesden, London, N.W.10.

Whodunnit?

I am an interested reader of 'Whodunnit' in your free supplement.

I have noticed that when the guilty people are trying to prove their 'guilt-lessness' they always hold their forearm out horizontally. I think this proves their guilt. In the Bible, Proverbs Chapter 6, verses 12-13, it says the following : 'A naughty person, a wicked man, walketh with a froward mouth. He winketh with his eyes, he speaketh with his feet, he teacheth with his fingers'. What do you think? – *Reg Mason, Halifax, Yorks.* [*I'm sure the horizontal forearm doesn't prove anyone's guilt, Reg, but I like your quotation from Proverbs. Ed.*]

Lists of prizewinners in EAGLE Competitions can be had on application to: EAGLE Reader Services, Long Lane, Liverpool 9. Please enclose a stamped addressed envelope.

THE RECOGNITION
of H.M. Queen Elizabeth II

When George VI died on 6 February 1952 the accession to the throne by Elizabeth II happened immediately, but it was not until June of the next year that the country was able to celebrate her Coronation. The ceremony on 2 June 1953 allowed an outbreak of joy and merriment. *Eagle* lavished many weeks and pages on the new reign.

With articles on the Royal household, and the state of the Empire in this time of change, the weeks of build-up culminated in a special Coronation Issue. L. Ashwell Wood was given free rein to fill a double-page spread with the Royal Naval Fleet while the route of the official ceremony was laid out in great detail and luxurious colour.

THE CORONATION NAVAL REVIEW

BRITISH NAVAL FLAGS

Royal Standard

Union Flag

Admiralty

White Ensign

Blue Ensign (R.N.R.)

Red Ensign (Merchant Navy)

Admiral

Vice-Admiral

Rear-Admiral

Commodore (1st class)

Commodore (2nd class)

Special numbered pennants (1 to 0)

1
2
3
4
5
6
7
8
9
0

Map showing the position of the Review Fleet at Spithead.

THE SOLENT
PORTSMOUTH
SPITHEAD
COWES
RYDE
ISLE OF WIGHT

At 3 p.m. on Monday 15th June H.M. the Queen and Admiral of the Fleet H.R.H. the Duke of Edinburgh, will leave Portsmouth Harbour in H.M.S. *Surprise* to review the fleet at Spithead. In accordance with tradition, the *Surprise* will be led out of the harbour by the Trinity House vessel *Patricia*. As the *Surprise* reaches Spithead, all saluting ships of the Review Fleet will fire a Royal Salute of 21 guns. The Royal procession will then be joined by other vessels including the liners *Orcades*, *Pretoria Castle* and *Strathnavar* with H.M. Government guests on board. The Royal Procession will pass through the lines of ships as indicated by the dotted line on our drawing. The ships

will be dressed overall with flags and 'manned', that is to say, the ships' companies will be lined up on the upper decks facing outboard. As Her Majesty passes each ship the ship's company will give three cheers. The *Surprise* will come to anchor ahead of *Glasgow* in line 'E', and at 5.30 p.m. there will be a Fly Past of over 300 naval aircraft. At 10.30 p.m. the ships will be illuminated and a firework display will be given at 11.0 p.m. In this *Eagle* drawing practically the entire Review Fleet of over 200 ships is illustrated, each ship in its correct place. The nine main lines are each seven miles long reaching from Spithead to east of Cowes.

KEY TO LETTERS OF LINES AND SHIPS

Line A: Headed by H.M.S. *Reward*, a fleet tug followed by Landing Craft and fishing vessels. *Line B:* Headed by H.M. Fleet Minesweeper *Rinaldo* followed by Boom Defence vessels and trawlers. *Line C:* Headed by H.M. Fleet Minesweeper *Coquette* followed by minesweepers, four lifeboats and, further along, submarines and motor vessels of the R.N.V.R. *Line D:* Headed by H.M. cruiser *Dido*, followed by H.M. cruiser *Cleopatra*, two fast minelayers and many destroyers and frigates. *Line E:* Headed by H.M. cruiser *Glasgow* followed by other cruisers, destroyers and frigates. *Line F:*

Headed by H.M. Battleship *Vanguard* (flagship of the fleet) followed by H.M. Aircraft carrier *Eagle*, eight other carriers, depot ships and submarines. *Line G:* Consists of foreign warships headed by the U.S. cruiser *Baltimore*. *Line H:* Headed by H.M. Aircraft Direction Vessel *Boxer* followed by Surveying ships, dockyard craft, Royal Fleet auxiliaries and Merchant ships. *Line K:* Headed by H.M. Fleet Minesweeper *Pluto* followed by tenders and merchant ships. Lines L and M are representatives of the Merchant Navy. Line N consists of fast patrol boats.

KEY TO NUMBERS

(1) H.M.S. *Surprise*, with Queen Elizabeth and the Duke of Edinburgh on board, forming the Royal Procession headed by the Trinity House vessel *Patricia*. (2) H.M. Government guest liners. (3) Track of the *Surprise* from Portsmouth Harbour. (4) Track of guest liners. (5) Track of the *Surprise*. (6) Return track of guest liners. (7) Return track of the *Surprise*. (8) Position of the *Surprise* for the Fly Past. (9) (10) (11) Areas for anchorage of yachts and other private craft. (12) Stokes Bay. (13) Portsmouth Harbour.

Special Flags used in Naval Signalling

Aeroplane
Ahead
Affirmative
Aircraft Carrier
Astern
Battle Cruiser
Battleship
Black
Blue Affirmative
Blue
Cruiser
Destroyer
Division
Fishery
Negative
Optional
Port
Preparative
Red
Flotilla
Starboard
Sub-Division
Submarine

L ASHWELL WOOD

EAGLE 1 January 1954

THE SILVER EAGLE BADGE

Mugs get a new name.

This week in EAGLE's sister paper, GIRL, we are launching a MUG's Badge scheme for girls. Their badge will be called the STAR ADVENTURER'S BADGE.

To make the EAGLE scheme of the same type, we are replacing the MUG's Badge by a SILVER EAGLE BADGE and STAR.

All present holders of the MUG's Badge may exchange it for a SILVER EAGLE BADGE, if they wish to do so, by returning their MUG's Badge to:– MUGS, EAGLE Reader Services, Long Lane, Liverpool 9, and enclosing their name and address.

The S.E.B. will be awarded in just the same way as the MUG's Badge for outstanding examples of courage and service among EAGLE Club Members. Claims should be written by an adult or by friends and addressed to the Editor. *Eaglers* should not send in claims on their own behalf.

We have prepared a new pamphlet called ALL ABOUT THE SILVER EAGLE BADGE AND STAR ADVENTURER'S BADGE, and we strongly advise you to send in for it. Address your request to SILVER EAGLE BADGE, (Pamphlet), EAGLE Reader Services, Long Lane, Liverpool 9.

When you write, please remember to enclose an envelope addressed to yourself and bearing a 2½d stamp in which we can forward the leaflet to you.

MUGS BECOME SILVER EAGLES

Ever since the early issues of *Eagle*, the editorial team had been awarding the seemingly dubious title of Mug of the Month to various readers for their bravery, courage, and all-round do-gooding-ness. In Issue 35 of Volume 4 (4 December 1953) nine-year-old Barry Ware had the honour of being the last ever recipient of the prize. The fact that he lived in "Hong Kong, China" [sic] indicates just how far *Eagle*'s wing-span reached. According to the report in that week's 'Eagle Club News', Barry had "spent a lot of his young life in hospital. There he has won everybody's affection by his cheerfulness. He is a member of the Hong Kong Wolf Cubs and is well-known everywhere for the courage he shows in spite of a rare bone disease."

To quote from Shakespeare: "Be not afraid of greatness: some are born great, some achieve greatness and some have greatness thrust upon them". – *Twelfth Night*, Act II, Scene V

And so on 1 January 1954 (Issue 1 Volume 5) the world was introduced to the Silver Eagle Badge. In that week's copy of *Eagle*'s sister paper *Girl* the Star Adventurer's Badge was being launched and the dropping of the Mug title was justified by the desire to "make the *Eagle* scheme of the same type", whatever that meant. Whatever the real reason, and given that one of the contemporary definitions of Mug was, "chump: a person who is gullible and easy to take advantage of", we can only guess, it was goodbye to the Mugs.

Having awarded Mug-dom to many people since it was introduced, *Eagle* was careful to make sure they were not forgotten. All Mugs were invited to exchange their Mug's badges for Silver Eagles by returning them to the reader services' offices. A special pamphlet was prepared explaining the new scheme and readers were "strongly" advised to send for it. Remembering of course to enclose an SAE. After all you'd be a mug not to.

JEFF ARNOLD IN *Riders of the Range*

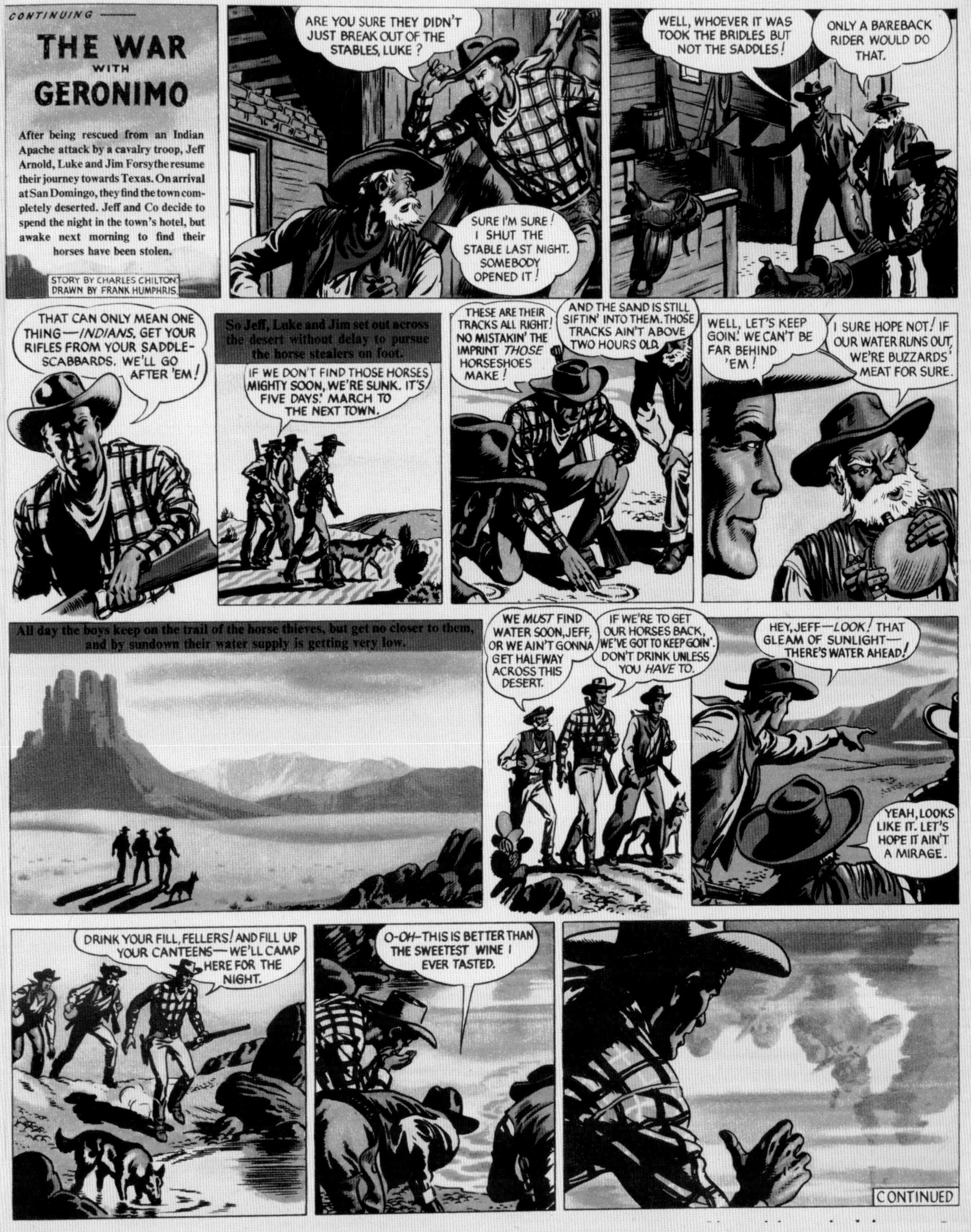
CONTINUING ——
THE WAR WITH GERONIMO
After being rescued from an Indian Apache attack by a cavalry troop, Jeff Arnold, Luke and Jim Forsythe resume their journey towards Texas. On arrival at San Domingo, they find the town completely deserted. Jeff and Co decide to spend the night in the town's hotel, but awake next morning to find their horses have been stolen.
STORY BY CHARLES CHILTON. DRAWN BY FRANK HUMPHRIS.
ARE YOU SURE THEY DIDN'T JUST BREAK OUT OF THE STABLES, LUKE?
SURE I'M SURE! I SHUT THE STABLE LAST NIGHT. SOMEBODY OPENED IT!
WELL, WHOEVER IT WAS TOOK THE BRIDLES BUT NOT THE SADDLES!
ONLY A BAREBACK RIDER WOULD DO THAT.
THAT CAN ONLY MEAN ONE THING—INDIANS. GET YOUR RIFLES FROM YOUR SADDLE-SCABBARDS. WE'LL GO AFTER 'EM!
So Jeff, Luke and Jim set out across the desert without delay to pursue the horse stealers on foot.
IF WE DON'T FIND THOSE HORSES MIGHTY SOON, WE'RE SUNK. IT'S FIVE DAYS' MARCH TO THE NEXT TOWN.
THESE ARE THEIR TRACKS ALL RIGHT! NO MISTAKIN' THE IMPRINT THOSE HORSESHOES MAKE!
AND THE SAND IS STILL SIFTIN' INTO THEM. THOSE TRACKS AIN'T ABOVE TWO HOURS OLD.
WELL, LET'S KEEP GOIN'. WE CAN'T BE FAR BEHIND 'EM!
I SURE HOPE NOT! IF OUR WATER RUNS OUT, WE'RE BUZZARDS' MEAT FOR SURE.
All day the boys keep on the trail of the horse thieves, but get no closer to them, and by sundown their water supply is getting very low.
WE MUST FIND WATER SOON, JEFF, OR WE AIN'T GONNA GET HALFWAY ACROSS THIS DESERT.
IF WE'RE TO GET OUR HORSES BACK, WE'VE GOT TO KEEP GOIN'. DON'T DRINK UNLESS YOU HAVE TO.
HEY, JEFF—LOOK! THAT GLEAM OF SUNLIGHT—THERE'S WATER AHEAD!
YEAH, LOOKS LIKE IT. LET'S HOPE IT AIN'T A MIRAGE.
DRINK YOUR FILL, FELLERS! AND FILL UP YOUR CANTEENS—WE'LL CAMP HERE FOR THE NIGHT.
O-OH-THIS IS BETTER THAN THE SWEETEST WINE I EVER TASTED.
CONTINUED

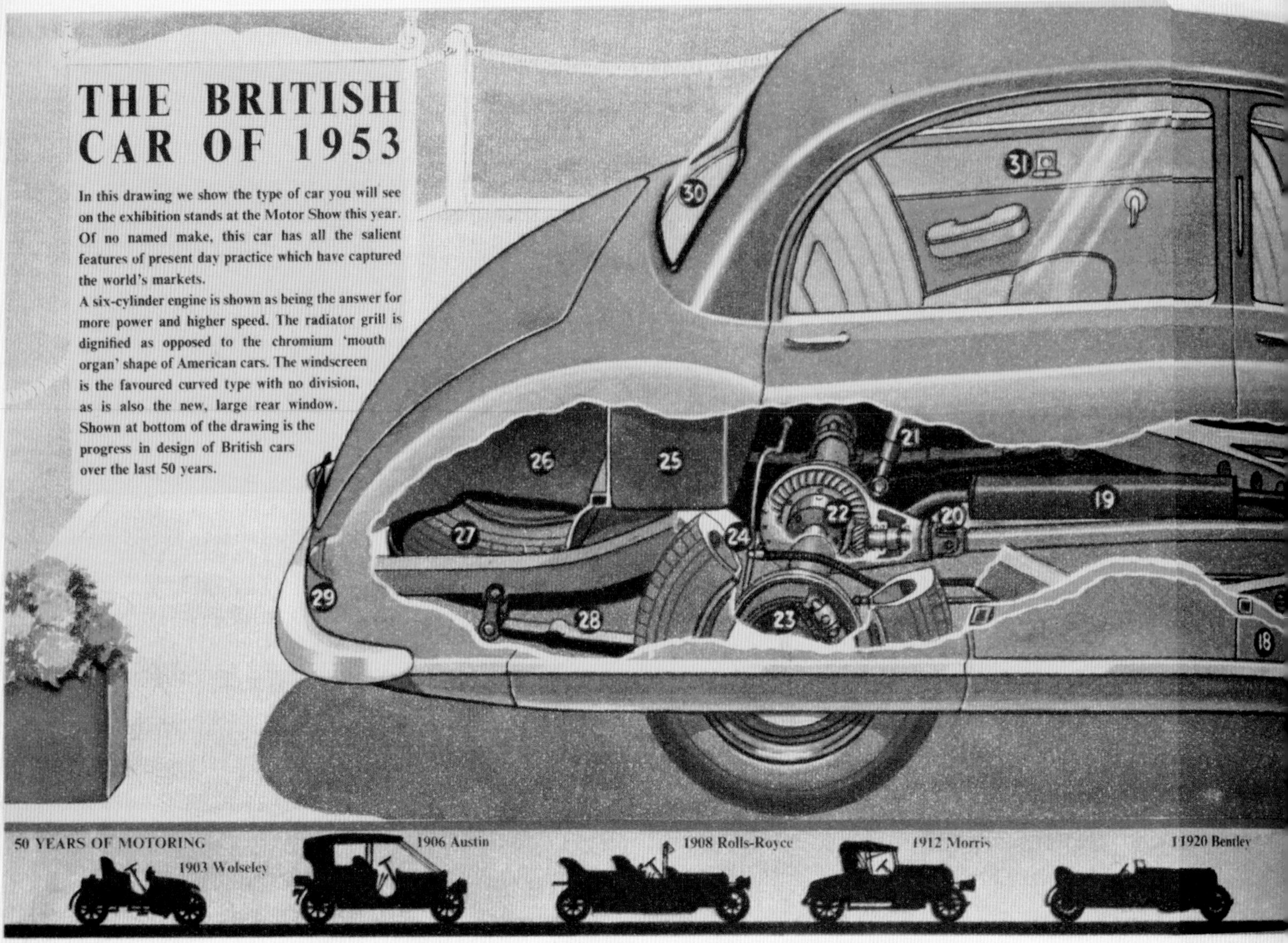
THE BRITISH CAR OF 1953
In this drawing we show the type of car you will see on the exhibition stands at the Motor Show this year. Of no named make, this car has all the salient features of present day practice which have captured the world's markets.
A six-cylinder engine is shown as being the answer for more power and higher speed. The radiator grill is dignified as opposed to the chromium 'mouth organ' shape of American cars. The windscreen is the favoured curved type with no division, as is also the new, large rear window. Shown at bottom of the drawing is the progress in design of British cars over the last 50 years.
30
31
26
25
21
22
20
19
24
27
29
28
23
18
50 YEARS OF MOTORING
1903 Wolseley
1906 Austin
1908 Rolls-Royce
1912 Morris
1920 Bentley

THE FAMILY SA

KEY TO SALIENT FEATURES

(1) Radiator air grill. (2) Radiator. (3) Ventilating and car heating unit. (4) Air cleaner for carburettor. (5) 12-volt battery for starter lighting and coil ignition. (6) Overhead valves. (7) Two rear pistons of 23 h.p., six cylinder engine. (8) Distributor head for coil ignition. (9) Dynamo for charging battery. (10) Independent coil spring front suspension. (11) Front hydraulic brake: two leading shoe type. (12) Worm and ball steering gear. (13) Single dry plate clutch. (14) Synchromesh gears with three forward and one reverse. (15) Front needle-roller bearing universal joint. (16) Propeller shaft. (17) All pressed-steel chassis. (18) All pressed-steel welded body. (19) Exhaust silencer. (20) Rear universal joint. (21) Telescopic shock absorber. (22) Hypoid (off-centre) spiral bevel drive and differential casing. (23) Leading and trailing shoe type hydraulic rear brake. This brake is also actuated mechanically by the hand brake lever. (24) Hydraulic Brake piping. (25) Petrol tank. (26) Luggage boot. (27) Spare wheel. (28) Rear suspension semi-elliptic springs. (29) Rear light (each side). (30) Large curved rear window. (31) Push-button door openers. (32) Steering column gear change lever. (33) Fewer instruments with large speed indicator. (34) Curved windscreen without a division.

1924 Humber   1928 Rover   1933 Standard   1938 Singer   Design 1953

LASHWELL WOOD

LOON

GREAT ESCAPES

THE COLDITZ STORY

TOLD BY GUY MORGAN: DRAWN BY P. NEVIN.

COLDITZ, A MEDIEVAL FORTRESS ON A 300-FT. CLIFF, FLOODLIT FROM EVERY ANGLE AND WITH GUARDS ALWAYS OUTNUMBERING PRISONERS, WAS GERMANY'S 'BAD-BOYS' CAMP FOR THE HARDENED ESCAPERS OF TWO WORLD WARS. ESCAPE-PROOF IN 1914-18, ITS RECORD WAS SOON BROKEN IN THE LAST WAR.

THESE TOOLS WILL, OF COURSE, BE CONFISCATED, CAPTAIN LAWTON.

THAT'S THE SPOT TO START TUNNELLING— WHERE HE'D LEAST SUSPECT IT— BANG UNDER HIS DESK!

ONE DAY, OBERSTABSFELDWEBEL (R.S.M.) GEPHARDT, CAMP SECURITY OFFICER, HAD CAPTAIN LAWTON INTO HIS OFFICE CONCERNING SOME TOOLS. LAWTON HAD AN IDEA. HE RECKONED THAT THE BEST PLACE TO START TUNNELLING WOULD BE FROM UNDER GEPHARDT'S DESK.

KEYHOLE →

BUT THE DOOR TO THE OFFICE WAS FITTED WITH A SPECIAL UNPICKABLE LOCK, WORKED BY MOVING & TINY PISTONS, EACH DIFFERENTLY, WITH ACCURACY OF 1/1000 TH OF AN INCH. A KEY AND KEYHOLE OF THE TYPE IN QUESTION ARE ILLUSTRATED ABOVE. UNDAUNTED, CAPT. VAN DOORNINCK OF THE DUTCH NAVY, USING WATCHMAKING TOOLS, MADE A SPECIAL MICRO-METER GAUGE TO MEASURE EACH PISTON'S MOVEMENT, AND THEN A KEY TO FIT THEM! HIS PATIENCE WAS REWARDED, FOR NOW THEY COULD ENTER THE OFFICE AND START WORK.

LOCKING THEMSELVES IN AT NIGHT, THEY TUNNELLED UNDER THE FLOOR OF GEPHARDT'S ROOM AND THROUGH AN 18-INCH WALL INTO A STORE-ROOM WHERE POLISH P.O.Ws WERE OFTEN BROUGHT FROM THE TOWN TO FETCH STORES.

ONE NIGHT, WHILE THEY WERE AT WORK, THERE WAS AN ALARM AND A GENERAL SEARCH WAS MADE BY THE GUARDS. LUCKILY, THEY DIDN'T THINK IT NECESSARY TO LOOK IN THE SECURITY OFFICER'S ROOM!

NO NEED TO SEARCH IN THERE—THE DOOR HAS A SPECIAL LOCK.

OBERSTABSFELDWEBEL

ONE MORNING, WEARING HOME-MADE POLISH UNIFORMS, FIVE BRITISH OFFICERS, LED BY VAN DOORNINCK IN THE UNIFORM OF A GERMAN N.C.O., MARCHED OUT OF THE CAMP FROM THE STORE-ROOM, CARRYING CIVILIAN CLOTHES WITH THEM IN THE BOXES. FOUR WERE RE-CAPTURED, BUT VAN DOORNINCK AND F/LT. BILL FOWLER REACHED SWITZERLAND SAFELY SIX DAYS LATER.

IT ISN'T TRUE !

That Camels Store Water In Their Humps

AS POLAR BEARS BELONG TO THE ARCTIC, SO CAMELS BELONG TO THE DESERT: TO THE SUN-SCORCHED PLAINS OF WATERLESS SAND WHERE WELLS MAY BE HUNDREDS OF MILES APART, WHERE, WITHOUT WARN-ING, BLINDING SANDSTORMS THREATEN DEATH.

EVEN TODAY, WITH AIR FREIGHTING AND CATERPILLAR-TRACKED VEHICLES, THE CAMEL CARAVAN IS STILL USED TO TRANSPORT MERCHANDISE ACROSS THE DESERT. IT IS OFTEN THOUGHT THAT THE HUMP OF THE CAMEL IS A SORT OF RESERVOIR OF WATER.

WHAT, IN FACT, HAS THE CAMEL'S HUMP GOT TO DO WITH ITS ABILITY TO GO LONG PERIODS WITHOUT WATER ? THE ANSWER IS — NOTHING.

FABULOUS STORIES HAVE BEEN TOLD ABOUT THE CAMEL'S AB-ILITY TO LIVE WITHOUT WATER. IN FACT THE LONGEST RECORD WITHOUT WATER IN WHICH THE CAMEL HAS SURVIVED IS TEN DAYS; THIS WAS A SOMALI CAMEL, A STRAIN NOTED FOR ITS HARDINESS. BUT IN A TERRIBLE MARCH FROM SUEZ TO ABU KLEA IN EGYPT IT WAS REPORTED THAT ALL CAMELS WITHOUT WATER FOR SIX DAYS DIED.

IF THE HUMP WAS CONNECTED WITH WATER STORAGE, THE BACTRIAN CAMEL WHICH INHABITS MONGOLIA AND TURK-ESTAN AND WHICH HAS TWO HUMPS, SHOULD BE ABLE TO LAST MUCH LONGER WITHOUT WATER THAN THE SINGLE-HUMPED VARIETY. BUT THIS IS CERTAINLY NOT THE CASE.

THE CAMEL'S HUMP IS, IN FACT, JUST A HUGE LUMP OF FAT. WHEN FOOD IS SHORT IT PRO-VIDES A MASS OF EMERGENCY NOURISHMENT. BUT, WHEN THE CAMEL IS GOING TO BE OUT FOR MORE THAN THREE DAYS, IT CARRIES ITS RESERVE OF WATER IN TWO PANNIER BAGS; CERTAINLY NOT IN THE HUMP.

CIRCUS prizewinners

The 24 winners of our Circus Competition were brought to London to spend the day at Bertram Mills Circus, Olympia.

Their day started with a visit 'behind the scenes' of the circus where they were introduced to the various artists. Two of the *Eaglers*, Barry Hope and Kenneth Young, helped Freddy Knie to rehearse his horses for the afternoon performance. Then they had lunch with Mr Cyril Mills, our Editor and other personalities. In the afternoon, they had ringside seats at the circus and how they enjoyed themselves. After a huge tea, they were seen on to their trains for home. All voted it was a truly wonderful day.

Eagler Barry Hope takes over the Ringmaster's job!

Here's an odd sleeping partner for Eagler Kenneth Young!

EAGLE 5 *March* 1954

Three of these mobile dental clinics, combining a dental surgery and laboratory, on wheels, have been brought into service by the Kent County Council for use in areas where village schools are remote from the usual services in towns.

The clinics cater for children of all ages and, in addition, for nursing mothers, who receive dental services free of charge.

A detachable 'mechanical horse' (or prime mover), which is a 28 h.p. Austin 3-5 ton articulated short chassis, moves all three clinics about the county in turn, from village to village.

Each clinic is fitted with the finest modern equipment and consists of a waiting room for six people, reached by portable steps on the nearside of the vehicle, a surgery and a combined recovery room and laboratory. They have their own X-ray apparatus and facilities for the development of X-ray films and for a technician to make dental appliances.

Advice is given on the correct way to clean teeth and gums after eating sweets and sticky foods, and why you should – 'Clean them twice a day and so prevent decay'.

LKL 807

THE DENTIST CO

EAGLE 5 March 1954

A MOBILE DENTAL CLINIC
(FOR VILLAGE SCHOOLS)

KEY TO CLINIC

(1) 28 h.p. Austin (the prime mover). (2) Spare wheel. (3) Articulated chassis. The clinic is jacked up and left at a school whilst the prime mover goes off to move another one. (4) Wardrobe. (5) Waiting Room. (6) Entrance door (with portable steps from ground). (7) Drug cupboard. (8) Electrical control cabinet. (9) Electric light and double insulated skin which surrounds the whole vehicle. (10) Electric drill. (11) Dental unit with warm water syringes, cuspidor, switches and instrument table with Bunsen gas burner. (12) Adjustable dental chair. (13) Electric sterilizer. (14) Instrument cupboard (cut away). (15) Fresh water tanks. These are used when main water supply is not available for connection. (16) Calor gas cylinder for water heating. (17) Air compressor for forcing water from tanks. (18) Water pipes. (19) Wash basin with hot and cold water. (20) Nitro-oxygen anæsthetic machine. (21) Adjustable arms of X-ray machine enabling it to be moved to any position. (22) X-ray machine. (23) Fire-extinguisher. (24) Dark room lamp, used when developing X-ray films. (25) Developing time clock. (26) Cylinders of fixer and developer. (27) Dental lathe. (28) Sink. (29) Dental and X-ray accessory storage. (30) Work bench. (Folds upwards when recovery couch is in use.) (31) Recovery or rest couch. (32) Rear doors. (33) Plugged-in electric cable from grid system. The whole clinic is electrically operated and, as most villages are now on the grid system of electricity supply, the clinic may be plugged in. In case electricity supply is not available, a portable petrol-driven motor generator is carried.

L ASHWELL WOOD

MES TO VISIT

RAILWAY WONDERS

ITALIAN "DIRETTISSIMA" ROUTES ARE SPECIALLY DESIGNED FOR HIGH-SPEED TRAVEL AND THE MOST DIRECT COURSE POSSIBLE IS TAKEN. THEY INCORPORATE THE MAXIMUM NUMBER OF STRAIGHT STRETCHES AND CURVES OF LARGE RADIUS. MANY TUNNELS AND BRIDGES WERE NECESSARY IN ORDER TO KEEP GRADIENTS TO THE MINIMUM. THE CARMETO TUNNEL, ON THE BOLOGNA-FLORENCE ROUTE, SHOWN HERE (BEFORE OVERHEAD ELECTRIFICATION WAS INSTALLED) IS A TYPICAL EXAMPLE.

A STREAMLINED ELECTRIC 3-CAR "RAPIDO" OF THE ITALIAN STATE RAILWAYS. THESE TRAINS ARE CAPABLE OF VERY HIGH SPEEDS. IN JUNE, 1939, AN ITALIAN 3-CAR ELECTRIC TRAIN AVERAGED 102 M.P.H. FROM FLORENCE TO MILAN, A DISTANCE OF 195 ¾ MILES. (BELOW) ANOTHER ITALIAN ELECTRIC STREAMLINER, WHICH HAS IDENTICAL ENDS. THE DRIVER SITS IN THE DOME OF THE FRONT CAR AND PASSENGERS USE THE FRONT END BELOW AS A GLASS-ENCLOSED LOUNGE. IT IS SHOWN CROSSING A TYPICAL ITALIAN VIADUCT ON A "DIRETTISSIMA" ROUTE.

A "DIRETTISSIMA" IS BUILT WITHOUT FEAR OF NATURAL OBSTACLES THROUGH WHICH IT HAS TO PASS, AND ON THE BOLOGNA-FLORENCE ROUTE THIS NECESSITATED THE BORING OF THE GREAT APENNINE TUNNEL, 11 MILES 879 YARDS LONG — THE SECOND LONGEST IN THE WORLD. IT IS OFTEN CONSIDERED TO BE THE GREATEST EXAMPLE OF TUNNEL CONSTRUCTION IN EXISTENCE, FOR IT IS BUILT FOR A DOUBLE TRACK, WHEREAS THE SIMPLON (WORLD'S LONGEST) HAS SINGLE TRACK TUNNELS. THE APENNINE COST THE LIVES OF 97 MEN, SUCH WERE THE TREMENDOUS DANGERS AND DIFFICULTIES THAT HAD TO BE OVERCOME DURING ITS CONSTRUCTION. A TRAIN IS SHOWN HERE EMERGING FROM THE STRIKING NORTHERN PORTAL.

RAILWAY WONDERS

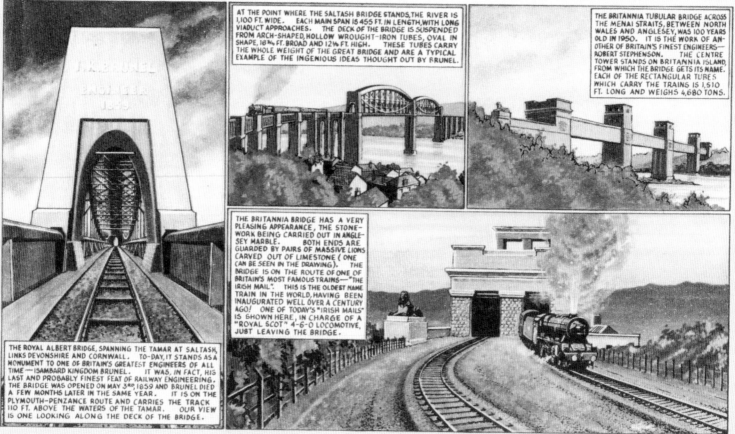

AT THE POINT WHERE THE SALTASH BRIDGE STANDS, THE RIVER IS 1,100 FT. WIDE. EACH MAIN SPAN IS 455 FT. IN LENGTH, WITH LONG VIADUCT APPROACHES. THE DECK OF THE BRIDGE IS SUSPENDED FROM ARCH-SHAPED, HOLLOW WROUGHT-IRON TUBES, OVAL IN SHAPE, 16 ¾ FT. BROAD AND 12 ¼ FT. HIGH. THESE TUBES CARRY THE WHOLE WEIGHT OF THE GREAT BRIDGE AND ARE A TYPICAL EXAMPLE OF THE INGENIOUS IDEAS THOUGHT OUT BY BRUNEL.

THE BRITANNIA TUBULAR BRIDGE ACROSS THE MENAI STRAITS, BETWEEN NORTH WALES AND ANGLESEY, WAS 100 YEARS OLD IN 1950. IT IS THE WORK OF ANOTHER OF BRITAIN'S FINEST ENGINEERS — ROBERT STEPHENSON. THE CENTRE TOWER STANDS ON BRITANNIA ISLAND, FROM WHICH THE BRIDGE GETS ITS NAME. EACH OF THE RECTANGULAR TUBES WHICH CARRY THE TRAINS IS 1,510 FT. LONG AND WEIGHS 4,680 TONS.

THE BRITANNIA BRIDGE HAS A VERY PLEASING APPEARANCE, THE STONEWORK BEING CARRIED OUT IN ANGLESEY MARBLE. BOTH ENDS ARE GUARDED BY PAIRS OF MASSIVE LIONS CARVED OUT OF LIMESTONE (ONE CAN BE SEEN IN THE DRAWING). THE BRIDGE IS ON THE ROUTE OF ONE OF BRITAIN'S MOST FAMOUS TRAINS — "THE IRISH MAIL". THIS IS THE OLDEST NAME TRAIN IN THE WORLD, HAVING BEEN INAUGURATED WELL OVER A CENTURY AGO! ONE OF TODAY'S "IRISH MAILS" IS SHOWN HERE, IN CHARGE OF A "ROYAL SCOT" 4-6-0 LOCOMOTIVE, JUST LEAVING THE BRIDGE.

THE ROYAL ALBERT BRIDGE, SPANNING THE TAMAR AT SALTASH, LINKS DEVONSHIRE AND CORNWALL. TO-DAY, IT STANDS AS A MONUMENT TO ONE OF BRITAIN'S GREATEST ENGINEERS OF ALL TIME — ISAMBARD KINGDOM BRUNEL. IT WAS, IN FACT, HIS LAST AND PROBABLY FINEST FEAT OF RAILWAY ENGINEERING. THE BRIDGE WAS OPENED ON MAY 3RD 1859 AND BRUNEL DIED A FEW MONTHS LATER IN THE SAME YEAR. IT IS ON THE PLYMOUTH-PENZANCE ROUTE AND CARRIES THE TRACK 110 FT. ABOVE THE WATERS OF THE TAMAR. OUR VIEW IS ONE LOOKING ALONG THE DECK OF THE BRIDGE.

RAILWAY WONDERS

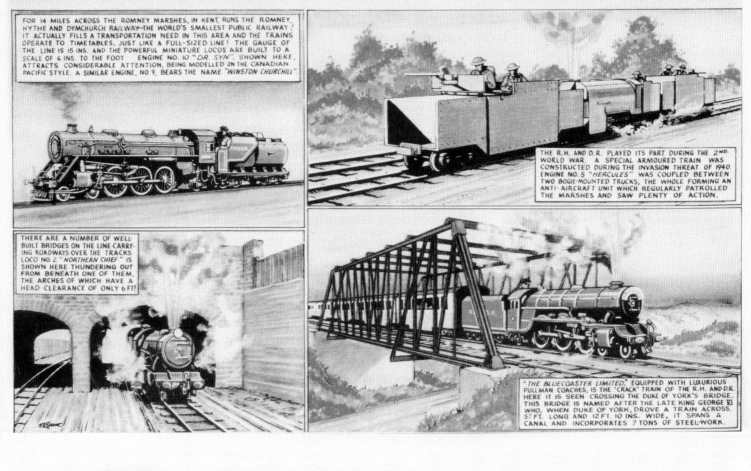

FOR 14 MILES ACROSS THE ROMNEY MARSHES, IN KENT, RUNS THE ROMNEY, HYTHE AND DYMCHURCH RAILWAY—THE WORLD'S SMALLEST PUBLIC RAILWAY! IT ACTUALLY FILLS A TRANSPORTATION NEED IN THIS AREA AND THE TRAINS OPERATE TO TIMETABLES, JUST LIKE A FULL-SIZED LINE! THE GAUGE OF THE LINE IS 15 INS. AND THE POWERFUL MINIATURE LOCOS ARE BUILT TO A SCALE OF 4 INS. TO THE FOOT. ENGINE NO. 10 "DR. SYN", SHOWN HERE, ATTRACTS CONSIDERABLE ATTENTION, BEING MODELLED ON THE CANADIAN PACIFIC STYLE. A SIMILAR ENGINE, NO. 9, BEARS THE NAME "WINSTON CHURCHILL".

THE R.H. AND D.R. PLAYED ITS PART DURING THE 2ND WORLD WAR. A SPECIAL ARMOURED TRAIN WAS CONSTRUCTED DURING THE INVASION THREAT OF 1940. ENGINE NO. 5 "HERCULES" WAS COUPLED BETWEEN TWO BOGIE-MOUNTED TRUCKS, THE WHOLE FORMING AN ANTI-AIRCRAFT UNIT WHICH REGULARLY PATROLLED THE MARSHES AND SAW PLENTY OF ACTION.

THERE ARE A NUMBER OF WELL-BUILT BRIDGES ON THE LINE CARRYING ROADWAYS OVER THE TRACKS. LOCO NO. 2 "NORTHERN CHIEF" IS SHOWN HERE THUNDERING OUT FROM BENEATH ONE OF THEM, THE ARCHES OF WHICH HAVE A HEAD CLEARANCE OF ONLY 6 FT!

"THE BLUECOASTER LIMITED," EQUIPPED WITH LUXURIOUS PULLMAN COACHES, IS THE 'CRACK' TRAIN OF THE R.H. AND D.R. HERE IT IS SEEN CROSSING THE DUKE OF YORK'S BRIDGE. THIS BRIDGE IS NAMED AFTER THE LATE KING GEORGE VI WHO, WHEN DUKE OF YORK, DROVE A TRAIN ACROSS. 57 FT. LONG AND 12 FT. 10 INS. WIDE, IT SPANS A CANAL AND INCORPORATES 7 TONS OF STEEL-WORK.

RAILWAY WONDERS

(12) The Railway that went to sea!

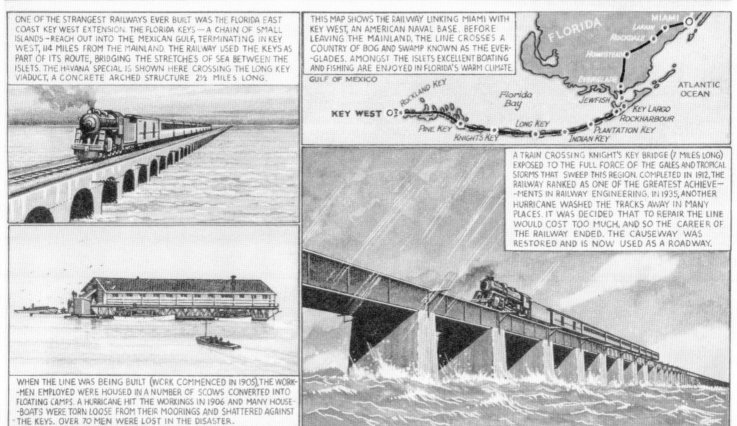

ONE OF THE STRANGEST RAILWAYS EVER BUILT WAS THE FLORIDA EAST COAST KEY WEST EXTENSION. THE FLORIDA KEYS—A CHAIN OF SMALL ISLANDS—REACH OUT INTO THE MEXICAN GULF, TERMINATING IN KEY WEST, 114 MILES FROM THE MAINLAND. THE RAILWAY USED THE KEYS AS PART OF ITS ROUTE, BRIDGING THE STRETCHES OF SEA BETWEEN THE ISLETS. THE HAVANA SPECIAL IS SHOWN HERE CROSSING THE LONG KEY VIADUCT, A CONCRETE ARCHED STRUCTURE 2½ MILES LONG.

THIS MAP SHOWS THE RAILWAY LINKING MIAMI WITH KEY WEST, AN AMERICAN NAVAL BASE. BEFORE LEAVING THE MAINLAND, THE LINE CROSSES A COUNTRY OF BOG AND SWAMP KNOWN AS THE EVER-GLADES. AMONGST THE ISLETS EXCELLENT BOATING AND FISHING ARE ENJOYED IN FLORIDA'S WARM CLIMATE.

FLORIDA — MIAMI — LARKIN — ROCKDALE — HOMESTEAD — EVERGLADE — JEWFISH — KEY LARGO — ROCKHARBOUR — PLANTATION KEY — INDIAN KEY — GULF OF MEXICO — KEY WEST — ROCKLAND KEY — PINE KEY — KNIGHTS KEY — LONG KEY — Florida Bay — ATLANTIC OCEAN

A TRAIN CROSSING KNIGHT'S KEY BRIDGE (7 MILES LONG) EXPOSED TO THE FULL FORCE OF THE GALES AND TROPICAL STORMS THAT SWEEP THIS REGION. COMPLETED IN 1912, THE RAILWAY RANKED AS ONE OF THE GREATEST ACHIEVE-MENTS IN RAILWAY ENGINEERING. IN 1935, ANOTHER HURRICANE WASHED THE TRACKS AWAY IN MANY PLACES. IT WAS DECIDED THAT TO REPAIR THE LINE WOULD COST TOO MUCH, AND SO THE CAREER OF THE RAILWAY ENDED. THE CAUSEWAY WAS RESTORED AND IS NOW USED AS A ROADWAY.

WHEN THE LINE WAS BEING BUILT (WORK COMMENCED IN 1905), THE WORK-MEN EMPLOYED WERE HOUSED IN A NUMBER OF SCOWS CONVERTED INTO FLOATING CAMPS. A HURRICANE HIT THE WORKINGS IN 1906 AND MANY HOUSE-BOATS WERE TORN LOOSE FROM THEIR MOORINGS AND SHATTERED AGAINST THE KEYS. OVER 70 MEN WERE LOST IN THE DISASTER.

Look around with George Cansdale
(3) Fish

DRAWN BY BACKHOUSE

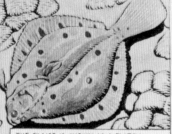

FISH LIVE IN ALMOST ANY WATER, FRESH OR SALT. THEIR GILLS TAKE OXYGEN FROM THE WATER, BUT SOME KINDS, LIKE THE AFRICAN LUNG-FISH, CAN LIVE IN A HOLE IN THE MUD AFTER THE LAKES HAVE DRIED UP. MOST FISH LAY GREAT NUMBERS OF EGGS. SOME, LIKE THE DOGFISH, HAVE LIVING YOUNG. FISH ARE AT THE SAME TEMPERATURE AS THE WATER AROUND THEM.

THIS WHALE SHARK IS THE BIGGEST KIND OF FISH, REACHING FIFTY FEET IN LENGTH AND WEIGHING MORE THAN AN ELEPHANT. AS IN ALL SHARKS AND DOGFISH, ITS SKELETON IS MADE OF HARD GRISTLE AND NOT OF PROPER BONE. THE SKIN IS TOUGH AND ROUGH. THIS HUGE FISH FEEDS ON SHRIMPS.

THIS VERY BEAUTIFUL NEON FISH COMES FROM SOUTH AMERICA AND IS ONE OF THE SMALLEST KINDS. IT IS VERY POPULAR IN TROPICAL AQUARIA.

THE PLAICE IS KNOWN AS A FLATFISH BECAUSE IT HAS BECOME VERY BROAD AND FLAT. THESE FISH LIVE ON THE BOTTOM OF RATHER SHALLOW WATER AND THEIR UPPER SURFACE GENERALLY HAS THE SAME COL-OUR AND PATTERN AS THEIR SURROUNDINGS.

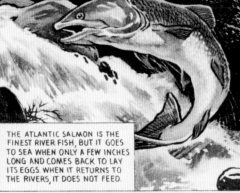

ALTHOUGH THE EEL MAY LOOK LIKE A SNAKE, IT IS A TRUE FISH. IT SPENDS MOST OF ITS LIFE IN FRESH WATER, BUT GOES TO SEA TO LAY ITS EGGS.

THE ATLANTIC SALMON IS THE FINEST RIVER FISH, BUT IT GOES TO SEA WHEN ONLY A FEW INCHES LONG AND COMES BACK TO LAY ITS EGGS. WHEN IT RETURNS TO THE RIVERS, IT DOES NOT FEED.

THE PIKE IS THE BIGGEST BRITISH FRESHWATER FISH. IT IS SOMETIMES CALLED A "RIVER WOLF" FROM ITS HABIT OF EATING OTHER FISH. IT SPENDS ALL ITS LIFE IN RIVERS AND LAKES.

ADVERTISER'S ANNOUNCEMENT

READERS' LETTERS

Pictures on the sky

RECENTLY I went to Switzerland and I saw a rocket-shaped object that was invented by a Swiss engineer to project pictures on the sky at night. I enclose a snap of it being taken out of the garage to be tested. – *Leslie R. Burke, Cricklewood, N.W.2.*

GEORGE CANSDALE VISIT

GEORGE CANSDALE paid a visit to our School recently and brought with him two pets, a bushbaby, and a small python; he allowed us to pass the python round, while the bushbaby jumped from shoulder to shoulder. Afterwards, he gave a very interesting lecture on natural history in the Gold Coast. – *J. N. Kirkman, Bolton, Lancs.*

UMBRELLA DOG

MY GRANDMA's dog was taken ill. As it was raining the day it was taken to the vet, it was carried under an umbrella. In a week's time there was the dog by the door, barking to go out, with an umbrella at his feet which was taken from the stand. He wanted to go for a walk in the rain. – *Kenneth Davies, Swansea, Glam.*

COOL ANYWAY

WHILE I was in Africa, I went out to call for my two-year-old brother to come in for his dinner. At last I found him, and where do you think he was? He was hidden in a big bucket with the water tap running on him. – *Julie Atkinson, Batley, Yorks.*

5/- is paid for each letter published. Readers who want a reply should enclose a stamped, addressed envelope.

George Cansdale was superintendent at London Zoo from the late Forties to the early Fifties and was a regular contributor to various comics and television programmes. His nature page in *Eagle* was generally accompanied by a drawing of him cuddling a monkey.

George was responsible for introducing a tortoise on the BBC's *Blue Peter*. The ancient reptile was named George in his honour and died aged 83. Coincidentally Cansdale was 83 when he died in August 1993.

Another of *Eagle's* occasional series on random subjects, this one covered vehicles such as the Mercedes-Benz Whale, a car built specifically to gain the land-speed record; and the Roadable from 1946 – a car to which wings and propeller could be added to turn it into a plane. On the sea, there was the Lakatoi, a craft from New Guinea, which was two canoes stuck together. And so it went.

Can you spot an engine-spotter?

You can spot an engine-spotter on most railway platforms throughout Britain. Engine-spotters are those bright boys and girls with little notebooks who hang around railway stations spotting all the different kinds of British engines.

Really *expert* engine-spotters don't just go by the numbers on the engines — they recognize the "look" of the engines and know them at a distance.

You can be an expert engine-spotter if you collect the new series of Kellogg's Corn Flakes Back Panels — a series of splendid colour prints of British Locomotives, with descriptions of each one shown.

Ask your mum to buy Kellogg's Corn Flakes regularly so you can collect this wonderful new series.

ODDITIES OF LAND, SEA AND AIR — AIR

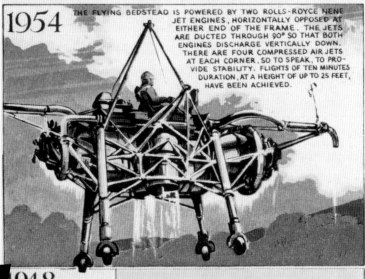

1954 THE FLYING BEDSTEAD IS POWERED BY TWO ROLLS-ROYCE NENE JET ENGINES, HORIZONTALLY OPPOSED AT EITHER END OF THE FRAME. THE JETS ARE DUCTED THROUGH 90° SO THAT BOTH ENGINES DISCHARGE VERTICALLY DOWN. THERE ARE FOUR COMPRESSED AIR JETS AT EACH CORNER, SO TO SPEAK, TO PROVIDE STABILITY. FLIGHTS OF TEN MINUTES DURATION, AT A HEIGHT OF UP TO 25 FEET, HAVE BEEN ACHIEVED.

1948 THIS IS THE CIERVA AIR HORSE, AT THAT TIME THE BIGGEST HELICOPTER IN THE WORLD. IT HAD THREE ROTORS WITH THREE BLADES EACH, SPACE FOR 24 PEOPLE OR THREE TONS OF CARGO, AND A ROLLS-ROYCE MERLIN ENGINE OF 1,640 H.P. DROVE IT. WHAT WITH FLYING BEDSTEADS, HORSES, ETC., THE OLD SAYING THAT "PIGS MIGHT FLY" STANDS A GOOD CHANCE OF COMING TO PASS.

G-ALCV

You write to the Editor

RICKSHAW'S DESCENDANT

WHILE my brother and I both enjoy reading the EAGLE and have done so since No. 1, we feel that you have slipped up over Rickshaws in Singapore. *No! No!* sir, not even for Storm Nelson and his crew! We know, as we have spent several years there and only returned to U.K. last year. The means of transport now used is the Rickshaw's descendant, the Trishaw. The enclosed photograph shows one on a bridge in Singapore with my mother, brother and myself standing nearby. – *Trevor Nightingale, Dumbarton, Scotland.*

THE MEKON IS HERE!

THE MEKON is now terrorizing our back garden, but luckily he is only in snow.

I spent all of last weekend making him. I had to make his body a bit thicker because his head toppled off a couple of times, one of them narrowly missing me. – *Clive Wilcocks, Farnham Common, Bucks.*

The EAGLE Brush

Concluding . . .

WEIGHT LIFTING WITHOUT WEIGHTS

By AL MURRAY
(the famous National Coach)

Al Murray demonstrates the Single-legged exercise

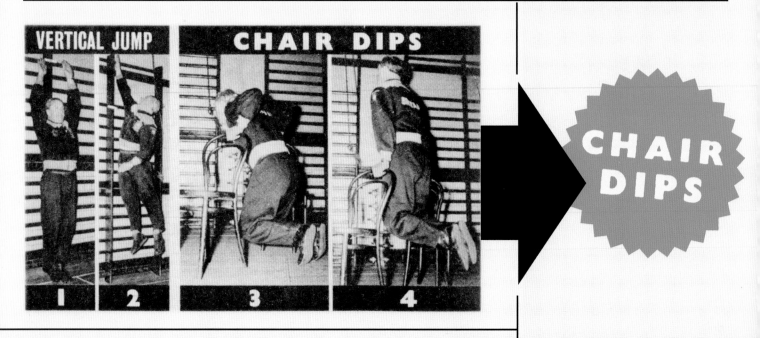

VERTICAL JUMP

CHAIR DIPS

1 2 3 4

CHAIR DIPS

More exciting news about EAGLE CLUB

WONDERFUL CHEAP HOLIDAYS

Are you coming?

In co-operation with the Youth Hostels Association EAGLE Club has organized some thrilling, cheap-but-good holidays for EAGLE Club members who are twelve and over. Details of walking and cycling tours are given below.

Study the places and dates carefully and see which one you want to join.

'THE CLIMBERS' Walking Tour of North Wales

In North Wales the hostels are full of climbers – some quite famous! Many "Everest" expeditions have trained above the slopes that you will scramble over. The most spectacular feat will be the attempt to climb Snowdon.

● Assembly Point : CHESTER

Tour D2 Aug 14th to 21st
Tour E2 Aug 21st to 28th
Tour F2 Aug 28th to Sept 4th

Inclusive cost from Assembly Point £3. 8. 0.

The 'PENNINE WALKERS' Tour

For those with an urge to climb some of the highest peaks in Britain – and to explore the remains of former underground rivers.

● Assembly Point : LEEDS

Tour B1 July 31st to Aug 7th
Tour D1 Aug 14th to 21st
Tour F1 Aug 28th to Sept 4th

Inclusive cost from Assembly Point £3. 6. 0

The 'WATER RATS' Cycling Tour of the Fens

For cyclists who also like swimming and messing about with boats this tour takes in Cambridge, Ely, Newmarket and Saffron Walden.

● Assembly Point : CAMBRIDGE

Tour A2 July 24th to 31st
Tour B2 July 31st to Aug 7th

Inclusive cost from Assembly Point £3. 3. 0.

The 'WEST RIDERS' Cycling Tour of the Yorkshire Dales

Castles, Caves, Swimming and Scrambling.

● Assembly Point : BRADFORD

Tour A1 July 24th to 31st
Tour C1 Aug 7th to 14th
Tour E1 Aug 21st to 28th

Inclusive cost from Assembly Point £3. 5. 6.

The 'TOPLINERS' Walking tour of the Lakelands

This tour takes you through some of Britain's finest mountain scenery: crags to climb, lakes to bathe in. It's a good stretch to the top, so bring your best pair of legs with you.

● Assembly point : KENDAL

Tour C3 Aug 7th to 14th

Inclusive cost from Assembly Point £3. 5. 6.

WHAT YOU HAVE TO DO

Discuss these holiday tours with your parents. You can assure them that you will be well looked after. There will be ten in each party in charge of an experienced Youth Hostels Association adult leader. You must arrange your own transport to and from the Assembly Point (where you meet), so choose a town convenient to you. If you are coming, fill in the Holiday Application form on page 11 as directed.

FURTHER ANNOUNCEMENTS WILL BE MADE NEXT WEEK ABOUT TOURS STARTING FROM LONDON, BIRMINGHAM and TYNESIDE

CRICKET

By arrangement with the M.C.C. and County Cricket Clubs, EAGLE Club members, on presenting a valid EAGLE Club card, will be allowed free admission after 4.30 p.m. to the county cricket grounds as listed in last week's EAGLE. ADDITIONAL: The same privileges will extend to the following County Cricket Clubs. Please add them to your list in last week's EAGLE and keep for reference.

SURREY C.C.C.
Free admission to the Oval Cricket Ground on dates to be announced in EAGLE.

WORCESTERSHIRE C.C.C.
Worcester and Kidderminster. (Excluding Bank Holidays and Benefit matches).

A further arrangement has been made with the M.C.C. regarding free admission to Minor County Championship Matches. We shall announce the matches and grounds concerned on EAGLE Club Page in the issue before the week in which the various fixtures take place.

Please Note *New Membership cards.* If you are already a member of EAGLE Club you should send your card (or name and address and birthday date if you have lost your card) to EAGLE Club, Eagle Reader Services Long Lane, Liverpool 9. Please enclose a stamped and addressed envelope (2½d stamp).

You will receive a new membership card which will be valid until April 1st, 1955. You cannot take part in these new Club activities until you have your new card. *If you want to join now.* If you are not yet a member, fill in the coupon on page 11 as directed. You require a postal order for 1/6 to join the Club. **Please Note**

THE EDITOR IS PRESIDENT OF THE CLUB: THESE FAMOUS MEN ARE YOUR VICE-PRESIDENTS.

| Neville Duke | Stirling Moss | Denis Compton | Stanley Matthews | Godfrey Evans | Trevor Bailey | Leonard Cheshire V.C. |

Keep this page carefully. You will need it for reference.

OUR VITAL W

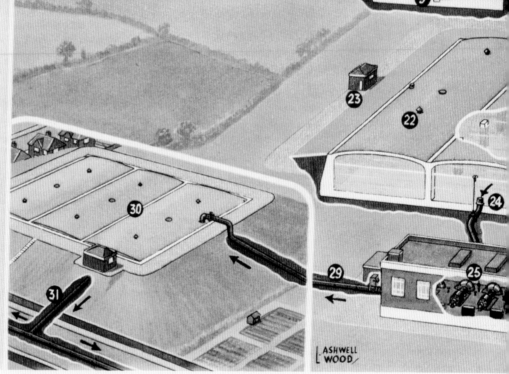

Pure water is one of the vital necessities of life. For the maintenance of health and cleanliness it is indispensable.

In this drawing we see how a modern city or town gets a supply of pure water, from the storage reservoir to your kitchen tap. All the various items are grouped together for convenience of illustration, but this would not be the case in actual practice. Some would be a considerable distance apart and also the piping arrangements would be much more complicated.

The storage reservoir would be filled either by water pumped from a river, as in London, or from a dammed-up valley or artificial lake miles away, the method used in the Manchester and Birmingham supply system.

SEQUENCE OF OPERATIONS.

(1) Large storage reservoir. (2) Outlets and valves at various levels. (3) Metering house where the flow is measured. (4) Outlet main or conduit. (5) Pumping house. (6) Water meter. The flow of water is constantly measured at different stages. (7) Chemical mixing house. (8) Settling tank. Here the chemicals take impurities to the bottom of the tank. (9) Screens. (10) Pumps forcing water to the primary filters. (11) Primary or quick filters. The water passes downwards through a layer of sand and graded shingle. (12) Water collects at bottom of channel. (13) Water meters and valves. (14) Water passes to the secondary or slow filters. (15) Slow filter beds. (16) The water slowly filters down through a layer of fine sand and various grades of gravel, which remove further impurities. (17) Sterilizing house. Here the filtered water is treated with one part per million of chlorine; that is, one gallon of chlorine to one million gallons of water. (18) Pumping house. (19) Water meter. (20) Water inlet to service reservoir. (21) Service reservoir. Here sterilization is completed and the pure water is stored ready for use. (22) Air vents. (23) Bottling house for water samples. A check on the purity of water is maintained at all times and samples sent to the laboratories for testing. (24) Pure water outlet. (25) Main pumping station. Here the pure water is pumped into the street mains and may also be pumped to other service reservoirs. (26) Final metering. (27) Street mains. These may be up to 48 inches in diameter. (28) Side street main of 6 inches diameter. Even smaller pipes lead off to the houses. (29) Main supply to distant service reservoir. (30) Service reservoir on high ground. (31) The pressure to supply mains is, in this case, maintained by gravity.

ASHWELL WOOD

WATER SUP

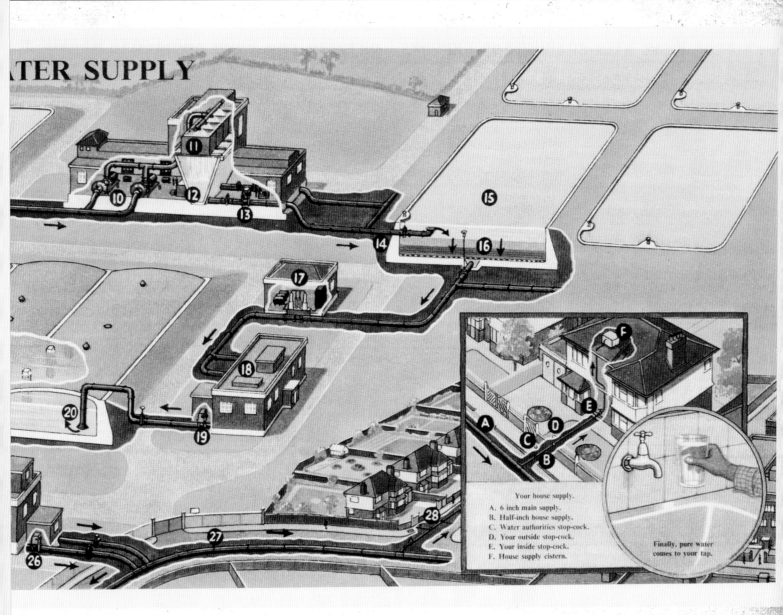

ATER SUPPLY

Your house supply.

A. 6 inch main supply.
B. Half-inch house supply.
C. Water authorities stop-cock.
D. Your outside stop-cock.
E. Your inside stop-cock.
F. House supply cistern.

Finally, pure water comes to your tap.

PLY

Fun in the shower at the end of a mission

Registered at the G.P.O. for transmission by Magazine post to Canada (including Newfoundland), Eagle Magazine with which is incorporated The Merry-Go-Round, printed in Great Britain by Eric Bemrose Ltd., Long Lane, Liverpool 9, for the Proprietors and Publishers, Hulton Press Ltd., 43/44 Shoe Lane, London, E.C.4. Sole agents for Australia and New Zealand, Gordon & Gotch (A/sia) Ltd.; South Africa, Central News Agency Ltd.; Sole agents for Israel, Pales Press Co. Ltd. Subscription Rate: Inland and abroad, 12 months 26/-, 6 months 13/-; Postage for single copies: 1½d. (Canada 1d.) You can have tapit sent to any address in this country or Overseas for one year for 26/-, and to Canada at a special rate of 13/10d. All readers in U.S.A. or Canada see will mail enquiries.

The 1,000 m.p.h. atomic-jet: Long-distance airliners would be pilotless and guided by radar and advanced electronics.
For internal routes, rocket-jets would be used in vertical rising convertiplanes (as shown on the left).
At the airport, sound-muffled take-off runs would be a feature and passengers would arrive by overhead monorail from the congested cities.
Trans-World Airlines, who have recently sponsored a similar interest in 'Aviation 30 years from now', celebrate their 30 years of service this year.

KEY TO PARTS: (1) Control tower radar-scanners. (2) Central control tower. (3) Underground subway and lifts. KEY TO CONVERTI-PLANE (Left): (4) Convertiplane rising vertically. Passengers in gyroscopic-mounted seats. (5) Rocket-jet power unit. (6) Rockets attached to tail controls for converting to level flight. (7) Firing pit. (8) Firing control, and loading and mooring tower (lowered). (9) Underground passenger subway. KEY TO ATOMIC-JET LINER (Centre): (10) Jet tail pipes inclined downwards into sound mufflers for take-off. (11) Atomic reactor and jet engines in shielded compartment against radiation. (12) Downward jets for vertical lift. (13) Swept back adjustable wings retracted. (14) Passengers' cabin. Seats lowered during acceleration at take-off. (15) Sleeping cabins. (16) Radar and electronic control apparatus. (17) Launching guide cradle. (18) Aircraft transporter. (19) Sound muffler and take-off run. KEY TO OTHER FEATURES: (20) Convertiplane with loading and mooring tower raised. (21) Convertiplane in level flight. (22) Swept back adjustable wings extended for take-off. (23) Downward jets giving continuous vertical lift. (24) Aircraft transporter. (25) Take-off run, with sliding doors closed ready for landing. (26) Underground maintenance hangars and lifts. (27) Radar scanners and aerials for guided control. (28) Observation lounge (1985 would also be the age of new glass – bendable and unbreakable). (29) Restaurant. (30) Underground subway to central control tower. (31) Passengers' entrance and exit ramp, to and from aircraft, with moving stairs. (32) Main aircraft control room, with pilot and co-pilot at the guiding controls and radar screens showing all aircraft movements. (33) Three-D cinema projecting moving cloud shapes and weather conditions. (34) Customs' Room. (35) Overhead monorail direct to airport.

L. ASHWELL WOOD

THE FUTURE

120

30 YEARS FROM NOW

A FUTURE COMMERCIAL AIRPORT

In this exclusive EAGLE feature, we endeavour to portray what a commercial airport might look like in 1985 – when Eagle will be 35 years old! This drawing is based on developments now pending and predictions of leading aeronautical scientists.

CITY AIRPORT

FOURPENCE-HALFPENNY

WITH THE MYSTERY SHIP LOCATED, LEX O'MALLEY AND DAN WASTE NO TIME IN ORGANIZING HER RECOVERY FROM THE DEEP AND SOON THE WORLD'S GREATEST NEWSPAPER BRINGS THE EAGERLY AWAITED HEADLINE . . .

EAGLE

COMPANION TO GIRL, SWIFT AND ROBIN

EVERY WEDNESDAY

19 AUGUST 1955 Vol. 6 No. 33

PENNY EUROPE : TEN CENTS PANAMERICA : FOUR ANNAS ASIA : ONE SUT PANAFRICA

DAILY WORLD POST

SIMULTANEOUSLY IN LONDON, NEW YORK, SAN FRANCISCO, TOKIO, DELHI, BAKU, ROME, BULAWAYO, SYDNEY, MARSVILLE AND MEKONTA

LONDON

SUBSCRIBER'S ROCKET MAIL COPY
ATLANTIC EDITION
DATE AS POSTMARK

THE HULTON PAPER

JUST RELEASED: THIS OFFICIAL SPACEFLEET PHOTOGRAPH IS FROM A TELE-FILM AUTO-RECORDED ON AN OBSERVER SCREEN. IT SHOWS THE MYSTERY SHIP A MOMENT BEFORE IT EXPLODED AND CRASHED INTO THE PACIFIC.

MYSTERY SHIP IS RAISED – OFFICIAL

SALVAGE FEAT MAY SOLVE SPACE RIDDLE

TOKIO, Tuesday.

THE salvage fleet assembled by R.N. and U.S.N. Units of the U.N. Naval Service has succeeded in raising the wreck of the mystery Intruder from the Tuscarora Deep. Working under conditions of strictest secrecy, experts from many nations teamed together under the leadership of Commander Lex O'Malley, R.N., to achieve the almost impossible – the raising of a wreck of considerable size from a depth of six miles.

COMMENT

The anxiety felt by most people at the sudden appearance of an unknown Spaceship, and its apparent ability to penetrate unseen through Earth defences, will be relieved to some extent by this morning's news.
Prompt action by the Royal Navy has more than justified "World Post's" successful campaign to keep that incomparable service in being at the time of the Universal Disarmament Convention.
Now that the ship has been raised, the Interplanetary Space Fleet has the opportunity to recover public esteem by answering 3 questions. HOW did the ship get through? WHERE did it come from – and WHY?

READ . . .

ILLUMINATED
THE FIRST 3-D COMIC WITH LUMINOUS PRINT
HULTON'S OF COURSE !

Novel and daring methods must have been employed to lift the ship from the ledge of Basalt on which it was found by Commander O'Malley, and Colonel Dan Dare of the Space Fleet. The wreck is being towed to Yokohama, where it will be disassembled by Space Fleet Experts and Rocketed to H.Q. for investigation.

DARE HAS SUPER-OPTIC SPEED THEORY

Space-Ace Colonel Dan Dare is reported to have advanced the theory that the strange ship which broke through Earth defences last week had achieved a speed faster than light! Professor Sigmund Sax, Director of Space Research Council, commented:– "Ridiculous! Dare should stick to flying and leave such matters to those better qualified to deal with them!" But the S.R.C. spokesman must face the fact that the man in the street is gravely concerned at the Council's failure to produce any explanation as to why the Solar Observation Corps completely failed to plot the course of the intruder prior to its sudden appearance on Space Fleet's Astroscope screens.

'LUCKY' LEX O'MALLEY DOES IT AGAIN

Commander Lex O'Malley, R.N., the colourful and unorthodox Irish submarine explorer, has earned new fame by his successful direction of the salvage operation. Author of two books on submarine exploration, the black-bearded Commander probably has more experience of the abyssal depths of the world's oceans than any other living man.

SALVAGED FOOD CAPSULES COULD SAVE 'MAN FROM NOWHERE' TOKIO, Late

Reported that Canisters of what appear to be some kind of food or vitamin capsules are being sent by special Rocket to London.
Discovered in the wreck when experts boarded her, it is hoped that they may help in the fight for the life of the "Man from Nowhere".

Three more survivors

Questioned by our correspondent on the spot, Sir Hubert Guest revealed a further three survivors were rescued from the ship's pressurized cabin. All have common racial characteristics with the "Man from Nowhere" found in Brazil's Mato Grosso shortly after the intruder crashed. The survivors are being rushed to London for interrogation.

'HIGHLY INTELLIGENT' SAYS HEMMING INSTITUTE

"Cranial form and brain structure indicate he is a creature of highest intelligence," said Sir Alan Cope, noted Anthropologist, after examining "The Man from Nowhere" at the Hemming Institute yesterday. A 3D model of the Stranger's head prepared by the Institute is shown at right.

Heli-Tennis 'Battle of the Century' opens

Lhasa was thronged today with excited crowds making their way to the Potala stadium for the long-awaited clash between the celebrated Frau Keller, the twin rotor "Menace from Mulhausen", and Pat Pulukovoski (Brooklyn Navy Yard) who favours the lighter "pulse jet" rig.

FRAU KELLER   PAT PULUKOVOSKI
CARTOONS BY MAY

One of the best benefits of joining the Eagle Club was free entry to sporting events, more specifically football and cricket matches. While the football freebies seemed to be limited to the lower leagues, cricket was much more generous. All the 17 major counties (Durham wasn't admitted till 1991) offered an open door policy to anyone carrying the yellow Eagle Club card.

After a short time though, it would appear that too many youngsters were taking advantage of the scheme and so it was limited to entry after 4.30 p.m. Even so, in a world where there is no such thing as a free lunch it must have been fabulous to stroll through the gates of Lord's, flash your yellow card, and sit down to watch Fred Trueman steaming in and hurling them down at Denis Compton. All for free, nothing, gratis, thanks to your friends at *Eagle*.

You write to the Editor

SPACESHIP DESIGNER

I AM enclosing a photograph of a supersonic spaceship which I have designed and made all myself. You can see the ramp and spaceship, which are painted with aluminium paint and look very realistic. – *John Malby, Grimley, Worcester.*

LUCKY CHAP

I HAVE some good news for you. I am living in a nice new house now. The council man came to tell my mummy and daddy on my daddy's birthday that we had a new house, and that my daddy had to go for the keys. It's smashing. I have a bedroom of my own now, and I can see fields and trees for miles, too. There is a big field at the bottom of our back garden where I can fly my kite and play football with my friends. – *Bryan Baker, Seaham, Co. Durham.*

BREAD FOR BAIT

ONCE when I was fishing in Wiltshire for trout, I got a bite; my bait was bread. I called to my father who was fishing nearby. He came and helped me play it. At last we got it in and it weighed 5 lb. 1 oz. We took it home. Now the fish is in a glass case in the dining room. – *Christopher Rawlence, Nr. Lingsfield, Surrey.*

5/- is paid for each letter published. Readers who want a reply should enclose a stamped, addressed envelope.

EAGLE CLUB NEWS

CRICKET FREE VIEWING!

Look! Here are the County XIs you will be able to see in action –

Derbyshire
Essex
Gloucestershire
Hampshire
Kent
Lancashire
Leicestershire
M.C.C. and Middlesex
Northamptonshire
Nottinghamshire
Somerset
Surrey
Sussex
Warwickshire
Worcestershire
Yorkshire

and all Minor County Matches, too !

WITH the Cricket Season just around the corner, we can now announce wonderful FREE VIEWING FACILITIES which have been arranged especially for EAGLE by the M.C.C. and the Management Committees of County Cricket Clubs. By using your YELLOW Club Card, you will be able to follow the fortunes of your favourite Cricket XIs throughout the whole of the Cricket Season.

You will be allowed into these Matches at certain times during the day, so you must watch EAGLE every week for announcements about the times of viewing and the Matches to be played.

Your cricketing Vice-Presidents are:
Denis Compton Trevor Bailey Godfrey Evans

It may be YOUR turn for a Birthday Gift this week!

IF YOUR birthdate appears in the list below and you are an EAGLE Club Member, you are entitled to a FREE birthday gift! Choose it from the following list: stamp album, jigsaw puzzle, stationery folder, adventure book, ball-point pen or propelling pencil.

Then state the gift of your choice clearly on a post-card, giving us your name, address and Club Number and also the date you were born, and post it to Birthday Present (108) EAGLE Club, Long Lane, Liverpool 9. Your post-card must reach us by Thursday, April 28th. Though the same birthdate may appear more than once, no Member may claim more than one gift.

OCT 17 1945
DEC 20 1944
JAN 29 1942
MAY 7 1943
JULY 20 1945
DEC 8 1946

2 more Circus Visits

HERE'S another FREE offer for Circus tickets for lucky Club Members living in or near NEWPORT and CARDIFF. We have twenty tickets for the Bertram Mills Circus visiting each of these towns on the following dates:–

Newport – Monday, May 2nd at 4.45 p.m.
Cardiff – Monday, May 9th at 4.45 p.m.

Write to EAGLE Circus Visits, Long Lane, Liverpool 9. The first 20 letters opened for each town will be the lucky ones. State your name, address, age, Club Number, and which show you prefer to see.

To join EAGLE CLUB, fill in this form

Please enrol me as a Member of the EAGLE Club

I ENCLOSE A P.O. VALUE 1/6d.   BLOCK CAPITALS, PLEASE

NAME......................................

ADDRESS ....

Date of Birth: Day.............Month.............Year.............

Post form with order for 1/6 to EAGLE Reader Services, Long Lane, Liverpool 9. P.O. should be made out to Hulton Press Ltd., and crossed '& /Co'.

Address this label to yourself in BLOCK LETTERS

NAME......................................

ADDRESS ....

EM

EAGLE SPORTS NEWS

● INFORMATION
● INSTRUCTION

Team of the year—1955
★ CHELSEA ★

Goalie McIntosh (Sheffield Wednesday) collects a high ball, challenged by Chelsea skipper Roy Bentley. By winning this match, Chelsea made certain of the Div. 1 title.

THE BIG KICK-OFF

"We believe in YOUTH at Chelsea"
says TED DRAKE

(interviewed by Kenneth Wheeler)

AS a player, Ted Drake gained every major honour; but none of his individual achievements mean as much to him as the success gained by Chelsea, the team he manages, in their Jubilee season of 1954-55.

Every Chelsea team won something! They brought no less than nine trophies to Stamford Bridge, including those for the First Division, London Combination and Metropolitan League Championships.

What was the secret of Chelsea's success? "Team spirit, and 100 per cent effort by everyone," says Ted Drake. "We're one big happy family at the Bridge, and we've learned to put the team first in all that we think and do.

"The youngest boy who sweeps the terraces is just as important to us as the longest-serving player. We want him to feel that he belongs, to learn from his seniors and strive for a place in the team. The training that he gets is of a kind that I hope my three sons may one day enjoy. Edward, he's 14, Robert (12); and Graham (9) all want to follow in my footsteps and become cricketer - footballers when they grow up, and I hope that they will show the necessary ability.

(Manager of the Year 1955)
TED DRAKE

"As a matter of fact," Ted Drake continued, "the success of our youngsters last season pleased me more than anything. Conducted by our Chairman, Mr Mears, who is also Chairman of the English Selection Committee, they visited Amsterdam last Easter to compete with the best Youth teams of Europe for the Z.S.G.O. Cup, which I'm proud to say they won.

"I'll give you an example of what it can mean to join Chelsea," said Ted Drake. "One morning last season I motored across London to discuss the future of a promising 15-year-old player who had just left school. I wanted to give him a job, and after a chat with his parents I was able to satisfy them about his prospects.

"Less than one hour later, this youngster was on the field at Stamford Bridge, wearing Chelsea colours and playing in a trial game as inside partner to Roy Bentley.

"That, surely, must be a world record in sport for any 15-year-old. And to cap it all, Roy Bentley took the boy to lunch and offered him all the help he could give.

"The boy's name – Peter Brabrook. He played in two big matches for us last year – and I'm convinced that he is going to make a big name for himself in soccer."

"LUCKY CHELSEA"

DURING their close-season tour of Spain and Portugal, the English team were sitting in the hotel lounge. "I think I'll skip tea," Roy Bentley told Nat Lofthouse. "I want to cut down on my eating before the big match." But Roy was persuaded to stay. If he had himself forgotten that it was his 31st birthday, the other England players hadn't! Presently the chef carried in a large birthday cake, baked in Roy's honour. "We've put a special message on it, instead of the usual greetings," said Trainer Jimmy Trotter. Roy read the message, piped on top of the cake with icing sugar. "LUCKY CHELSEA" it said.

How the game has changed… Chelsea 1955 – 'We believe in youth.'
Chelsea 2007 – still believe in youth, but other clubs'

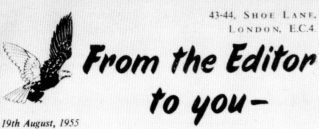

From the Editor to you–

43-44, SHOE LANE,
LONDON, E.C.4.

19th August, 1955

ON page 15 you will see the first announcement of our National Table Tennis Tournament for 1955/1956, and I hope as many of you as possible will take part.

This Table Tennis Tournament is not for experts only – it's for all of you who would like to have a try, so don't be bashful about joining in. Even if you aren't a very good player, you will learn a lot about Table Tennis and have a chance to meet some of the experts, who are eager to show you how to improve your play.

NOW for a word about that 'newspaper look' on EAGLE's front page (and it's for one week only!). You'll see an advertisement for a *Junior Helirig*, but please remember that *The Daily World Post* is a paper of the future and that the *Junior Helirig* hasn't been invented yet – so don't send in for one, please! Your enthusiastic letters about our present Dan Dare story show very clearly that "The Man from Nowhere" has captured your imagination! There's even more excitement to come.

Yours sincerely,

Marcus Morris

SPOTTERS' CORNER

THE A.E.C. REGAL Mk. IV coaches used by British European Airways are a familiar sight on the roads between Waterloo Air Terminal and London Airport. There are 50 of them, and they are the biggest single-deckers in the country, with seats for 37 passengers, and a luggage compartment under the raised rear half-deck big enough to hold up to three suitcases for each person. Between them, they carry about 1¼ million passengers each year.

Although specially designed, after careful study of the requirements by B.E.A. engineers and the London Transport Executive, the coaches use many of the same components and fittings as standard L.T. vehicles. Their bodies were built by Park Royal, and they have six-cylinder underfloor Diesel engines. They are painted in the standard B.E.A. colours with two shades of grey, white flash line and dark red trim.

WATCH FOR the "1½-deck" appearance resulting from the unstepped roof, which is unusual for a half-deck coach, and the insignia. Overall Length: 30 ft. Width: 8 ft. Unladen Weight: 8 tons, 3 cwt.

SUBMARINE ESCAPE — LATEST METHODS

New methods have recently been developed by which submariners have a much greater chance of escape should their craft be unable to surface. Amongst them is the "free-ascent" technique, which may be used up to depths of 300 ft. Another is the one-man escape chamber (A) which, following tests in the submarine *Solent*, is likely to be fitted in all new craft. The great advantages of this are speed of operations and the fact that a whole compartment does not have to be flooded, as with the use of the Twill escape trunk (see AA), which is now standard. In the compartments containing the latter is an air-supply manifold with individual leads, so that men may receive fresh air while awaiting their turn to come up. Drawing B shows a submarine bell in operation. These have proved most successful with the U.S. Navy, but can only be used if the submarine is on an even keel. H.M.S. *Kingfisher*, recently converted into a rescue ship, carries one of these. It weighs 10 tons, has a crew of 2 and can bring up 7 others each trip. BB shows the bell being lowered from the rescue ship, which has to be very carefully moored, for the former has to fit on to a special flange on the submarine's deck. Unfortunately

this flange – for structural reasons – cannot be fitted to our existing vessels. C shows one of the two marker-buoys by which a submarine reveals her position. The forward one is red and yellow, the after one all yellow. Each has a flag and a flashing light which is surrounded by cat's eye reflectors. D illustrates the "free-ascent" technique, in which submariners have now been trained. No breathing apparatus is worn, only goggles and nose clip. Initially the lungs are under pressure, but during the ascent the air in them expands as water pressure decreases. Each man is therefore trained to keep his mouth open then, so that excess air may be slowly expelled. The immersion suits are not needed for the ascent, but to provide warmth and buoyancy when on the surface. Inflatable, they have electric heating.

In drawing E, the dotted lines show the extent of the working space in a submarine. It is planned that new ones shall have two escape compartments, each large enough to take the whole crew and protected by a very strong bulkhead. In each, there will be a one-man escape chamber (A) and fittings for a rescue bell (B).

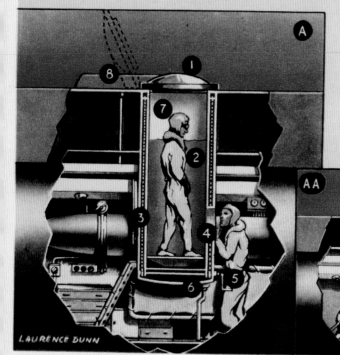

KEY TO NUMBERS
(Submarine Escape)

1. Escape hatch.
2. One-man escape chamber.
3. Entrance.
4. Observation window.
5. Handle for raising floor (if required).
6. Drain to bilges.
7. Air under pressure.
8. Housing for hatch controls.
9. Escape hatch.
10. Flange on deck, to fit base of bell.
11. Lifting gear, also air and electric leads.
12. Compressed-air motor for winding gear.
13. Upper hatch.
14. Lower hatch lid.
15. Tackle for raising lower hatch.
16. Water ballast tanks.
17. Flange for bell.
18. Marker-buoy cable.
19. "Iron man" observation chamber.
20. Recompression chamber.
21. Immersion suit, pressed close to body by water pressure.
22. Red electric light.
23. Immersion suit inflated (note peculiar quilted effect).
24. Buoyancy stole.
25-25. Large escape compartments.
26-26. Specially strengthened bulkheads.

LAURENCE DUNN

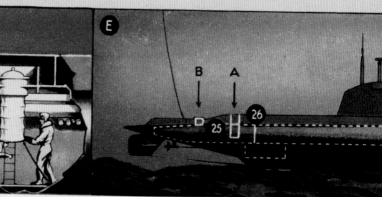

THE D

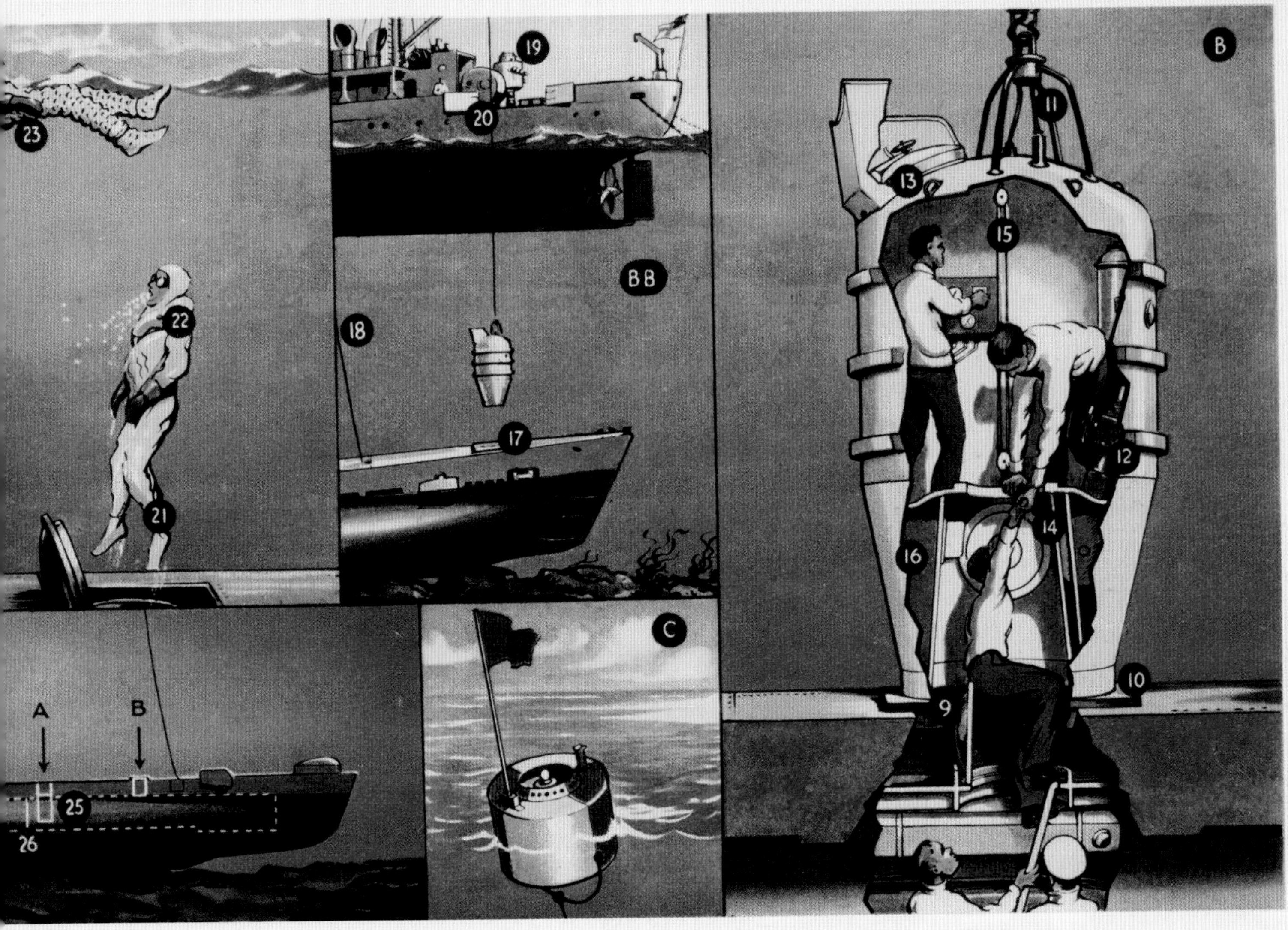
19
20
23
B
13
11
15
BB
18
22
17
12
21
14
16
C
10
9
A
B
25
26

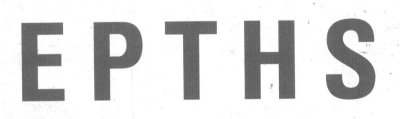

EPTHS

BREAKING THE SPACE BARRIER

Earth satellites that will circle the upper atmosphere of the earth at 18,000 m.p.h. will be in being by 1957, that is official. This will be a step nearer the realm of Dan Dare, the pioneer of spaceships and interplanetary travel.

America will send up these "basketballs" by means of multi-stage rockets to a height of about 250 miles. They will weigh 110 pounds and have a diameter of 19½ inches, twice the size of footballs, circling the earth every 90 minutes.

The object will be to find out about the upper atmosphere, the mysterious cosmic rays, the ultra-violet rays, etc., and automatically radio these recordings back to earth. After a short time, the satellite would be slowed down by the rarefied air. It would then spiral towards the earth and vaporize when it hit the heavier lower atmosphere. In this exclusive Eagle feature, "Operation Basketball" is made clear.

KEY TO MULTI-STAGE ROCKET: (1) Turbine of first stage rocket. (2) Fuel tanks, empty. (3) The spent first stage rocket falls away at about 80 miles altitude. (4) Attachment bolts automatically sheared. (5) Second stage rocket; sheared at about 160 miles' altitude. (6) Venture of second stage turbine. (7) Combustion chambers. (8) Turbine and pumps. (9) Liquid oxygen tanks. (10) Alcohol tank. (11) Double skin and cooling coils against frictional heat. (12) Third stage rocket; this will finally reach an altitude of 250 miles. (13) Shearing bolts. (14) Third stage turbine. (15) Fuel tanks. (16) The satellite mounted in a ring. (17) Instruments for recording information on the way up. These break away and come to earth by parachute. (18) The satellite is launched by explosive blast at about 250 miles altitude, when it then orbits the earth.

KEY TO THE EARTH'S ATMOSPHERIC BELT

A. Mount Everest, 29,003 feet.
B. The Troposphere (next to earth) and the Tropopause.
C. The Stratosphere.
D. Ordinary wireless waves are bent to earth by the Heaviside layer. Beam wireless waves are bent by the Appleton layer at about 170 miles' altitude.
E. The Ionosphere.
F. Limit of visible meteors.
G. Streamers of Aurora from here upwards.
H. The light of sky disappears into inky darkness beyond.
J. Satellite launched by rocket into outer space outside the atmospheric belt.
K. Outer space.
L. Electrons colliding with atoms of the upper atmosphere, resulting in cosmic rays.

HEIGHT IN MILES

L. ASHWELL WOOD

THE HE

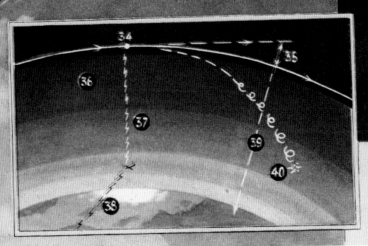

KEY TO REVOLVING SATELLITE: (19) Gamma ray recorder. (20) Antenna. (21) Sun's rays. (22) Sun ray collecting-rings. (23) Ultra-violet ray recorder. (23A) Electron recorder. (24) Alpha ray (X-ray) recorder. (25) Axis about which the satellite revolves. (26) Solar power turbines. (27) Magnetized tape recorder for radio transmitter. (28) Recording drum and gears. (29) Automatic radio transmitter and radar reflector. (30) Battery in protective wrapping. (31) Cosmic ray recorder. (32) Aurora recorder. (33) Short wave radio beams to earth. KEY TO INSET LEFT: (34) Satellite orbiting the earth at 18,000 m.p.h. (35) What keeps it up? The satellite's speed will tend to take it straight out into space, but gravity will be pulling it back to earth at the same time. The effect of these two opposing forces is to make the satellite travel in an orbit. (36) Upper atmosphere. (37) Short wave radio beams from satellite are picked up near the North Pole by aircraft. (38) Aircraft relays the radio information to earth. (39) Earth's gravitation pull. (40) Spent satellite spirals to earth and is vaporized by the heavy lower atmosphere.

IGHTS

👁 SPOTTERS' CORNER 👁

THE VOLKSWAGEN MICROBUS has become popular all over the world because of its combination of high per-formance and low running costs. It could hardly be described as handsome, but it offers as much comfort as the average 'station wagon' type of car and is far more roomy, having been designed from the start to carry as great a load as possible within its small dimensions.

Powered by the standard 36 b.h.p. Volks-wagen air-cooled four-cylinder engine, mounted at the rear of the chassis, the *Microbus* cruises safely at 50 m.p.h. and

has an average fuel consumption of 30 miles to the gallon. It carries eight per-sons and about 16 average-size suitcases, which can be loaded through the top-hinged rear door while passengers are entering the double side-doors. The interior is air-conditioned by a heater and adjustable roof-mounted ventilation system. The *de luxe* version has additional wrap-round rear windows, a sunshine roof and other refinements.

WATCH FOR the large Volkswagen badge on the snub nose, and the absence of any kind of radiator grille.

● Overall Length: 13 ft. 9 ins.   Width: 5 ft. 8 ins.   Loaded Weight: 36½ cwt. ●

P.C. 49 by ALAN STRANKS JOHN WORSLEY — **THE CASE OF THE NEW MEMBER**

CONTINUED:
P.C. 49 AND THE BOYS' CLUB GANG ARE TRAPPED AT THE BOTTOM OF A STEEP CLIFF BY "NUMBER ONE" AND MYSTICO, TWO CROOKS WHO HAVE STOLEN SECRET PAPERS AND LEFT MICK MULLIGAN TO DROWN IN A NEARBY CAVE.
AS NIGHT FALLS, P.C. 49 AND HIS YOUNG CHUMS PREPARE FOR ACTION...

YOU CHAPS HAVE PUT ME IN A STICKY SPOT. THOSE CROOKS ARE ARMED — AND I'VE GOT TO KEEP YOU UNDER COVER.

TIDE'S RISING FAST — WE'LL DROWN IF WE STAY HERE!

I'VE GOT TO FIND MICK! HE'S IN DANGER — I CAN FEEL IT IN MY BONES.

IT'LL BE PITCH DARK IN A FEW MINUTES.

NOT SO, O ELMER! SEE THAT FLASHING LIGHT?

THAT'LL BE LAMPREY LIGHT-HOUSE IF WE COULD GET A SIGNAL TO THE KEEPERS...

T-TOO MUCH T-TALK! "OVER THE T-TOP", SAY I!

P.C. 49 by ALAN STRANKS JOHN WORSLEY — **THE CASE OF THE SQUARE RING**

MY LORDS — EAGLERS — AND GENTLEMEN!
THIS IS A THIRTEEN-ROUND SERIAL, FEATURING P.C. 49, THE BOYS' CLUB GANG AND A NUMBER OF NEW FACES — SOME GOOD AND SOME NOT SO GOOD! PERMIT ME TO INTRODUCE...

ON MY RIGHT...

ON MY LEFT...

P.C. 49

TOBY

KID GLOVER (UNKNOWN WELTERWEIGHT)

KAYO KILLIGAN (REIGNING WELTER CHAMPION)

PAT

MICK

MAXIE MONKS (KAYO'S MANAGER)

GIGS

DOC WILDE (KID'S TRAINER)

DEUCE SPADE (A CROOKED GAMBLER)

GUMMY GULLETT (DEUCE'S STOOGE)

TIKI

SECONDS AWAY! ROUND ONE!

BUNNY

JEFF ARNOLD STARTS A SUPER NEW ADVENTURE! P.7

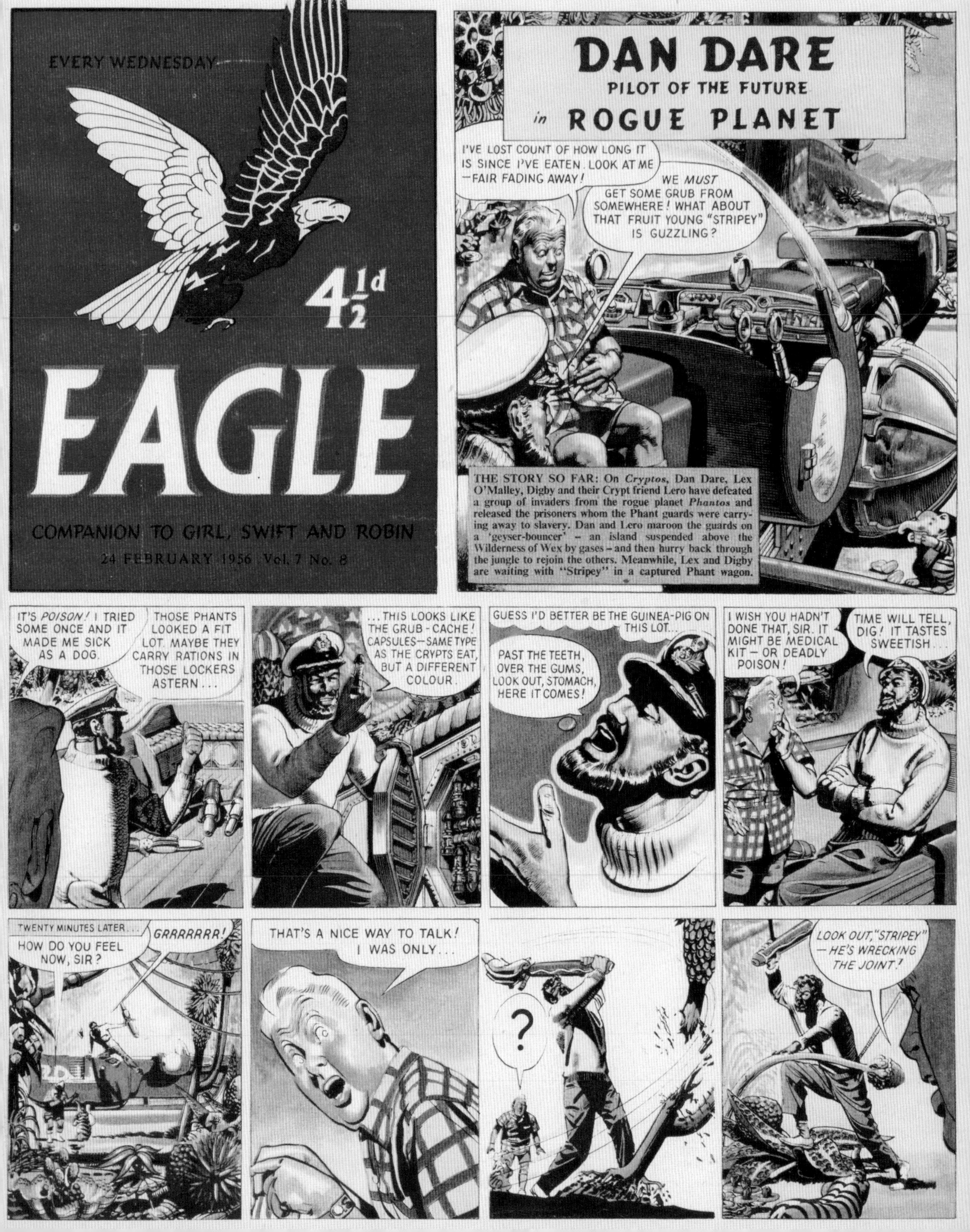
EVERY WEDNESDAY
4½d
EAGLE
COMPANION TO GIRL, SWIFT AND ROBIN
24 FEBRUARY 1956 Vol. 7 No. 8
DAN DARE
PILOT OF THE FUTURE
in ROGUE PLANET
I'VE LOST COUNT OF HOW LONG IT IS SINCE I'VE EATEN. LOOK AT ME —FAIR FADING AWAY!
WE MUST GET SOME GRUB FROM SOMEWHERE! WHAT ABOUT THAT FRUIT YOUNG "STRIPEY" IS GUZZLING?
THE STORY SO FAR: On Cryptos, Dan Dare, Lex O'Malley, Digby and their Crypt friend Lero have defeated a group of invaders from the rogue planet Phantos and released the prisoners whom the Phant guards were carrying away to slavery. Dan and Lero maroon the guards on a 'geyser-bouncer' – an island suspended above the Wilderness of Wex by gases – and then hurry back through the jungle to rejoin the others. Meanwhile, Lex and Digby are waiting with "Stripey" in a captured Phant wagon.
IT'S POISON! I TRIED SOME ONCE AND IT MADE ME SICK AS A DOG.
THOSE PHANTS LOOKED A FIT LOT. MAYBE THEY CARRY RATIONS IN THOSE LOCKERS ASTERN...
...THIS LOOKS LIKE THE GRUB-CACHE! CAPSULES—SAME TYPE AS THE CRYPTS EAT, BUT A DIFFERENT COLOUR.
GUESS I'D BETTER BE THE GUINEA-PIG ON THIS LOT...
PAST THE TEETH, OVER THE GUMS, LOOK OUT, STOMACH, HERE IT COMES!
I WISH YOU HADN'T DONE THAT, SIR. IT MIGHT BE MEDICAL KIT — OR DEADLY POISON!
TIME WILL TELL, DIG! IT TASTES SWEETISH...
TWENTY MINUTES LATER...
HOW DO YOU FEEL NOW, SIR?
GRRRRRRR!
THAT'S A NICE WAY TO TALK! I WAS ONLY...
?
LOOK OUT, "STRIPEY" —HE'S WRECKING THE JOINT!

The story of 'The Rogue Planet' hinges on the accidental discovery by Lex O'Malley of nutritional tablets which turn whoever consumes them into aggressive monsters. There are also tablets which can make a whole race into passive beings. In this tale the Crypts eat only yellow pills, while the Phants, the warrior race, live on purple pills. Fact being at least as strange as fiction, at around the same time this story was coming out, the American Army was experimenting on its own soldiers with various drugs, most notably lysergic acid diethylamide (LSD), to make the ultimate soldier.

Members of the studio producing the strips each week were continually used as models for the drawings. In this panel from 13 April 1956, Dan does a very passable impersonation of Digby to help Stripey understand his message.

EAGLE 27 July 1956

Our Painting Competition

Here is a selection from the best paintings in our recent National Painting Competition. Throughout, the standard was very high indeed and gained the admiration of the judges. See Editor's letter for full list of winners.

GROWING SHADOWS *by Paul Scholey (aged*

MARKET *by Douglas John Boyd (aged 16)*

IN HARBOUR *by Malcolm Dunnett (aged*

43-44, SHOE LANE,
LONDON, E.C.4

From the Editor to you—

15th June, 1956

FROM time to time you may have heard of boys or girls being hurt because they have picked up an explosive object in the fields or on the beaches, usually a relic of the last war.

Although clearing of wartime training and defence areas has been carried out very thoroughly, there is just a remote possibility of a buried missile being ploughed up to the surface or of an unexploded mine being washed up by the sea. The War Office have asked me to pass on these words of advice to you: –

Do not touch any strange metal object. Tell the police.

Do not enter a firing range or a training area. They are clearly marked by fencing and warning notices.

There is no need, of course, to go around the fields and beaches on tiptoe, fearing the worst and waiting for a great big bang! The chance of meeting with an explosive object is very remote indeed. BUT – if you *should* chance to see something that looks odd, remember – don't touch it, however exciting it looks.

Yours sincerely.

Marcus Morris

You write to the Editor

ROBERT'S PUP

I HAVE a one-month-old puppy named Satish. Every time I tap her nose she snaps at me, and she loves to crawl under the food cabinet. But when I call out "Ho, Ha, Ho, Ha, Ho," she rocks her head from side to side and then crawls out. Here is a photograph of me holding Satish, when she was a fortnight old, with my sister Shirley. – *Robert Pringle, Tripoli.* ED. – *Robert, you forgot to give us your full address. Would you kindly send it to us in order that we may send you your prize?*

5/- is paid for each letter published.
Readers who want a reply should en-
close a stamped, addressed envelope.

CRICKET CLUB

LAST November, a few of my friends and myself decided to form a 'Colts' Cricket Club and, with the help of an M.C.C. Youth Coach, we grew in membership, until now we have 25 members. Last week Mr Fred Titmus, the Middlesex and England cricketer, very kindly accepted the offer of being Club President. He also said that he would try to come to our trial match.

Later I had the honour of being photographed with Mr Titmus. – *Brian Collins, Enfield, Middlesex.*

WE'RE IN THE ARMY NOW!

I AM a reader of the EAGLE and have just joined the Army. In the Education Centre here, they have pinned the centre pages of the EAGLE showing the working parts of lorries, ships, etc. It is an excellent way of teaching drivers, and mechanics, how to strip and repair machines. – 23470087 *C. R. James, Aldershot, Hampshire.*

EAGLE 27 *July* 1956

INDUSTRIAL LANDSCAPE *by John Braben* (aged 11)

THE CRESCENT *by Jeremy David Annett (aged 14)*

TRAFALGAR SQUARE
by Frank Elsey (aged) 15

A special letter from the Editor

43-44, SHOE LANE,
LONDON, E.C.4.

27th July, 1956

THE picture shows just a fraction of the best paintings from which the judges, headed by Sir William Richardson, President of the Royal Academy, chose the top prizewinners in our National Painting Competition. The finalists were: – *Groups 14, 15, 16:* Douglas Boyd of Weybridge; Jeremy Annett of London; Charles Prosser of Harrogate. *Group 12 and 13:* Paul Scholey of Retford, Notts; Christopher Tilley of Launceston, Cornwall. *Group 10 and 11:* John Stevens of Ewell, Surrey; and Martin Lange of Margate.

Douglas Boyd and Jeremy Annett win the trip to Italy. I shall tell you more about that later.

I feel extremely proud of the tremendous show your paintings made and congratulate not only the winners but every one who tried.

Yours sincerely,

Marcus Morris

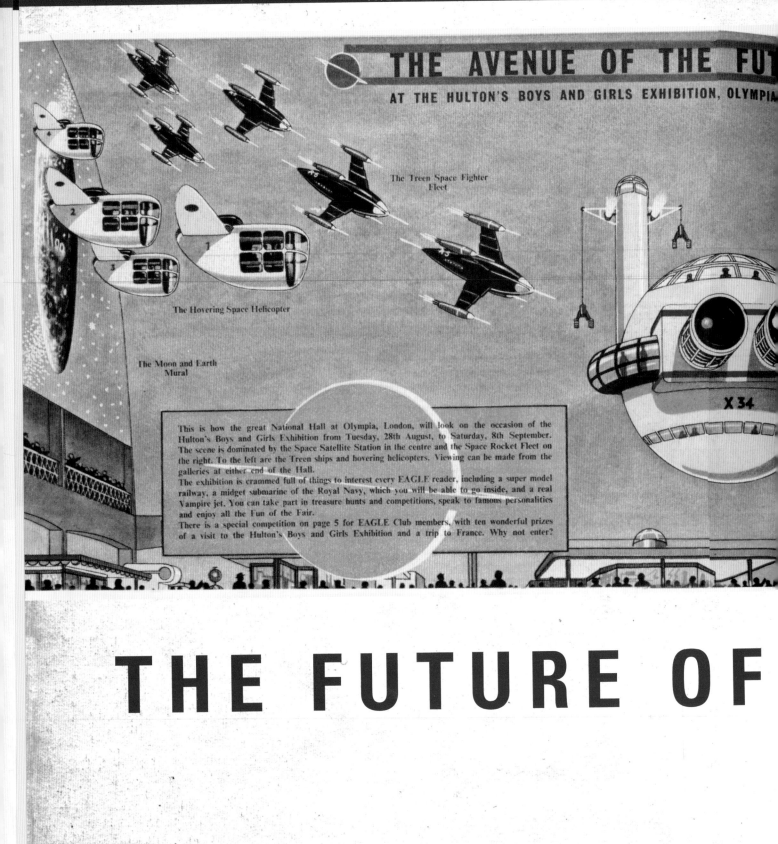

THE AVENUE OF THE FUT

AT THE HULTON'S BOYS AND GIRLS EXHIBITION, OLYMPIA

The Treen Space Fighter
Fleet

The Hovering Space Helicopter

The Moon and Earth
Mural

This is how the great National Hall at Olympia, London, will look on the occasion of the
Hulton's Boys and Girls Exhibition from Tuesday, 28th August, to Saturday, 8th September.
The scene is dominated by the Space Satellite Station in the centre and the Space Rocket Fleet on
the right. To the left are the Treen ships and hovering helicopters. Viewing can be made from the
galleries at either end of the Hall.
The exhibition is crammed full of things to interest every EAGLE reader, including a super model
railway, a midget submarine of the Royal Navy, which you will be able to go inside, and a real
Vampire jet. You can take part in treasure hunts and competitions, speak to famous personalities
and enjoy all the Fun of the Fair.
There is a special competition on page 5 for EAGLE Club members, with ten wonderful prizes
of a visit to the Hulton's Boys and Girls Exhibition and a trip to France. Why not enter?

X 34

THE FUTURE OF

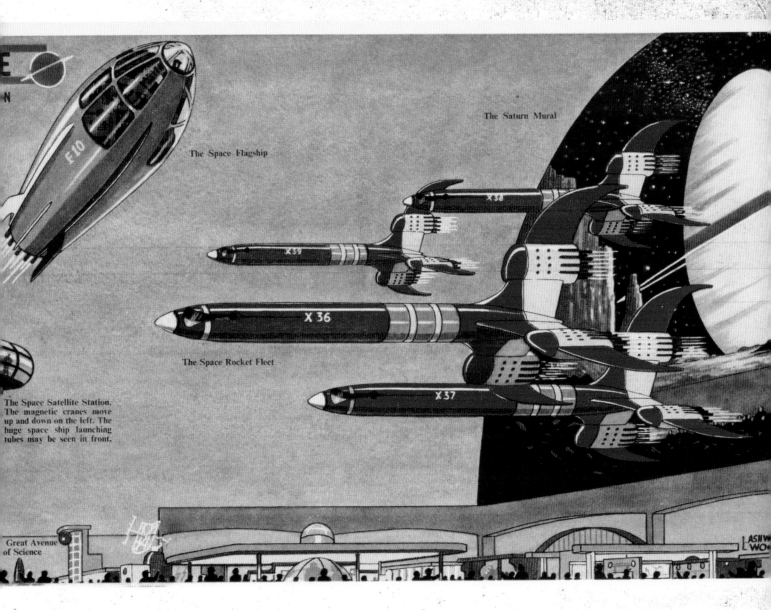

E 10

The Space Flagship

The Saturn Mural

X 39

X 36

X 37

The Space Rocket Fleet

The Space Satellite Station. The magnetic cranes move up and down on the left. The huge space ship launching tubes may be seen in front.

Great Avenue of Science

ASHW WO

THE WORLD

SILVER EAGLER OF THE YEAR

John Wilson

PICKING the Silver Eagler of the Year has been especially difficult this year. We have had many outstanding claims come in — some for single acts of courage, some for exceptional initiative, some for magnificent records of social service, some for that quieter kind of courage which overcomes the setbacks of illness, disability or accident. But, in the end, we were in no doubt that the special honour of Silver Eagler of the Year for 1956 should be accorded to John Wilson, aged 12, of Muirkirk, Ayrshire.

One of a family of seven, John has undertaken, during the last six years, the heavy extra burdens arising from the fact that his father, unfortunately, has poor health. Recently his mother also became ill. Refusing to be discouraged by this extra setback, John redoubled his efforts, answering any demand upon him that the critical situation called for. Heavily pressed in this way, some boys would have thought that here was an excuse for going easy on their school work. Not John. His school record is as splendid as his record at home. John's claim is strongly supported by a county councillor, a doctor, John's head-teacher, and his minister. We think that John lives up to the high standards we expect of a Silver Eagler of the Year.

✲✲✲✲✲✲✲✲✲✲✲✲✲✲✲✲✲✲✲✲✲

In addition to the awards already published, the following boys established a claim for a Silver Eagle Badge during the course of 1956.

Melvyn Jones

Peter Richardson

Michael Beck

Peter Goodall

Hector Newnham

Raymond Bunyan

Leonard Thwaites   Michael Horne   Martin Redman

John Hatch   David Sharpe

MELVYN JONES
of East Croydon. For his kindness to animals.

JOHN HATCH
of Wokingham, Bucks. For promptness and initiative in an emergency.

MICHAEL HORNE
of Baughurst, Hants. For outstanding service to his Church.

MARTIN REDMAN
of Edgeworth, Lancs. For courage in overcoming a physical disability.

DAVID SHARPE
of Gt. Malvern, Worcs. For courage and fortitude in facing sickness.

PETER GOODALL
of West Molesey, Surrey. For social service.

LEONARD THWAITES
of Dunscroft, Doncaster. For promptness and initiative in an emergency.

RAYMOND BUNYAN
of Luton, Beds. For a high standard of unselfishness and service at home.

PETER RICHARDSON
of Lancing, Sussex. For determination and courage in facing sickness.

HECTOR NEWNHAM
of Milton, Clackmannanshire. For grit and determination in facing illness.

MICHAEL BECK
of Boscombe, Hants. For determination and courage in facing illness.

✩✰✩✰✩✰✩✰✩✰✩✰✩✰✩✰✩✰✩✰✩✰✩✰✩✰✩✰✩✰✩

A Note to Parents . . .

. . . and also to teachers, clergymen, doctors, youth leaders and others in a position to recognize exceptional qualities in young people. We invite you to let us know about members of the EAGLE Club who deserve consideration for the Silver Eagle Badge. If you have a boy in mind who has a record which you think justifies a claim, please write to us at EAGLE Reader Service, Long Lane, Aintree, Liverpool 9, enclosing a stamped and addressed envelope, and we shall be very glad to forward to you the special booklet describing the Silver Eagle Award in full detail.

✩✰✩✰✩✰✩✰✩✰✩✰✩✰✩✰✩✰✩✰✩✰✩✰✩✰✩✰✩✰✩

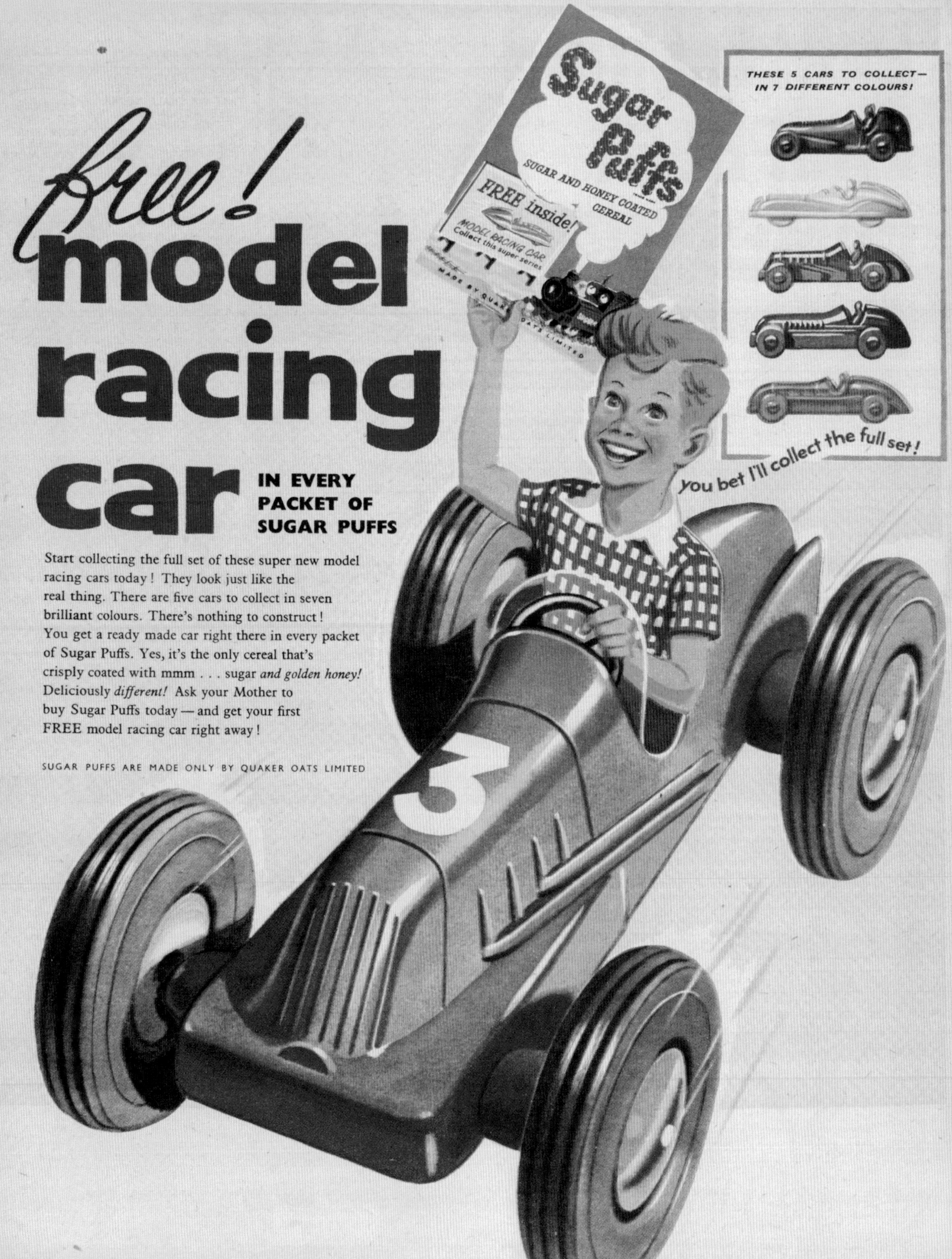
free!
model racing car
IN EVERY PACKET OF SUGAR PUFFS
Start collecting the full set of these super new model racing cars today! They look just like the real thing. There are five cars to collect in seven brilliant colours. There's nothing to construct! You get a ready made car right there in every packet of Sugar Puffs. Yes, it's the only cereal that's crisply coated with mmm . . . sugar *and golden honey!* Deliciously *different!* Ask your Mother to buy Sugar Puffs today — and get your first FREE model racing car right away!
SUGAR PUFFS ARE MADE ONLY BY QUAKER OATS LIMITED
Sugar Puffs
SUGAR AND HONEY COATED CEREAL
FREE inside!
MODEL RACING CAR
Collect this super series
MADE BY QUAKER OATS LIMITED
THESE 5 CARS TO COLLECT— IN 7 DIFFERENT COLOURS!
you bet I'll collect the full set!
3

SUPER BICYCLES AND BOOKS TO BE WON! SEE PAGE II

EAGLE

EVERY WEDNESDAY

4½d

COMPANION TO GIRL, SWIFT AND ROBIN

6 SEPTEMBER 1957 Vol. 8 No. 36

DAN DARE
PILOT OF THE FUTURE
in REIGN OF THE ROBOTS

THE STORY SO FAR
Earth is in the grip of the Mekon, who is trying to force Dan to help him conquer the universe. Dan and Co. know that their only chance is to find and destroy the power station of the Elektrobots, mechanical monsters controlled by the Mekon's voice vibrations. Dan escapes in the Mekon's ship and evades pursuit by a Treen squadron. As he bores deeper into uncharted space, Dan sees . . .

JUMPING JETS! I MUST HAVE STRUCK THE GRAVE-YARD OF EVERY SHIP THAT EVER WENT OFF-BEAM SINCE SPACEFLIGHT BEGAN...

FRANK HAMPSON
PRODUCTION

The Mekon's proud boast that 'no human brain can defeat' the mind reading vidi-sphere, was easily proven wrong by Digby's willpower, and his sheer love of food.

FISH AND CHIPS!

WITH LASHINGS OF SALT AND VINEGAR!

HE STILL THINKS OF FOOD... INCREASE THE POWER.

TURKEY AND TRIMMINGS— AH! THAT'S GOOD, WHAT'S THERE FOR AFTERS, CHRISTMAS PUD?

THE MYSTERY OF THE LOCH NESS MONSTER! SEE PAGE 4

In this cover from the classic adventure 'Reign of the Robots', one of London's icons, Big Ben, fills the background. It was this use of familiar buildings and places which made Dan Dare seem so real to the reader. By keeping the stories grounded in everyday reality, the reader was continually challenged to remember what was real and what was not.

It had long been a dream of Frank Hampson to draw the life of Jesus. In the story, scripted by Marcus Morris, Hampson poured his all onto the pages, displaying all his trademark style and eye for detail. It was to be his last great contribution to the comic he had helped create.

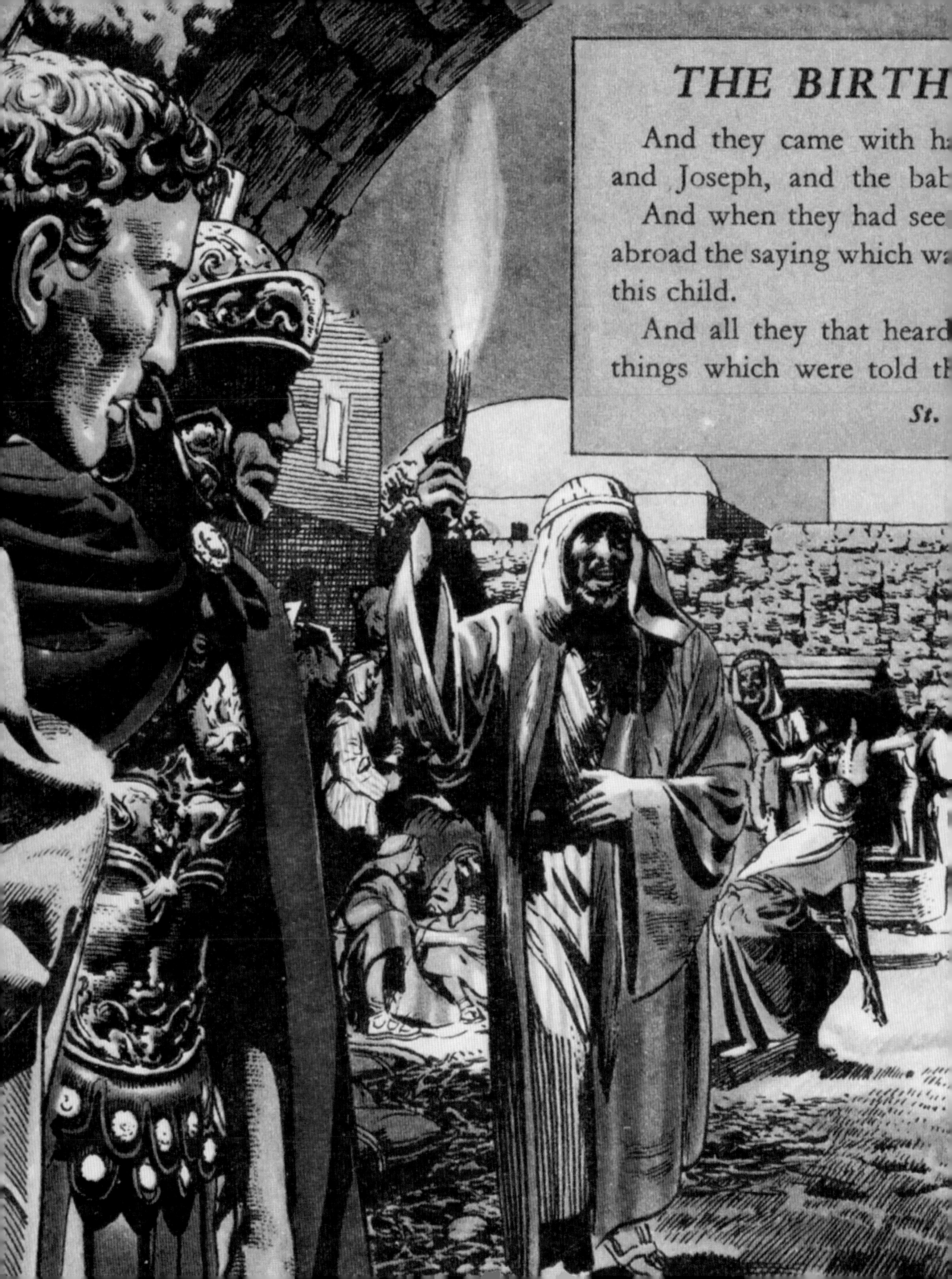

THE BIRTH

And they came with ha
and Joseph, and the bab
And when they had see
abroad the saying which wa
this child.

And all they that heard
things which were told th

St.

OF JESUS

e, and found Mary,
lying in a manger.
t, they made known
told them concerning

t wondered at those
n by the shepherds.

ke 2, vs. 16, 17 and 18

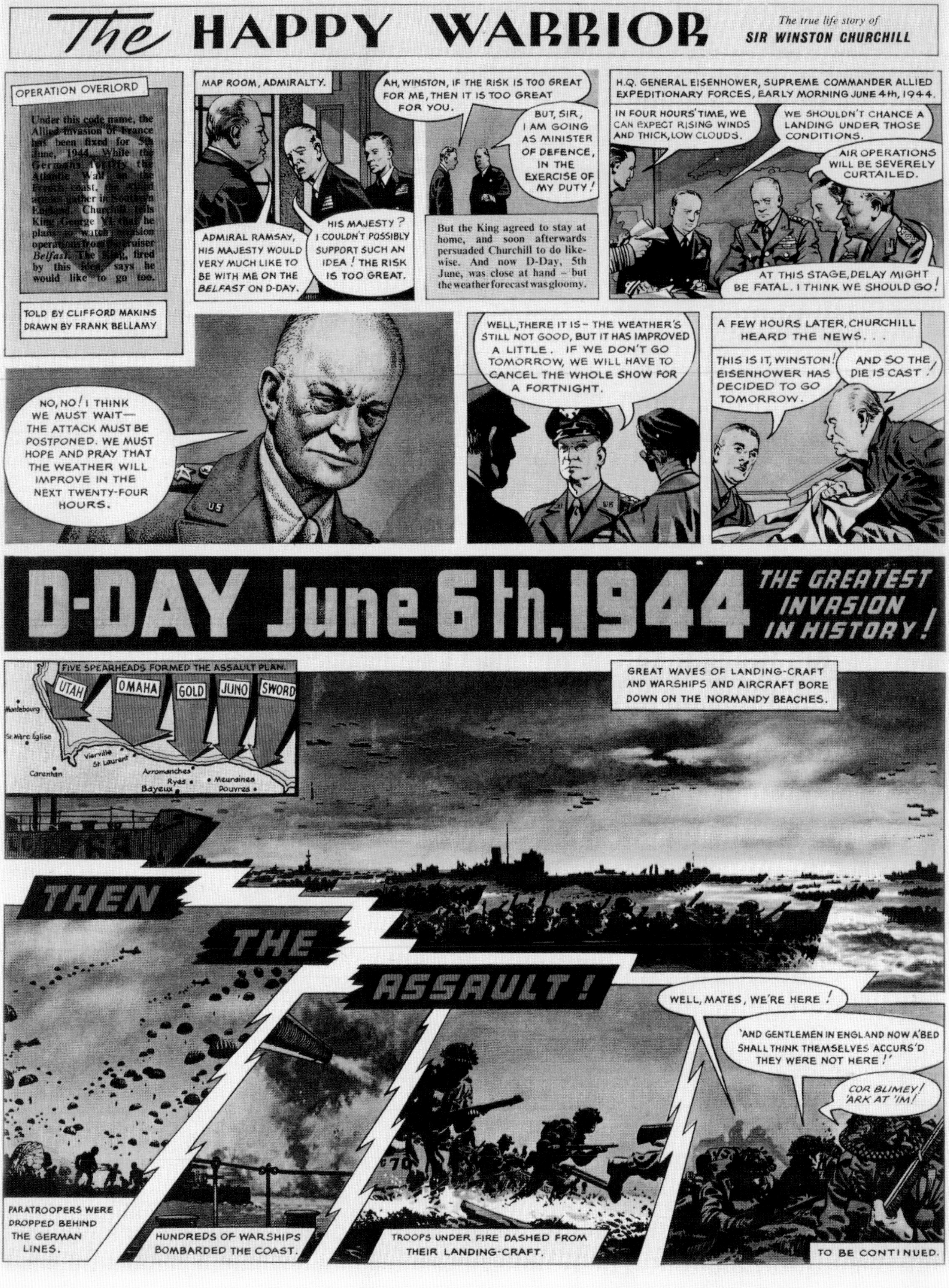
The HAPPY WARRIOR
The true life story of
SIR WINSTON CHURCHILL
OPERATION OVERLORD
Under this code name, the Allied invasion of France has been fixed for 5th June, 1944. While the Germans fortify the Atlantic Wall on the French coast, the allied armies gather in Southern England. Churchill tells King George VI that he plans to watch invasion operations from the cruiser Belfast. The King, fired by this idea, says he would like to go too.
TOLD BY CLIFFORD MAKINS
DRAWN BY FRANK BELLAMY
MAP ROOM, ADMIRALTY.
ADMIRAL RAMSAY, HIS MAJESTY WOULD VERY MUCH LIKE TO BE WITH ME ON THE BELFAST ON D-DAY.
HIS MAJESTY? I COULDN'T POSSIBLY SUPPORT SUCH AN IDEA! THE RISK IS TOO GREAT.
AH, WINSTON, IF THE RISK IS TOO GREAT FOR ME, THEN IT IS TOO GREAT FOR YOU.
BUT, SIR, I AM GOING AS MINISTER OF DEFENCE, IN THE EXERCISE OF MY DUTY!
But the King agreed to stay at home, and soon afterwards persuaded Churchill to do likewise. And now D-Day, 5th June, was close at hand – but the weather forecast was gloomy.
H.Q. GENERAL EISENHOWER, SUPREME COMMANDER ALLIED EXPEDITIONARY FORCES, EARLY MORNING JUNE 4th, 1944.
IN FOUR HOURS' TIME, WE CAN EXPECT RISING WINDS AND THICK, LOW CLOUDS.
WE SHOULDN'T CHANCE A LANDING UNDER THOSE CONDITIONS.
AIR OPERATIONS WILL BE SEVERELY CURTAILED.
AT THIS STAGE, DELAY MIGHT BE FATAL. I THINK WE SHOULD GO!
NO, NO! I THINK WE MUST WAIT— THE ATTACK MUST BE POSTPONED. WE MUST HOPE AND PRAY THAT THE WEATHER WILL IMPROVE IN THE NEXT TWENTY-FOUR HOURS.
US
WELL, THERE IT IS – THE WEATHER'S STILL NOT GOOD, BUT IT HAS IMPROVED A LITTLE. IF WE DON'T GO TOMORROW, WE WILL HAVE TO CANCEL THE WHOLE SHOW FOR A FORTNIGHT.
A FEW HOURS LATER, CHURCHILL HEARD THE NEWS...
THIS IS IT, WINSTON! EISENHOWER HAS DECIDED TO GO TOMORROW.
AND SO THE DIE IS CAST!
D-DAY June 6th, 1944
THE GREATEST INVASION IN HISTORY!
FIVE SPEARHEADS FORMED THE ASSAULT PLAN.
UTAH
OMAHA
GOLD
JUNO
SWORD
Montebourg
St. Mère Église
Carentan
Vierville
St. Laurent
Arromanches
Ryes
Meuraines
Bayeux
Douvres
GREAT WAVES OF LANDING-CRAFT AND WARSHIPS AND AIRCRAFT BORE DOWN ON THE NORMANDY BEACHES.
THEN THE ASSAULT!
WELL, MATES, WE'RE HERE!
'AND GENTLEMEN IN ENGLAND NOW A'BED SHALL THINK THEMSELVES ACCURS'D THEY WERE NOT HERE!'
COR BLIMEY! 'ARK AT 'IM!
PARATROOPERS WERE DROPPED BEHIND THE GERMAN LINES.
HUNDREDS OF WARSHIPS BOMBARDED THE COAST.
TROOPS UNDER FIRE DASHED FROM THEIR LANDING-CRAFT.
TO BE CONTINUED.

LIVE & LEARN with MR. THERM

LET'S HAVE A GAS AIRING-CUPBOARD...

An alcove in a bathroom, or on a landing, can be put to excellent use by converting the space into a gas-heated airing-cupboard, says Mr. Therm . . .

LIKE THIS!

. . . like this one. The same method may be applied to converting an existing cupboard. Before you start, go to your gas showrooms for the airing cupboard gas-heater, and arrange for the gas supply to be installed at the bottom of the cupboard; this includes a control tap, with a restrictor which enables the gas fitter to set the heater's correct gas rate. If the cupboard contains a cold water tank and pipes, make sure that they are well insulated to avoid condensation.

SKIRTING

Start with the base. Make two side pieces, slightly shorter than the depth of the alcove and the same height as the skirting. Cut notches in top edges and front, using a small saw and chisel. Nail to skirtings at side of alcove. Then fit 1 in. by 2 in. battens in the notches and nail them in place.

Cover both the top and front of the base frame with pegboard. Glue the meeting surfaces of frame and pegboard, and secure with ⅛ in. oval nails spaced 4 ins. apart. Make allowance for a ventilation opening of at least 3 sq. ins. at the top and bottom of the cupboard, says Mr. Therm.

ASBESTOS PLUGGING

A batten is fixed to the wall each side of the alcove, running from base to ceiling. Secure with 2½ in. screws driven into holes which have been filled with asbestos plugging, as shown here. Leave a 1 in. space at the front.

The front frame is 1 in. by 2 in. softwood. The foot is left open, but an extra rail is fitted across at a distance of 12 ins. below the top. Half joint the four frame members, secure joints with glue and screws, and screw front frame to side battens. Cover top panel with pegboard. NEXT WEEK, Mr. Therm will show you how to finish your gas-heated airing-cupboard.

CHRISTOPHER·TEMPLE

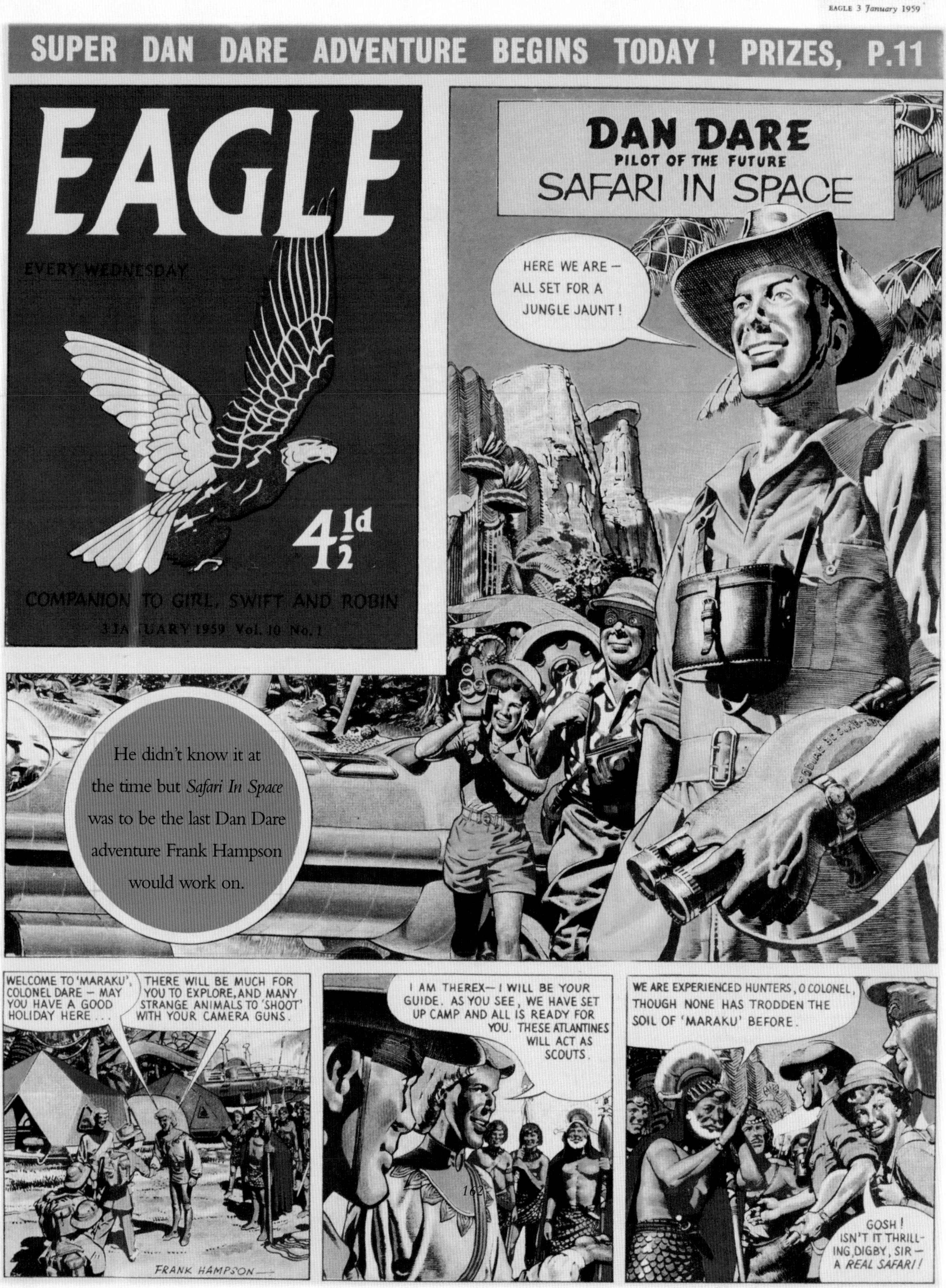

EAGLE 3 January 1959
SUPER DAN DARE ADVENTURE BEGINS TODAY! PRIZES, P.11
EAGLE
EVERY WEDNESDAY
4½d
COMPANION TO GIRL, SWIFT AND ROBIN
3 JA UARY 1959 Vol. 10 No. 1
DAN DARE
PILOT OF THE FUTURE
SAFARI IN SPACE
HERE WE ARE — ALL SET FOR A JUNGLE JAUNT!
WELCOME TO 'MARAKU', COLONEL DARE — MAY YOU HAVE A GOOD HOLIDAY HERE...
THERE WILL BE MUCH FOR YOU TO EXPLORE, AND MANY STRANGE ANIMALS TO 'SHOOT' WITH YOUR CAMERA GUNS.
FRANK HAMPSON
I AM THEREX — I WILL BE YOUR GUIDE. AS YOU SEE, WE HAVE SET UP CAMP AND ALL IS READY FOR YOU. THESE ATLANTINES WILL ACT AS SCOUTS.
WE ARE EXPERIENCED HUNTERS, O COLONEL, THOUGH NONE HAS TRODDEN THE SOIL OF 'MARAKU' BEFORE.
GOSH! ISN'T IT THRILLING, DIGBY, SIR — A *REAL SAFARI*!

He didn't know it at the time but *Safari In Space* was to be the last Dan Dare adventure Frank Hampson would work on.

EAGLE CLUB

South London T.T. Tournament

Scores of boys converged on two Boys' Clubs in Kennington Oval to spend the day vying with each other for the honour of being the South London Regional EAGLE JUNIOR TABLE TENNIS CHAMPION.

With willing help and assistance from the National Association of Boys' Clubs and officials from the English Table Tennis Association our Tournament got off to an early start, and it was soon apparent that the standard of playing was going to be extremely good. Johnny Leach, the Tournament's Chief Coach, was again impressed by the skill of the competitors, and found that the under 13's as well as the seniors showed they had a sound knowledge of the game. The winner of the Senior Section was D. Bloy, Runner-up W. Williams. For the Junior Section the winner was D. Johnson, Runner-up M. A. Blok.

Just a reminder to all those who have not yet received their final playing instructions; don't think that you have been forgotten or that your Entry Form has been lost. This is not the case — you will all be informed about your own particular Tournament in good time. Watch for further news soon.

Junior Winner, D. Johnson, and Junior Runner-up, M. A. Blok, proudly display their trophies.

Johnny Leach congratulates D. Bloy, Senior Regional Champion.

NEW YEAR GREETINGS

Our Vice-Presidents are scattered over the world, but they have remembered to send a personal message to every EAGLE Club Member. They wish you all a Happy New Year with good sportsmanship at work, play and on the field. Stick to the rules in your Club Card, they say, think of the other chap — and you can't go wrong.

Left to right: Neville Duke, Stirling Moss, Denis Compton, Stanley Matthews, Godfrey Evans, Trevor Bailey and Leonard Cheshire, V.C.

Is *YOUR* Birthdate here this week?

SEPT. 13th 1940 – DEC. 14th 1942
MAY 9th 1941 – APR. 20th 1943
AUG. 3rd 1944 – JAN. 27th 1940

You are entitled to a FREE birthday gift if you are an EAGLE Club Member and your birthdate appears in the list above. Choose it from the following list: stamp album, jigsaw puzzle, stationers folder, adventure book, ball-point pen or propelling pencil. Then state your choice on a post-card, giving your name, address, Club Number and the date you were born, and post it to: Birthday Present (92) EAGLE Club, Long Lane, Liverpool 9.

Your post-card must reach us by Thursday, January 6th. Though the same birthdate may appear more than once, no Member may claim more than one gift.

Manchester Soccer Demonstration

Our first F.A. soccer-coaching demonstration was an outstanding success! Hundreds of Manchester EAGLE Club Members thoroughly enjoyed themselves and took a keen interest in the films and practical coaching demonstrations put on for them.

Excitement really became high when star players from Manchester City and Manchester United took part in one or two friendly competitions, each of which was designed to demonstrate the arts of ball control.

The finale of a heading tennis match brought the EAGLE Club Members to their feet, and the cheering during each rally of this thrilling and skilful game almost brought the house down!

Fagan, McAdams, and Savage of the City signing autographs.

John Berry, Jack Rowley of the United have a heading tennis rally.

EAGLE READER — are you a member of EAGLE Club? There are many privileges to be had by joining; free viewing and coaching for football and cricket, free treats to many entertainments and special cheap-but-good holiday schemes where you can enjoy the companionship of other EAGLE Club Members.

It costs only 1/6d. to join — and there's a coupon on page 11.

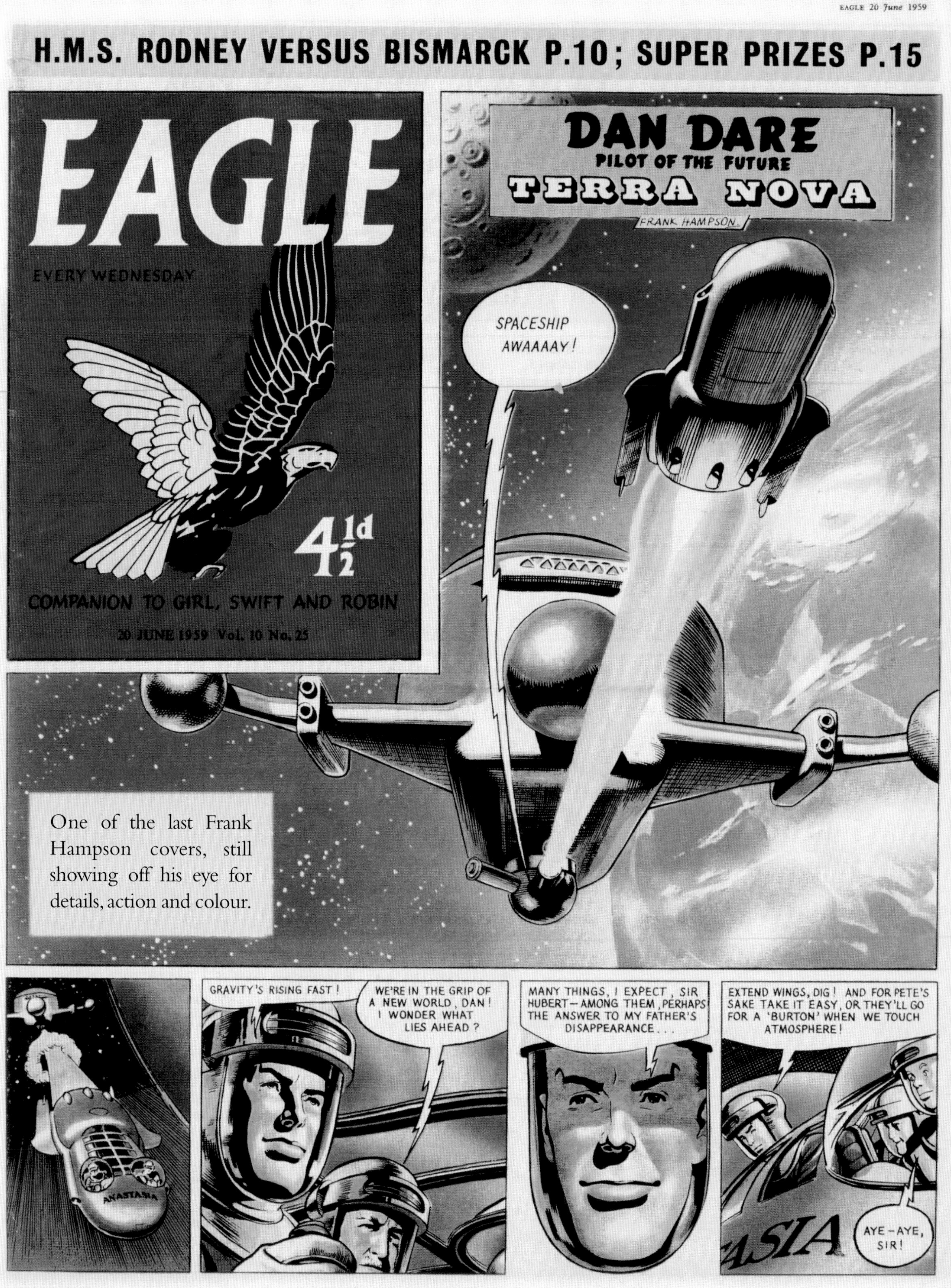
EAGLE 20 June 1959
H.M.S. RODNEY VERSUS BISMARCK P.10; SUPER PRIZES P.15
EAGLE
EVERY WEDNESDAY
4½d
COMPANION TO GIRL, SWIFT AND ROBIN
20 JUNE 1959 Vol. 10 No. 25
DAN DARE
PILOT OF THE FUTURE
TERRA NOVA
FRANK HAMPSON
SPACESHIP AWAAAAY!
ANASTASIA
GRAVITY'S RISING FAST!
WE'RE IN THE GRIP OF A NEW WORLD, DAN! I WONDER WHAT LIES AHEAD?
MANY THINGS, I EXPECT, SIR HUBERT—AMONG THEM, PERHAPS, THE ANSWER TO MY FATHER'S DISAPPEARANCE . . .
EXTEND WINGS, DIG! AND FOR PETE'S SAKE TAKE IT EASY, OR THEY'LL GO FOR A 'BURTON' WHEN WE TOUCH ATMOSPHERE!
AYE-AYE, SIR!

One of the last Frank Hampson covers, still showing off his eye for details, action and colour.

Hobbies Corner

Cheese making — THEN

Cheese is one of the oldest foods known to man. Mention of it has been found in early Greek literature, when it was produced in nearly the same way as housewives make it now-adays. Some of the English varieties of cheese that we eat today were being made during the Middle Ages, and this illustration shows it being prepared in the Mid-Eighteenth century.

Cheese making — NOW

During the last war, a uniform cheese was produced suitable for cutting into the tiny ration allowance. Since 1954, when restrictions were removed, the cheese-makers have turned their skill to making the famous English varieties again. To-day, however, only 5% of the cheese produced is made on the farm; the rest is made in factories, where cleanliness is all important.

SOME HOME-PRODUCED VARIETIES

COLLECTING CHEESE LABELS

Fromology (the science and study of cheese) is the accepted name for the hobby of collecting cheese labels and, although this pastime is young in comparison with others, it has a wide scope and tremendous interest. A neatly-arrayed album page can look very colourful and attractive, and a further advantage is the small amount of outlay needed to start your collection.

Methods of obtaining specimens vary. Let your friends and relatives know that you are interested in cheese labels. They will catch some of your enthusiasm and will find pleasure in adding to your collection, possibly bringing you back some foreign examples from Continental holidays. Writing to cheese-makers is not generally fruitful, although it may be worth while to visit your local grocer. Other sources are pen-friends and label-dealers.

The Fromologists' Circle was founded in 1952, and now has over 5,000 members. If you write, mentioning EAGLE, to: M. Storey, 331, Horbury Rd., Wakefield, Yorks., enclosing a stamped, addressed envelope, he will send 10 FREE labels and a Bulletin.

MOUNTING YOUR LABELS

Care must be taken when preparing your labels for mounting, as any damage will reduce their value. Difficulty is sometimes experienced when removing them from the silver paper. An easy method in these cases is to insert a strip of thin card between the label and the foil, moving it to and fro and leaving the glue adhering to the label rather than the silver paper. Soaking in water is not a good idea, as quite often this spoils the label's lustre and freshness.

An album with large pages - preferably loose leaves retained by ring clips - is recommended, as this will give a better 'display area' and the opportunity to insert more pages when necessary. You will find that the use of black pages will enhance the coloured labels, while some of the more flimsy types will look crisper on white.

For mounting, nothing beats the stamp hinge, as it allows rearrangement without damage.

NEXT WEEK: MATCH-BOX LABELS

MAGIC IN METER

BY DENNIS MALLET

The story we are now to tell, Thanks to GAS, turns out quite well!

© Gas Council

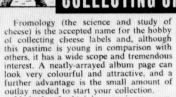

"It's New Year's Eve! All on parade! What Resolutions have we made?" When good old Dad addressed us thus, Mum answered first: "No flap, no fuss...

"Is what I want on Washing Day— I'll wash our things the *Thermal* way!

"Quite right," responded Dad, "Hear, hear! And fresher food's a good idea. I vow to see that waste is never Seen round here in muggy weather!"

Then Gran chipped in: "My room shall be As warm as warm—just wait and see!"

"I'll learn to cook," said sister Sue, "The simplest way—that's what I'll do!"

Then everybody looked at *me*. I meekly said: "I guarantee...

"To wash myself with special care— Provided *Mr Therm* is there!"

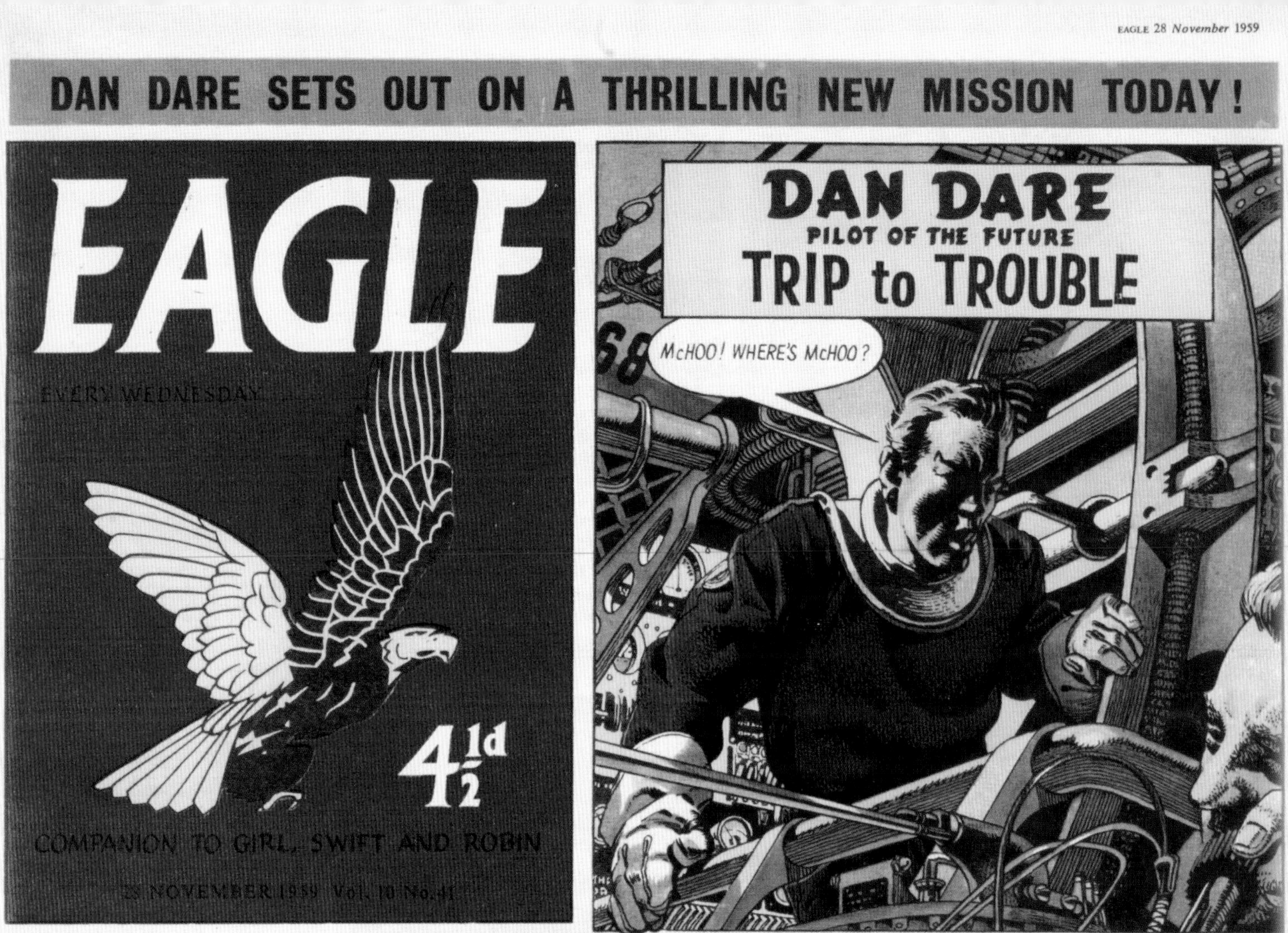
EAGLE 28 November 1959
DAN DARE SETS OUT ON A THRILLING NEW MISSION TODAY!
EAGLE
EVERY WEDNESDAY
4½d
COMPANION TO GIRL, SWIFT AND ROBIN
28 NOVEMBER 1959 Vol. 10 No. 41
DAN DARE
PILOT OF THE FUTURE
TRIP to TROUBLE
McHOO! WHERE'S McHOO?

By now Frank Bellamy has taken over from Hampson. His style is cleary evident when you compare this cover to his drawing on the Happy Warrior

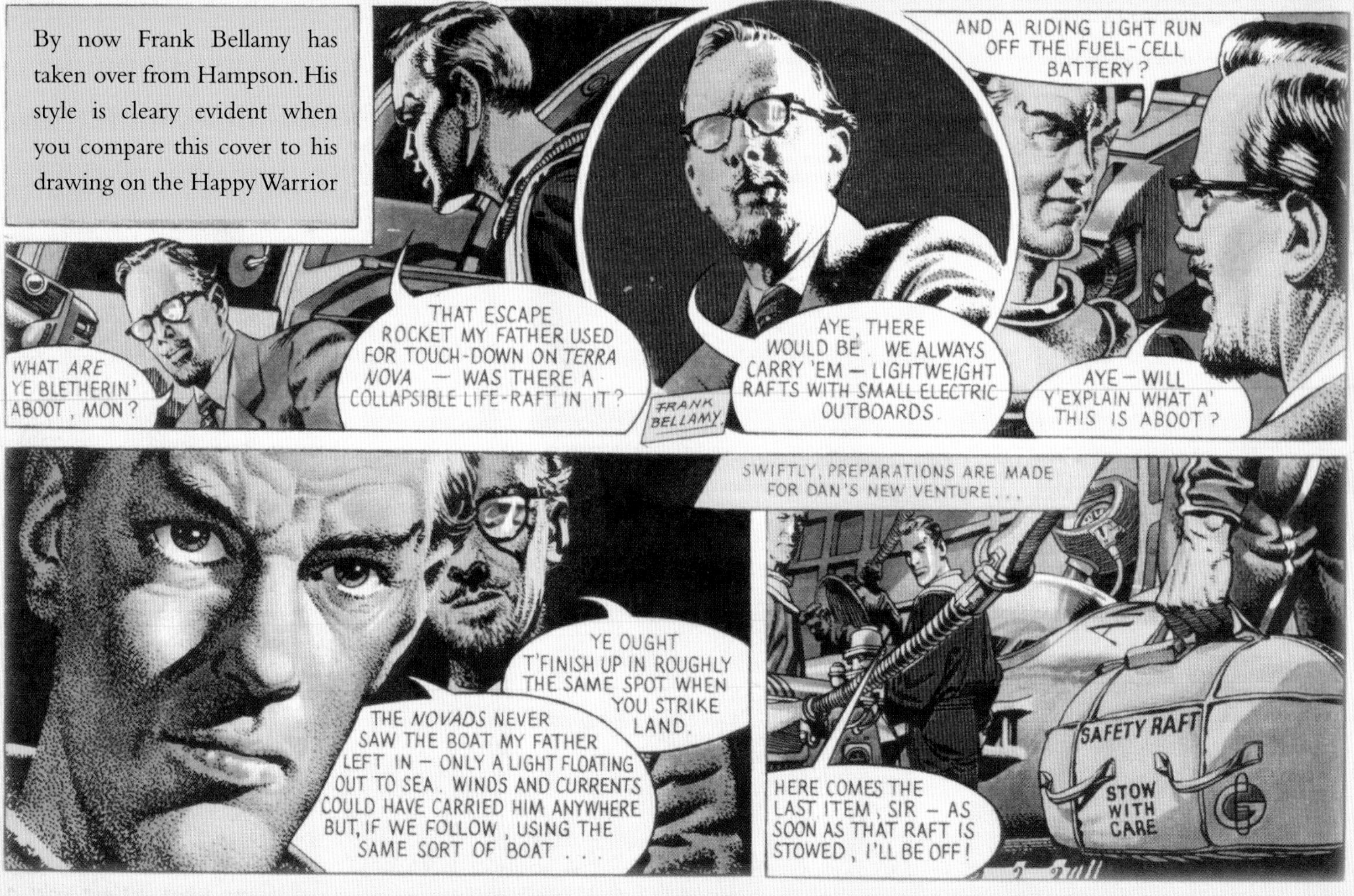
AND A RIDING LIGHT RUN OFF THE FUEL-CELL BATTERY?
WHAT *ARE* YE BLETHERIN' ABOOT, MON?
THAT ESCAPE ROCKET MY FATHER USED FOR TOUCH-DOWN ON *TERRA NOVA* — WAS THERE A COLLAPSIBLE LIFE-RAFT IN IT?
FRANK BELLAMY
AYE, THERE WOULD BE. WE ALWAYS CARRY 'EM — LIGHTWEIGHT RAFTS WITH SMALL ELECTRIC OUTBOARDS.
AYE — WILL Y'EXPLAIN WHAT A' THIS IS ABOOT?
YE OUGHT T'FINISH UP IN ROUGHLY THE SAME SPOT WHEN YOU STRIKE LAND.
THE *NOVADS* NEVER SAW THE BOAT MY FATHER LEFT IN — ONLY A LIGHT FLOATING OUT TO SEA. WINDS AND CURRENTS COULD HAVE CARRIED HIM ANYWHERE BUT, IF WE FOLLOW, USING THE SAME SORT OF BOAT . . .
SWIFTLY, PREPARATIONS ARE MADE FOR DAN'S NEW VENTURE . . .
SAFETY RAFT
STOW WITH CARE
HERE COMES THE LAST ITEM, SIR — AS SOON AS THAT RAFT IS STOWED, I'LL BE OFF!

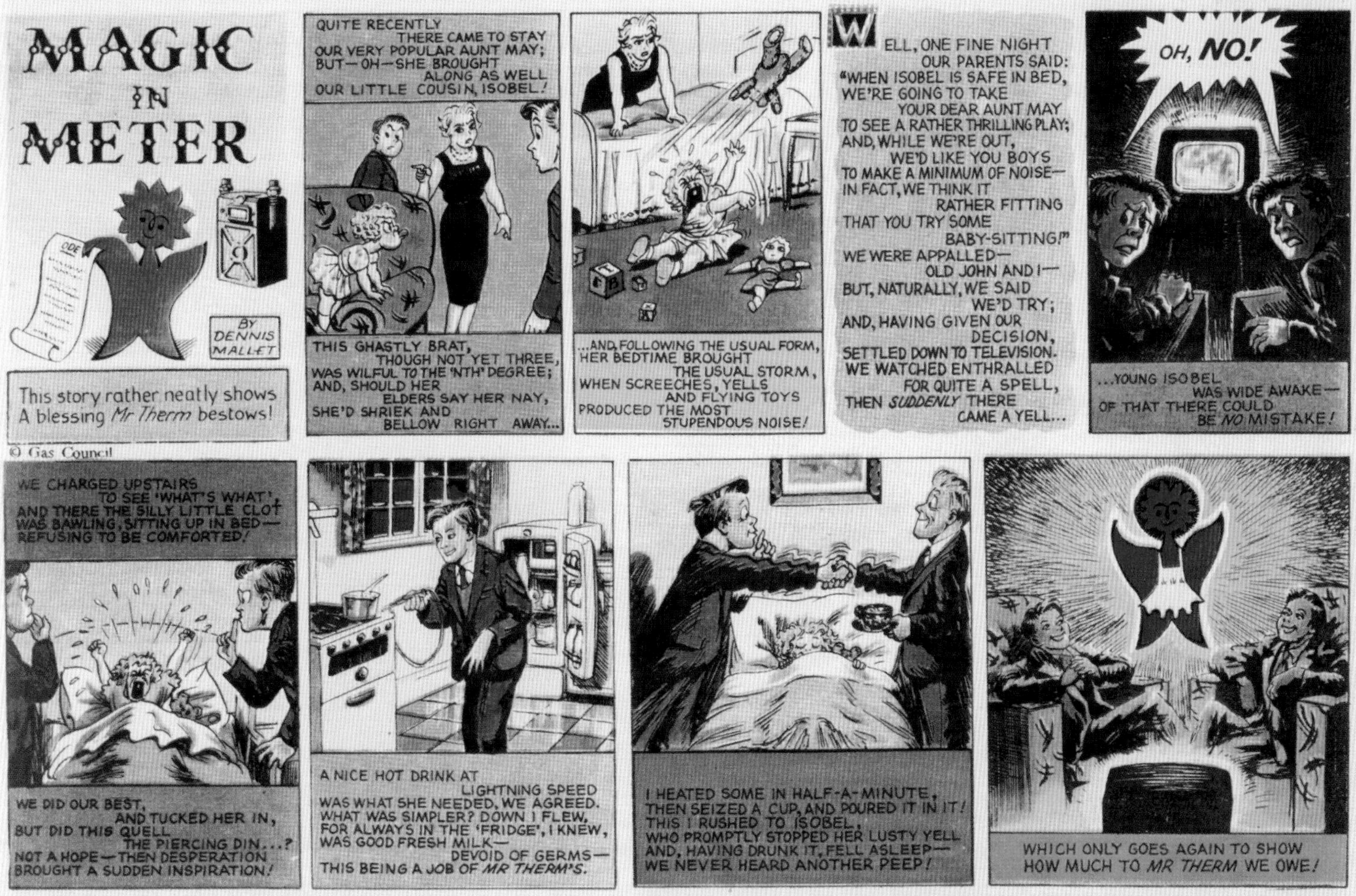
MAGIC IN METER
BY DENNIS MALLET
This story rather neatly shows A blessing *Mr Therm* bestows!
© Gas Council
QUITE RECENTLY THERE CAME TO STAY OUR VERY POPULAR AUNT MAY; BUT—OH—SHE BROUGHT ALONG AS WELL OUR LITTLE COUSIN, ISOBEL!
THIS GHASTLY BRAT, THOUGH NOT YET THREE, WAS WILFUL TO THE 'NTH' DEGREE; AND, SHOULD HER ELDERS SAY HER NAY, SHE'D SHRIEK AND BELLOW RIGHT AWAY...
...AND, FOLLOWING THE USUAL FORM, HER BEDTIME BROUGHT THE USUAL STORM, WHEN SCREECHES, YELLS AND FLYING TOYS PRODUCED THE MOST STUPENDOUS NOISE!
WELL, ONE FINE NIGHT OUR PARENTS SAID: "WHEN ISOBEL IS SAFE IN BED, WE'RE GOING TO TAKE YOUR DEAR AUNT MAY TO SEE A RATHER THRILLING PLAY; AND, WHILE WE'RE OUT, WE'D LIKE YOU BOYS TO MAKE A MINIMUM OF NOISE— IN FACT, WE THINK IT RATHER FITTING THAT YOU TRY SOME BABY-SITTING!" WE WERE APPALLED— OLD JOHN AND I— BUT, NATURALLY, WE SAID WE'D TRY; AND, HAVING GIVEN OUR DECISION, SETTLED DOWN TO TELEVISION. WE WATCHED ENTHRALLED FOR QUITE A SPELL, THEN *SUDDENLY* THERE CAME A YELL...
OH, NO!
...YOUNG ISOBEL WAS WIDE AWAKE— OF THAT THERE COULD BE *NO* MISTAKE!
WE CHARGED UPSTAIRS TO SEE 'WHAT'S WHAT' AND THERE THE SILLY LITTLE CLOT WAS BAWLING, SITTING UP IN BED— REFUSING TO BE COMFORTED!
WE DID OUR BEST, AND TUCKED HER IN, BUT DID THIS QUELL THE PIERCING DIN...? NOT A HOPE—THEN DESPERATION BROUGHT A SUDDEN INSPIRATION!
A NICE HOT DRINK AT LIGHTNING SPEED WAS WHAT SHE NEEDED, WE AGREED. WHAT WAS SIMPLER? DOWN I FLEW, FOR ALWAYS IN THE 'FRIDGE', I KNEW, WAS GOOD FRESH MILK— DEVOID OF GERMS— THIS BEING A JOB OF *MR THERM'S*.
I HEATED SOME IN HALF-A-MINUTE, THEN SEIZED A CUP, AND POURED IT IN IT! THIS I RUSHED TO ISOBEL, WHO PROMPTLY STOPPED HER LUSTY YELL AND, HAVING DRUNK IT, FELL ASLEEP— WE NEVER HEARD ANOTHER PEEP!
WHICH ONLY GOES AGAIN TO SHOW HOW MUCH TO *MR THERM* WE OWE!

A FLOATING FIR

THE FLOATING

ENGINE

The great array of factories, wharves and warehouses that line the banks of London's river Thames are in congested areas which make it difficult to bring up a large number of fire engines by road in the event of a big fire.

By means of this remarkable London County Council firefloat, named *Massey Shaw*, fires can be fought from the river itself.

The two Diesel propelling engines are of 160 h.p. each, giving her a speed of 12 knots. The engines also drive the powerful Merryweather 8 in. turbine pumps through clutches. The pumps themselves have a delivery pressure of 125 lb per sq. in. each and can be operated together to give a pressure of 250 lb. per sq. in.

Water is supplied by them to 8 delivery heads on the deck, 4 each side, and to the powerful monitor, which can throw a jet of water to a great height. Only 4 delivery heads are shown in use.

The *Massey Shaw* has a length of 78 ft; beam 12 ft. 6 ins. and a draught of only 3 ft. 9 ins.

KEY TO HOW IT WORKS
(1) Water suction inlets. (2) Two-way suction head. (3) Suction pipe to pumps. (4) Turbine pump, driven by Diesel engine. (5) Delivery pipe to deck. (6) Four-way delivery head to hoses. (7) One of four hose nozzles in use. (8) Delivery pipe to monitor. (9) Powerful monitor, which can be rotated and elevated. (10) 160 h.p. Diesel engine which is also used for pro-

pelling the ship. (11) Port side 160 h.p. Diesel engine. (12) Port side turbine pump. (13) Port side system of pipes is the same as the starboard side and all are interconnected. (14) Engine room telegraph receiver. (15) Diesel engine driving electricity generator. (16) Propeller shaft tunnel. (17) Starboard propeller. (18) Engine exhaust.

KEY TO OTHER PARTS
(19) Galley. (20) Crew's quarters. (21) First-aid hose reel. (22) Engine room telegraph. (23) Steering and control platform. (24) Hose and equipment room. (25) Hand capstan. (26) Hand windlass. (27) Bow fender. (28) Shallow draught of 3 ft. 9 in. allowing vessel to get close inshore.

L. ASHWELL WOOD

FIRE ENGINE

MAN IN

SPACE

For its first test flights, the X-15 is powered by two small four-barrel rocket engines. Later, a single Reaction Motor rocket of 60,000 lbs. thrust will be fitted. Made of special heat-resisting metals, the X-15 has a wing-span of 22 ft. and is 50 ft. in length.

One of the most exciting aeroplanes ever built is now at the U.S.A.F.'s top-secret Edwards Air Force Base, California, for its initial flight tests. Known as the North American X-15, it is designed to fly at over 3,600 m.p.h. and to climb to a height of at least 100 miles, where it will be above 99.9% of the atmosphere. Later it may be put into a satellite orbit with the help of a giant booster-rocket.

First pilot of the X-15 is 37-year-old North American test pilot Scott Crossfield, who was the first man to fly at twice the speed of sound. His specially-designed aluminium-coated pressure suit is insulated, ventilated by cooling air and inflatable, to enable him to breathe and to prevent his blood boiling when he is at great heights.

Inside this building, Scott Crossfield has been able to learn what it is like to fly the North American X-15 without leaving the ground, by using the world's biggest whirling-arm centrifuge.

Below, Scott Crossfield is pictured stepping into the gondola on the end of the great centrifuge rotor arm.

The gondola is fitted out as a dummy X-15 cockpit, in which Crossfield can experience the accelerations of a real flight and check positions of the controls and instruments. The X-15 will be launched from a B-52 mother-plane to zoom four times higher than any previous manned aircraft, gathering data for space flight and to discover how space vehicles can re-enter the atmosphere without being burned up by friction.

you write to the Editor

'BANDIT' SPEAKING

HERE IS a picture of our dog, 'Bandit', chewing over the international situation on the telephone with a friend. He is becoming very intellectual! He is a Staffordshire bull terrier, a breed which is only now becoming popular in England. – David Lindy, Littlehampton.

THANKS, Mr. THERM

THE Live and Learn series by Mr. Therm has been a great help in providing me with some good fun in building cupboards under the sink, and also the fold-up table. – Graham Fields, Eastbourne.

AN EAGLE PRIZE

I HAVE just finished reading the EAGLE novel, entitled Storm Nelson and the Sea Leopard, which I found most absorbing and exciting. I won it in a recent EAGLE competition, and thoroughly recommend it for all ages. – S. Adams, Carlisle.

STICK 'EM UP!

AS MY brother and I are joining EAGLE Club, we thought you would like to see our photograph. Mum took it while we played a 'Jeff Arnold' game. It is our favourite story in EAGLE. – Laurence Eddy, Rhondda, Glamorgan.

5/- is paid for every letter published. Readers who want a reply should enclose a stamped, addressed envelope.

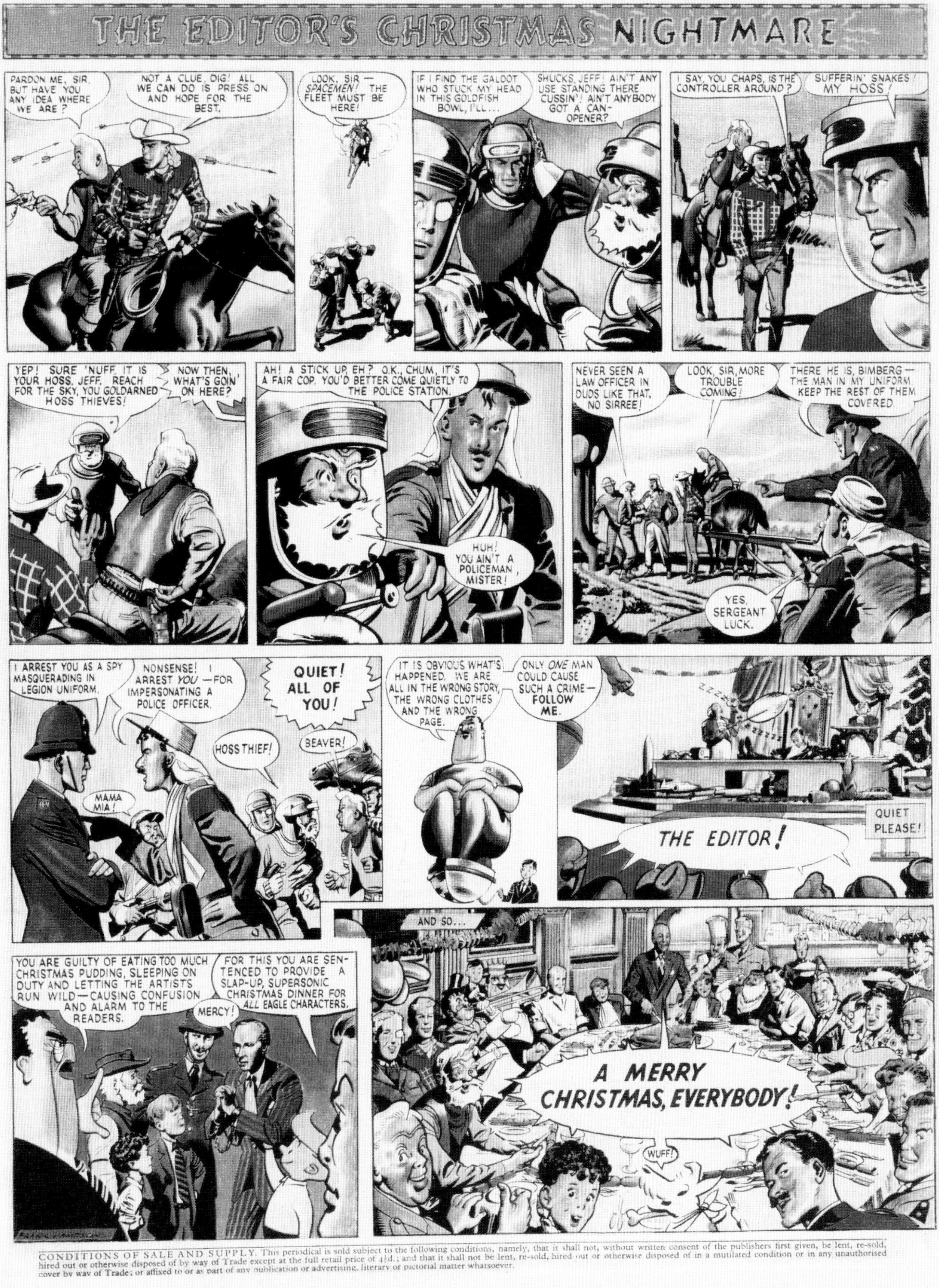
THE EDITOR'S CHRISTMAS NIGHTMARE
PARDON ME, SIR, BUT HAVE YOU ANY IDEA WHERE WE ARE?
NOT A CLUE, DIG! ALL WE CAN DO IS PRESS ON AND HOPE FOR THE BEST.
LOOK, SIR — SPACEMEN! THE FLEET MUST BE HERE!
IF I FIND THE GALOOT WHO STUCK MY HEAD IN THIS GOLDFISH BOWL, I'LL...
SHUCKS, JEFF! AIN'T ANY USE STANDING THERE CUSSIN'! AIN'T ANYBODY GOT A CAN-OPENER?
I SAY, YOU CHAPS, IS THE CONTROLLER AROUND?
SUFFERIN' SNAKES! MY HOSS!
YEP! SURE 'NUFF, IT IS YOUR HOSS, JEFF. REACH FOR THE SKY, YOU GOLDARNED HOSS THIEVES!
NOW THEN, WHAT'S GOIN' ON HERE?
AH! A STICK UP, EH? O.K., CHUM, IT'S A FAIR COP. YOU'D BETTER COME QUIETLY TO THE POLICE STATION.
HUH! YOU AIN'T A POLICEMAN, MISTER!
NEVER SEEN A LAW OFFICER IN DUDS LIKE THAT, NO SIRREE!
LOOK, SIR, MORE TROUBLE COMING!
THERE HE IS, BIMBERG — THE MAN IN MY UNIFORM. KEEP THE REST OF THEM COVERED.
YES, SERGEANT LUCK.
I ARREST YOU AS A SPY MASQUERADING IN LEGION UNIFORM.
NONSENSE! I ARREST YOU — FOR IMPERSONATING A POLICE OFFICER.
QUIET! ALL OF YOU!
HOSS THIEF!
BEAVER!
MAMA MIA!
IT IS OBVIOUS WHAT'S HAPPENED. WE ARE ALL IN THE WRONG STORY, THE WRONG CLOTHES AND THE WRONG PAGE.
ONLY ONE MAN COULD CAUSE SUCH A CRIME — FOLLOW ME.
ZZZZ
QUIET PLEASE!
THE EDITOR!
AND SO...
YOU ARE GUILTY OF EATING TOO MUCH CHRISTMAS PUDDING, SLEEPING ON DUTY AND LETTING THE ARTISTS RUN WILD — CAUSING CONFUSION AND ALARM TO THE READERS.
FOR THIS YOU ARE SENTENCED TO PROVIDE A SLAP-UP, SUPERSONIC CHRISTMAS DINNER FOR ALL EAGLE CHARACTERS.
MERCY!
A MERRY CHRISTMAS, EVERYBODY!
WUFF!
FRANK HAMPSON

AFTERWORD

During my 20 years' involvement in the intellectual property the *Eagle* and Dan Dare, I can vividly recall one treasured moment back in 2000 at the production offices of one of Hollywood's leading computer animation studios. It was a unique experience for me in this whole *Eagle* story.

As the executive producer of the CGI television series *Dan Dare – Pilot of the Future*, I was sitting in front of a team of over 50 American animation technicians, writers, and production executives, who were literally about to bring Dan Dare to life in 26 episodes of state-of-the-art computer animation. The average age of this team was less than 30, and they were all highly experienced and talented in their profession in LA, with a string of animated hit shows behind them.

In front of me on the table I laid out a selection of original artwork to give them all an understanding and flavour of where Dan Dare and the *Eagle* began back in the 1950s. This original artwork featured a selection of the original strips held in our archives, together with cover designs by Frank Hampson, Frank Bellamy, and Keith Watson. I was about to explain the unique talent of all the individuals who had been involved in the *Eagle*. However, this creative team seated around me, already knew the history well, they were avid fans of what was created in the fifties. They adored the quality, the design and the vivid colours of the artwork of Frank Hampson and all the artists associated with the comic. They were simply in awe of this artwork, and remember it was the year 2000 and the artwork I was showing was from the fifties and sixties, almost 50 years prior. I knew then that with the British and American writers, the animators, and the production team in front of me, I was about to embark on an amazing experience in producing Dan Dare in the new millennium to a huge global audience. Southport had arrived in California. It was a thrilling and enlightening experience, and the series has now been sold to over 130 countries – so the *Eagle* and Dan Dare is now very much alive to a new worldwide audience, and more is to come.

The whole *Eagle* story is nothing less than remarkable. To think that Marcus Morris and Frank Hampson sat and worked together with a small team, in their Southport studio, built detailed models of the characters and vehicles, and had the imagination to create wonderful, pure adventure stories that the youth of Britain could relate to, is simply inspiring. Soon after publication, the success story began to gather serious momentum. Nearly one million copies were being sold of the *Eagle* comic every week. The youth of Britain simply stopped on a Friday awaiting the next issue of the *Eagle*. As you will have now read: what evil and intriguing plots did the Mekon have up his sleeve? What was the next PC49 or Riders of the Range adventure going to be? What revelations were about to be revealed of the inner workings of the Vulcan bomber and the Nautilus submarine, in the amazing 'cutaways'? And what was Professor Brittain about to explain?

The Eagle Club was truly a 'must have' membership. To be a member enrolled you into adventure, excitement, thrills, and exclusive opportunities. The *Eagle* captured the imagination of a generation in the UK, during the fifties and sixties, in a truly exciting way – exactly what Harry Potter has achieved for a new global generation today.

Personally, I believe that the *Eagle* created the original real Super Hero 'Dan Dare – Pilot of the Future'. Alongside Superman, Batman, Spiderman, and Captain America, Dan simply towers! He will always do so.

I have often thought about what the creators of the *Eagle* would have thought had they entered the name Dan Dare or the *Eagle* into the Internet search bar today and seen the results. It is simply amazing. From a small studio in Southport, to the worldwide web, the story is remarkable and, more importantly, ongoing.

This book has captured the flavour of the quality, adventure, innovation, and excitement of outstanding comic entertainment. It is the first of several new publishing ventures for everybody young and old to enjoy. Next year look out for Dan and the *Eagle* moving into the 1960s.

The words in Elton John's and Bernie Taupin's song, 'Dan Dare (Pilot of the Future)', say it all: 'Can you tell me how old Dan might have done it, if he had been here now'. Well he is certainly here now, together with the *Eagle,* as this wonderful adventure continues.

COLIN FREWIN, AUGUST 2007
CHIEF EXECUTIVE
DAN DARE CORPORATION LIMITED

AUTHOR BIOGRAPHY

Daniel Tatarsky was born in Liverpool nearly 15 years after *Eagle*. Researching this book has allowed him to fall in love with the comic's characters and style in the same way that readers first did back in the 1950s. He is also an actor, and one day he hopes to play Dan Dare's sidekick Digby. The *Eagle Annual of the 1950s* is his second book. He has also written *Flick to Kick: An Illustrated History of Subbuteo.*

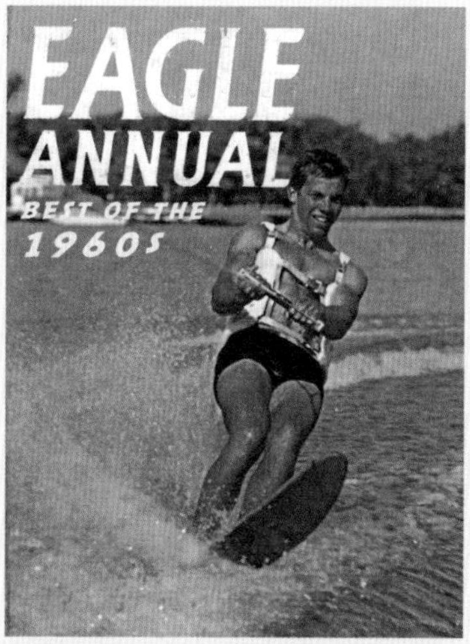
EAGLE
ANNUAL
BEST OF THE
1960s

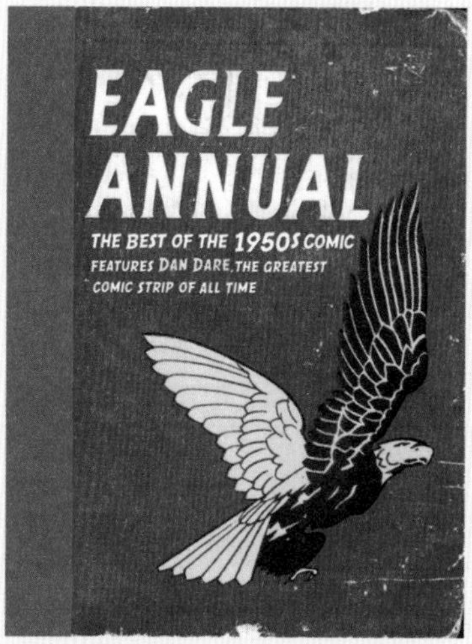
EAGLE
ANNUAL
THE BEST OF THE 1950s COMIC
FEATURES DAN DARE, THE GREATEST
COMIC STRIP OF ALL TIME

FROM ALL GOOD BOOKSHOPS AND RETAIL OUTLETS.

THE EAGLE ANNUAL: BEST OF THE 1960s

A GREAT, NEW EAGLE ANNUAL WILL BE ON SALE NEXT AUTUMN, AND IT'S SMASHING: THE EAGLE ANNUAL: BEST OF THE 1960s, FULL OF STORIES, STRIPS, GAMES AND HOBBY HINTS, AS WELL AS SUPER NEW ADVENTURES FROM THE REGULAR EAGLE CAST: DAN DARE, HARRIS TWEED, JEFF ARNOLD AND THE REST OF THE GANG.

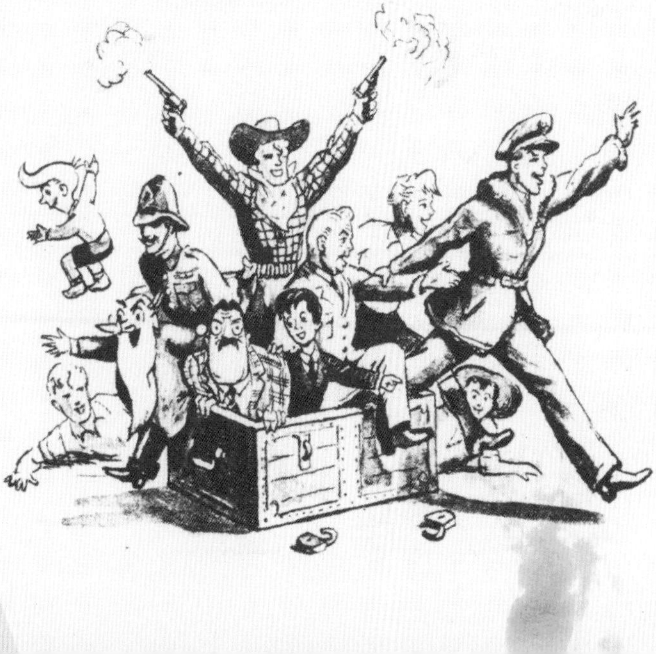